*This exhibition and catalog have been made possible
through the generous support of*

Kansallis Banking Group
Finnair
Pohjola Group
Finnish Foundation for the Visual Arts
Yhtyneet Paperitehtaat
Cultor
Haka Corporation
Aamulehti
Finlandia Vodka

CICA

Center for International Contemporary Arts
c/o Mr. Robert W. Kleinschmidt
Tocqueville Asset Management L.P.
1675 Broadway, New York, NY 10019

September 30, 1993

Dear Educator,

Please accept the enclosed set of catalogues from the Center for International Contemporary Arts (CICA). It is our hope that these will be a welcome addition to your institution's library.

The Center for International Contemporary Arts opened to the public in 1989, in New York City. In three years, CICA mounted seven ambitious exhibitions representing the work of artists from Japan, Great Britain, the United States and Finland. We strived to promote contemporary art from around the world and to increase awareness within the New York artistic community of exciting and important developments in the visual arts at the international level.

Unfortunately, due to the financial climate in the arts, CICA was closed last year. We have made every attempt to see that our resources go to respected institutions in order to continue the work in which we were engaged. Our library can be accessed through the library at the Museum of Modern Art, the Japanese Art books are located at the New York Public Library. Our permanent collection and archives can be viewed at the Archer M. Huntington Art Gallery at the University of Texas in Austin.

Sincerely,

Ms. Esa Epstein and Dr. Reiko Tomii

enclosures

Kimmo Kaivanto

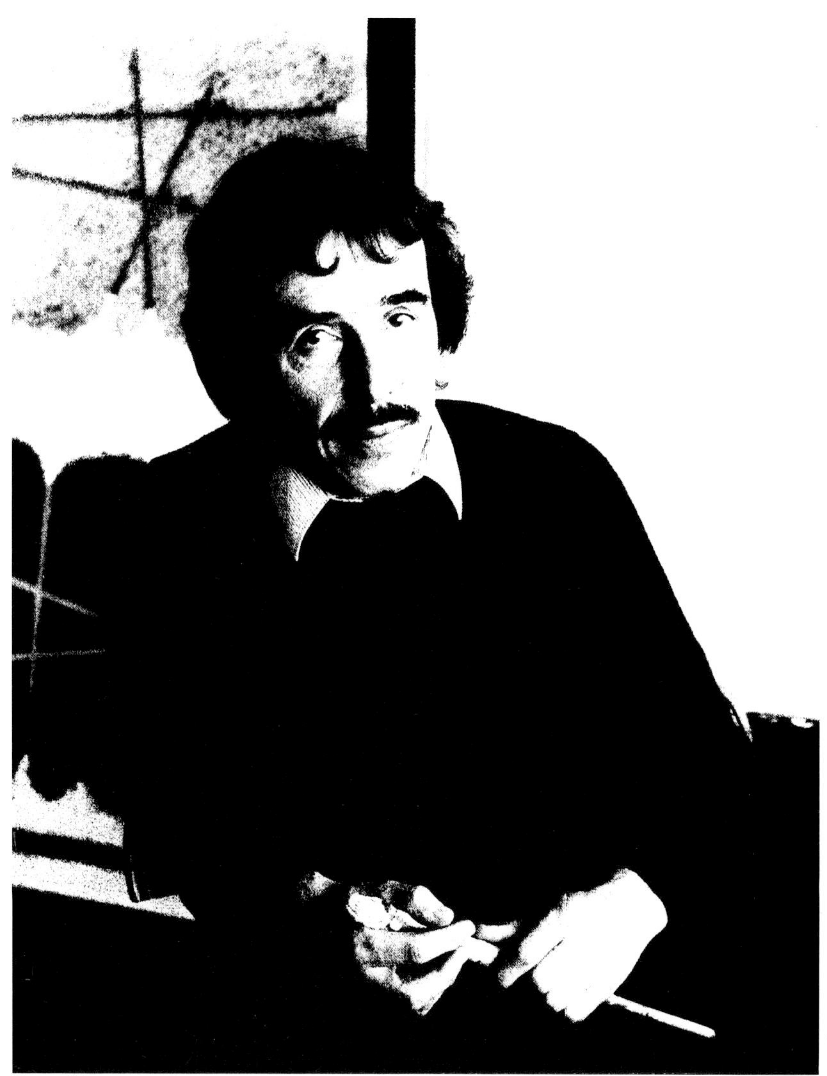

Kimmo Kaivanto, 1982. Photo by Olavi Kaskisuo.

Kimmo Kaivanto

Edited by
Bhupendra Karia

CICA

Center for International Contemporary Arts
New York

Published by the Center for International Contemporary Arts
in conjunction with the exhibition *Kimmo Kaivanto*
March 25, 1992 — June 6, 1992

Project Director and Curator
Bhupendra Karia

Senior Research Associate
Reiko Tomii, Ph.D.

Research Associates
Esa Epstein
Heikki Saros

Catalogue design
Peter Joseph

Translation from Swedish of Erik Kruskopf text
Martha Gaber Abrahamsen

Copy editor (Erik Kruskopf text)
Kathleen Friello

Exhibition Associate
John Doyle

Photography
Lasse Koivunen

Additional photography
Kare Bondsdorff
Hannu Teriö
Pekka Kuparinen
Petri Nuutinen
Simo Rista
Olavi Kaskisuo

Library of Congress Catalogue Card Number 92-070679
ISBN 0-9623764-8-5
Printed and bound in the United States of America

Contents

Acknowledgements

Among the most demanding elements of mounting a retrospective exhibition is the gathering of research material and supporting documentation. Although the artist is an indispensable source of first-hand information about his or her life and work, most artists have neither the time, nor inclination to keep systematic records. Embarking on this series on Scandinavian artists, our researchers were expecting to spend long hours digging through libraries and sleuthing around archives. But this exhibition turned out to be pleasantly different. As preliminary research demanded clarification and amplification, and faxed queries to Helsinki assumed relentless regularity, Mr. Kaivanto proved to be one of those rare artists who not only keeps meticulous records but can also produce the exact document from his vast and well-organized personal archive. Our deep appreciation and thanks are due to Mr. Kaivanto and his devoted assistant, Mr. Heikki Saros, for their cooperation. Throughout the long months we spent researching this exhibition, they consistently guided us to the needed information, regardless of how obscure or tangential it might have seemed. Whatever could not be located at the moment was carefully noted down and sent on by mail or fax, or conscientiously conveyed over the telephone. Yet through all the intensive sessions, Mr. Kaivanto and his wife, Sari Roiha, remained ever the gracious hosts: always thanking *us* for spending long hours researching and rummaging through his life's work and papers, ensuring a supply of fresh coffee and refreshments; responding to the most mundane of questions with exemplary patience.

Dr. Erik Kruskopf, who agreed to write the catalogue essay on short notice despite his other commitments, has been equally dedicated. From the time the first draft of his manuscript was delivered to his translator, Mrs. Abrahamsen, last fall, to the frantic stages of final editing and preparing the manuscript for publication, he continued to field a barrage of questions with good humor and efficiency. Our thanks are also due to Mr. Jari Björklöv, for compiling a well-researched bibliography on the artist, and to Ms. Marja Sakari of the Central Art Archives, Helsinki, for her supervision and cooperation.

This series on Finnish contemporary art could not have been realized without the enthusiastic cooperation of the board of directors of the Finnish Foundation for the Visual Arts, New York, and the single-minded dedication of the foundation's Executive Director, Ms. Marjukka Kaminen. My special appreciation to Mr. Severi Blomstedt, Chairman, and Ms. Päivi Lahtila, Executive Director of the Finnish Foundation in Helsinki for their wholehearted cooperation in this project.

On behalf of the trustees and the staff of CICA I offer my sincere thanks to Ms. Outi Polón of the Ministry for Foreign Affairs, Helsinki, who once again provided logistical coordination, looked after CICA's staff in Helsinki, and responded with unfailing courtesy and efficiency to our numerous requests for assistance. Ms. Marja-Liisa Linder, curator, Tampere Museum of Art, deserves special thanks for guiding me through Tampere city's public collections and for the enormous time and effort she dedicated to tracking down historical photographs in picture archives.

For their continuing support and encouragement, I am grateful to CICA's committee of consulting scholars, including Ms. Marketta Seppälä, Director of the Pori Museum; Mr. Timo Vuorikoski, Director of the Sara Hildén Art Museum in Tampere; Ms. Maaretta Jaukkuri, Chief Curator, the Ateneum; Mr. Markku Valkonen of Helsingin Sanomat; Ms. Soili Sinisalo, Director, the

Ateneum in Helsinki; Ms. Sirkka Valanto, Acting Director of the Central Art Archives; Prof. Leena Peltola, scholar and art historian; Dr. Staffan Carlén, Director, the Nordic Arts Centre; and Ms. Katriina Salmela-Hasán, Curator, the Museum of the City of Helsinki.

Numerous individuals and institutions in Finland and in the United States have enriched CICA's library resources on Finnish art with gifts of books, catalogues and reference works, which added immeasurably to the project and for which I am deeply grateful.

On behalf of the trustees, I gratefully acknowledge the generous grants and support received from various corporations and agencies. Without this crucial assistance, it would have been impossible to embark on this ambitious project. Thanks and appreciation are due to Mr. Peter Moden, President; Mr. Timo Aittola, Vice President; and Ms. Sole Öhberg, Assistant Treasurer, respectively, of Kansallis Banking Group for their continuing support of this project. Finnair in New York has generously provided travel arrangements for numerous research trips to Finland, and Finnair in Helsinki has assumed the responsibility for transporting artworks. The Pohjola Group has underwritten a portion of the insurance needs for this exhibition.

The Ministry for Foreign Affairs in Helsinki has provided local assistance and liberal support to our research staff who traveled to Finland, not to mention crucial administrative support throughout this project, for all of which I am deeply indebted.

I want to express my sincere thanks and gratitude to all private collectors and institutions including the Sara Hildén Art Museum, Tampere; the Museum of Contemporary Art, Finnish National Gallery, Helsinki; Tampereen Alvesäästopankki; Mr. Erkki Reponen; Ms. Kaija Junnila; Prof. Leena Pelota; the City of Tampere; Kansallis-Osake-Pankki, Helsinki; and the artist for the loan of Kimmo Kaivanto's works for this exhibition. For photographs of artworks and installations as well as for permission to reproduce such photographs, I thank the Central Art Archives, Helsinki; Sara Hildén Art Museum, Tampere; Amos Anderson Art Museum, Helsinki; and The Kuntsi Collection, Vaasa.

I am grateful to the trustees of the Center for International Contemporary Arts for nurturing these ambitious programs and for their continuing encouragement and support. The staff and interns of CICA have served the project with diligence and dedication. I continually marvel at the energy they devote to the unending chores surrounding such complex projects. Their dedication to CICA's guiding principles, and their striving for excellence in the most challenging conditions, have been both gratifying and inspirational. I owe a particular debt of gratitude to Peter Joseph and Reiko Tomii for contributing their enormous labors and talent towards realizing this exhibition and catalogue. By cheerfully assuming ever increasing administrative responsibilities, Esa Epstein and Jessica Oppenheim have made it possible for all of us to focus our efforts on research and development leading to this project, for which I am sincerely thankful. Our thanks are also due to Dave and Doug Roberts of the E. H. Roberts, for producing the beautifully printed catalogues on time despite the impossible schedule. On behalf of the trustees and staff, I offer my appreciation to Irene Chow, Kathleen Friello, John Doyle, Brooke Molinaroli, Bettina Roost-Ehm and Tom Martinelli for additional support.

B. K.

Ode to Blue Joy

by
Erik Kruskopf

In the summer of 1775, the Swedish king Gustavus III paused on a visit to the eastern part of his vast empire, which then included Finland, to admire the spectacular scene where Lake Näsijärvi empties into Lake Pyhäjärvi sixty feet below. The Tammerkoski rapids are not particularly noteworthy except in the context of the Finnish flatlands (fig. 1). However, when the thirty-three-year-old king decreed the free town of Tampere to be founded on this spot in 1779,[1] he had more than its scenic beauty in mind: he clearly envisioned water-powered industries to prosper here. The king himself inaugurated its first industry, a distillery he gave as a gift to Tampere (fig. 2).

Soon, a wood and paper mill was also established in Tampere. A decade after the Finnish territory was ceded to Russia in 1809, Finland's Grand Duke, Tsar Aleksandr I, invited an enterprising Scot, James Finlayson, who had settled in St. Petersburg, to set up a cotton mill here in 1820. The textile mill was soon followed by a foundry in 1842, and a linen mill, a woolen mill and a knitwear factory in 1856. By 1877, Finlayson had become a model employer providing not only jobs for 200 workers (forty percent of Tampere's population in 1860) but also a church, a school, a hospital, a library, a skating-rink, and a child-care facility for his employees (fig. 3). Tampere became the first city in Finland to be electrically lighted in 1882, the same year Thomas Edison lighted New York's Wall Street. By the time an ambitious young cobbler, Emil Aaltonen, arrived from the countryside to establish Finland's first footwear factory there in 1905, this medieval marketplace had been transformed into a bustling industrial and trading center and the second-largest city in Finland (fig. 4).

Cultural wealth, however, accumulated slowly. More than a century elapsed from the town's founding before the first art exhibition, organized by the newly-formed Tampere Art Society (Tampereen taideyhdistys), was held in the Tampere town hall in 1898. Although the political crisis brought on by the February Manifesto of 1899 interrupted the Art Society's activities, an important architectural project soon provided a showcase for the work of two important Finnish artists.[2] Magnus Enckell (1870-1925) and Hugo Simberg (1873-1917) executed stained glass windows and wall decorations for St. John's Evangelical Church, designed by Lars Sonck (1870-1956) and constructed between 1902 and 1907 (fig. 5).[3] Enckell's altarpiece and Simberg's mural, *Wounded Angel*, are recognized as seminal works in the history of Finnish art.

The Historical Museum of Tavastland (Hämeen Museo)[4] was founded in 1908, under the directorship of Gabriel Engberg (1872-1953), a local painter who would play an important role in the art scene of Tampere. But cultural activities once again came to a virtual standstill as the country was engulfed by the five-month-long Civil War which broke out following Finland's declaration of independence from Russia on December 6, 1917 (figs. 6, 7).[5] Life was never quite the same after Tampere, the last bastion of the labor-dominated Red faction in the Civil War, was subdued by General Mannerheim. Old institutions suddenly began to appear stodgy and retrogressive to the younger generation, and the progressive Tampere Artists' Association (Tampereen taiteilijaseura) was launched in 1920 under Engberg's leadership. Within two years, the new Association had organized a competition for a monument to the poet laureate Alexis Kivi (1834-1872),

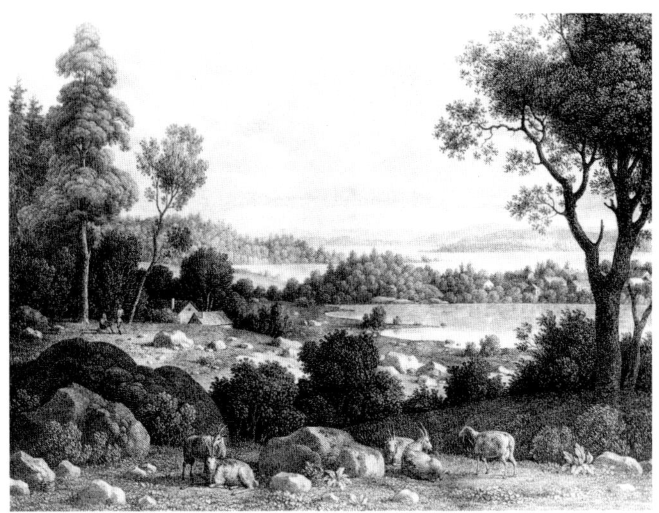

Figure. 1. Tampere, c. 1818, lithograph after drawing by Carl von Kügedl-gen. Courtesy of Museovirasio, National Board of Antiquities, Finland

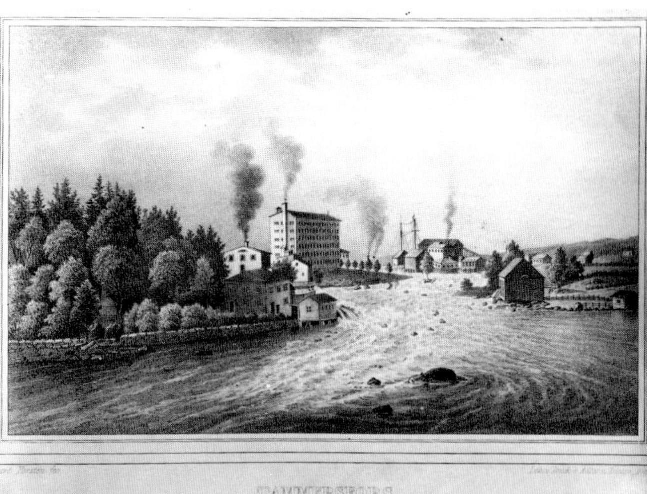

Figure. 2. Tampere, c. 1845-52, lithograph by Adler von Dietzl after Lennart Forstén. Courtesy of Museovirasio, National Board of Antiquities, Finland

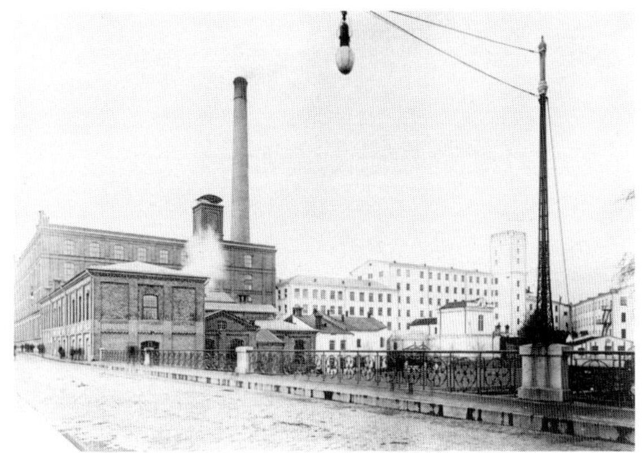

Figure. 3. Finlayson factory, c. 1910. Photo courtesy of Tampere Museum Photo Archive

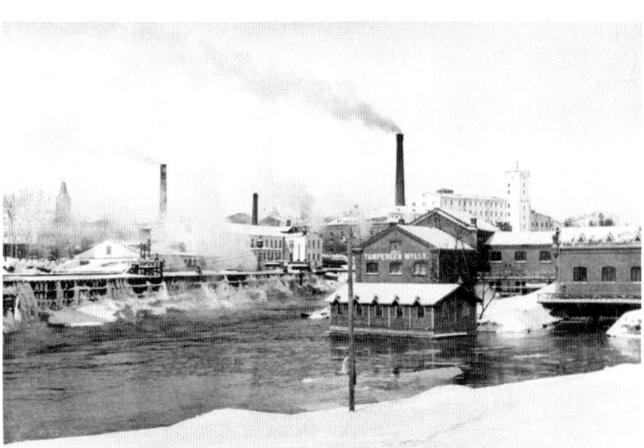

Figure. 4. A view of Tammerkoski rapids and Tampere Mill at the turn of the century. Photo by Gustin Lojander

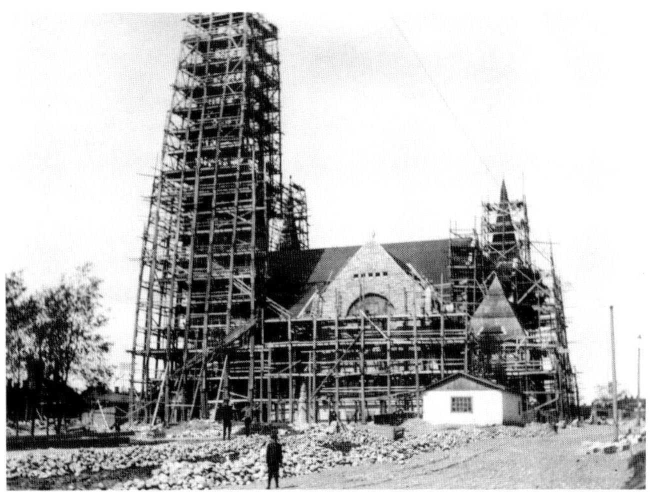

Figure. 5. Tampere Cathedral under construction, c. 1905

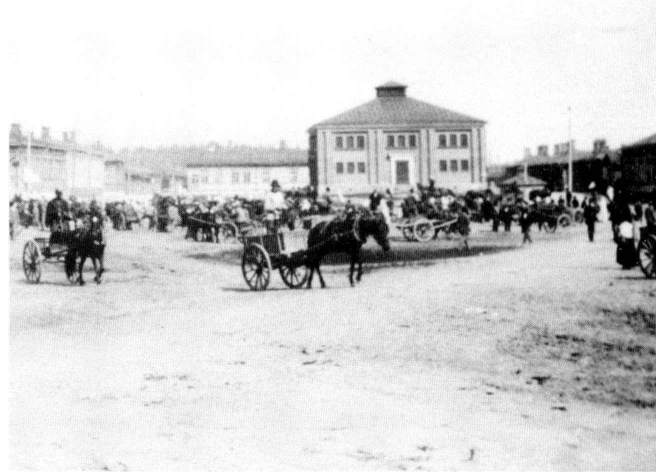

Figure. 9. Granary designed by Carl Ludwig Engel in 1828 was converted into Tampere Museum in 1931. Photo by J. Silke, courtesy of Tampere Seura ry

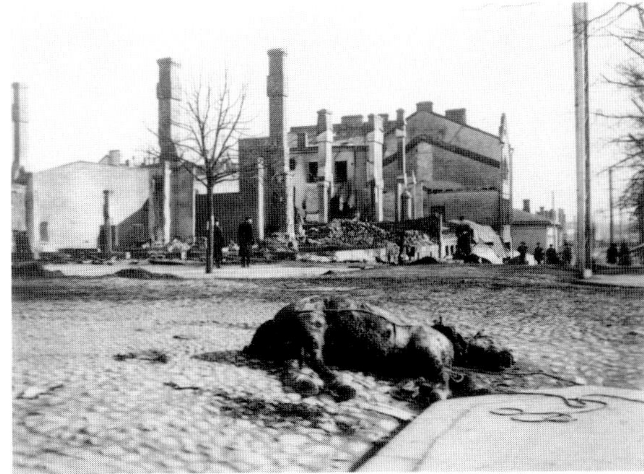

Figure. 6. Death and destruction in Tampere during the Civil War, 1918. Photo *Aamulehti*, courtesy of Tampere Museum Photo Archive

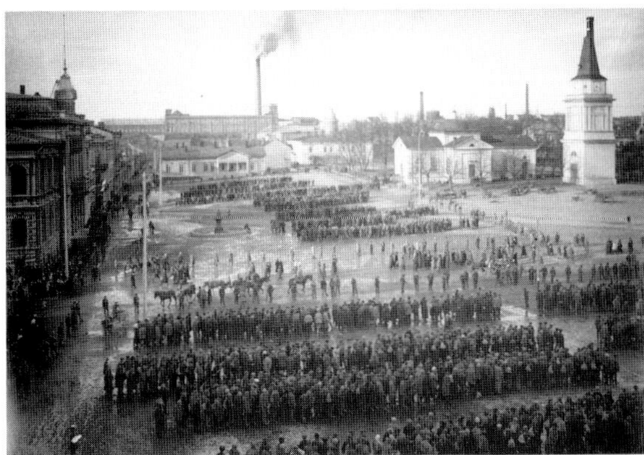

Figure. 7. Red prisoners in Tampere Square at the end of Civil War, 1918. Photo *Aamulehti*, courtesy of Tampere Museum Photo Archive

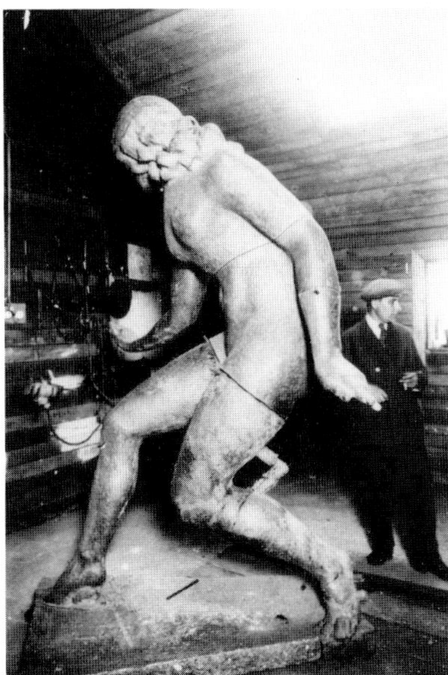

Figure. 8. Sculptor Wäino Aaltonen in his studio working on the Alexis Kivi monument, 1928. Photo by V. Kanninen, courtesy of *Aamulehti*

and awarded the commission to the twenty-eight-year-old sculptor Wäino Aaltonen (1894-1966) (fig. 8). In 1930, the first exhibition by Association members opened in the temporary hall of the public library, establishing a tradition of annual group shows which survives to this day. All this had the desired effect of jolting the old guard into action. The Tampere Art Society launched a drive to set up an art museum for the town, and a century-old granary designed by Carl Ludwig Engel, the German-born architect in charge of the Helsinki master plan, was converted into a museum in 1931 (fig. 9).

◆

It was in this industrial city that Kimmo Kaivanto was born on May 25, 1932, the second of four children. His parents were also born in Tampere. His father, Vilho Kaivanto (1904-1972), worked as a storehouse manager. His mother, Laina Elina Wallenius (1905-1985) was a skilled retoucher of photographic negatives and occasionally did window displays for the photo store for which she worked. Kimmo's schooling consisted of six years of public elementary school at Tammelan kansakoulu and three years of high school at Tampereen II Lyseo. Growing up during the harsh years of the Winter War (1939-1940) followed by five years of Finland's involvement in World War II, made a deep impression on the young Kaivanto. His father was drafted into the army, and the Kaivanto family lived through nine Russian bombing raids on Tampere, coping with the shortages and privations of war as best they could (figs. 10, 11).

Kaivanto gave free reign to his emotions in a series of drawings. These sketches, made when he was eleven, give the first indication of his interest in the expressive power of visual imagery. Page after page of his diaries from 1943 to 1948 is crammed with colored illustrations, cartoon strips, and family episodes, all amazingly well rendered for someone so young and without any training in art. One of his cartoon strips, a rather naive but action-filled story of a flying war hero, was even published in the monthly, *Jokapoika* (Every Boy), in 1944 (fig. 12).

The illustrated journal kept by the youthful Kaivanto, far from being the personal and private record of a precocious child, served as a family chronicle (figs. 13-15). At times, the family sat around the hearth reading the episodes Kimmo had depicted. But most of all, the journal was kept for their father so he could share some of the domestic incidents that took place during his absence: how Kimmo was scolded for accidentally flooding the bathroom and ruining the rug; how the carefully rationed bread was always gone whenever the older son Pekka (b. 1929) went on a picnic with his friends; how each family member fared on skis during the last snowfall. One page shows the slim journal sitting on a shelf in the basement, where his mother had deposited it for safekeeping during bombing raids on Tampere. Thus it was sharing and communication, rather than the venting of private angst and emotions, that was at the heart of this endeavor–precisely the elements that distinguish Kaivanto's mature work. The same simple and straightforward desire to communicate is also evident in the numerous hand-drawn postcards the young boy sent to his father at the front (figs. 16, 17).

Drawing was a means of expression for the entire family; his mother was an amateur painter and his brother, Pekka and two sisters, Kirsti Maria (b.1940) and Tuija (1933-1948) zealously sketched everything in sight. Kirsti even practiced commercial art for several years. In fact, this artistic strain ran deeper still: Lambert Hjalmar Kaivanto, Kimmo's paternal grandfather, a carpenter and an accomplished carver, had assisted in the execution of ornamental woodwork and decoration in St. John's Cathedral.[6] It is significant that the largely self-taught Kimmo would go on to do some of his most important work in conjunction with architectural projects.

Kaivanto was not only impatient with school and formal art studies, but also demonstrated a youthful grit and eagerness to get on with the real challenge of making a living. Graduating from high school at seventeen, he obtained a summer job as a trainee with Tampere's newly-formed advertising agency, Mainos Lehmus. Since the agency offered a wide array of services from sign painting to window display in addition to the conventional advertising functions, Kaivanto quickly acquired a host of new skills. He also made the acquaintance of two other artists, Martti Peurasalo (1920-1984) and Pentti Toivonen (1921-1973), both recruited by the advertising agency that summer. Peurasalo and Toivonen were neither avant-garde nor yet professionally recognized, but the fervor with which they spoke of carving out careers as artists was infectious. To the impressionable young Kaivanto, their determination and the bohemian lifestyle held all the glamor of life as an artist. He fondly acknowledges that the days and nights they spent talking about their high ideals and the practical problems of a life dedicated to art marked a turning point in his career. From there on he, too, was determined to make a career out of his hobby.

Tampere's cultural scope was defined by its industrial base and colored by its predominantly working-class population. Thus a characteristic theme of Tampere art was the life of its workers. This has been particularly true in literature, as exemplified by the pioneer writers of the Pispala school. Pispala, a suburb of laborers' shacks and narrow, winding streets on the slopes of the Pyynikki ridge, was dominated by a proletarian character well into the 1950s (figs. 18, 19). Lauri Viita (1916-1965), the son

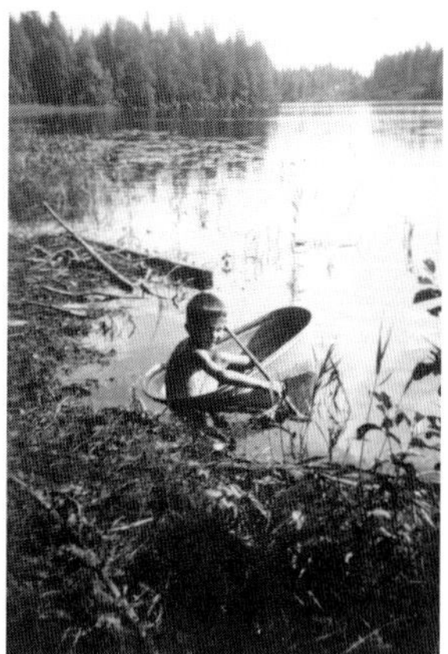

Figure. 10. Kaivanto in Kyynärä-jaärvi, 1937

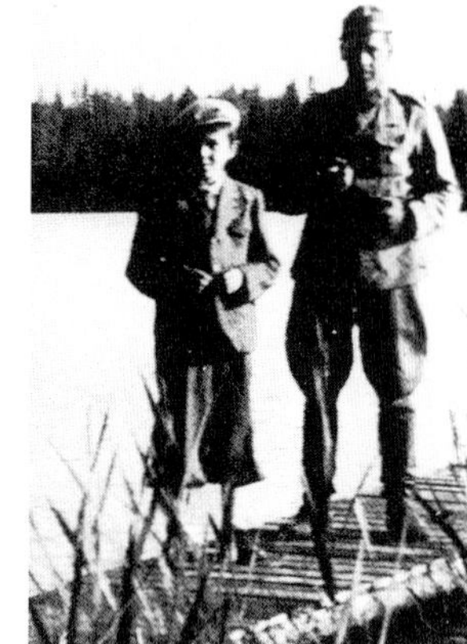

Figure. 11. Kaivanto at age ten with his father in military uniform, c. 1942

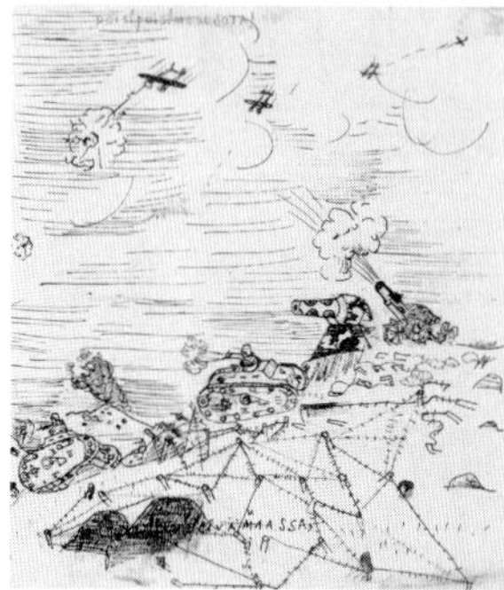

Figure. 12. Kimmo Kaivanto. Drawing, ink on paper, c. 1942

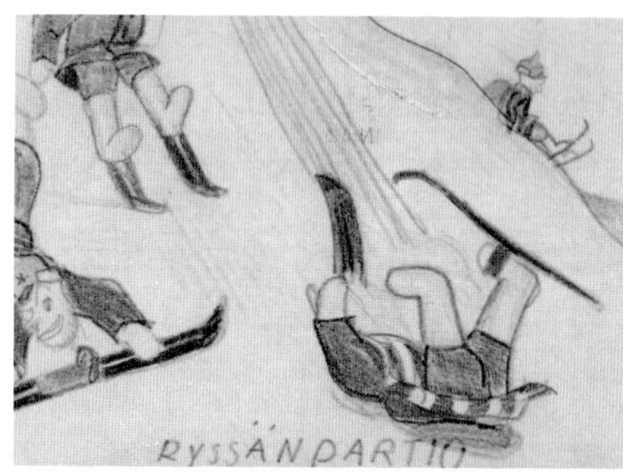

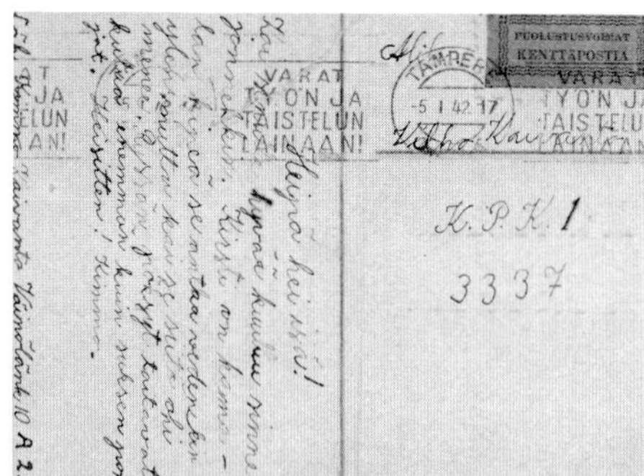

Figures. 16, 17. Kaivanto's postcard titled "Russian Troops," sent to his father on January 5, 1942. Text reads:

Hello Father! // I suppose you are well, wherever you are. Kirsty is awfully sick, she even throws up the water she drinks, but I suppose she will get over it. The Russkies are such poor skiers that their trousers wear out faster than their skis, I think // Bye then! Kimmo

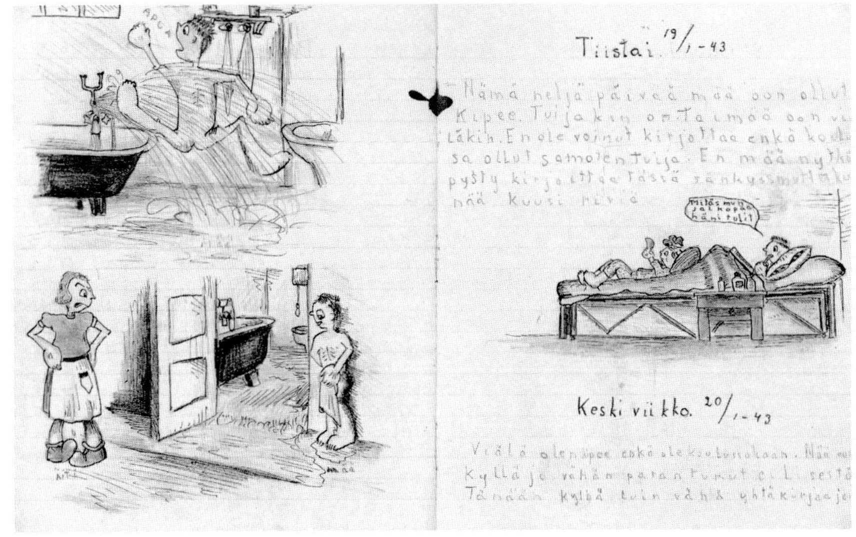

Figure. 13. Kaivanto's journal entries for January 15, 19 and 20, 1943. Text for the Jan. 15 entry (on the verso, not illustrated) reads:

Friday 15/1-43 / The past eight days have been so boring that I have not even written the diary. But something did happen this evening. Before having my bath, I wanted to scrub the bathtub. First I turned on both taps, then I pushed the lever for the hand shower. But the handle fell off and a whole lot of water gushed out and flooded the floor. The water reached all the way to the entrance hall. I was so upset that I did not think of turning off the faucets. Mom knocked on the door and Pekka also came in when I opened the door and he put the handle back with great effort. Mother was livid because I tried to scrub the tub; she had already done that.

Text for Jan. 19 entry reads:

Tuesday 19/1-43 / I have been sick for the last four days. Tuija also. Perhaps I'm still sick. I have not been able to write, I have not gone to school, neither has Tuija. Even now I'm able to write only six lines in bed // What are you doing in my bed?

Figure. 14. Kaivanto's journal entry for May 29, 1943. Text reads:

Piatsu [Pekka] plans to go on an overnight trip again. He is in his pajamas preparing his picnic lunch, as you see in the picture. Overnight trips are his specialty, especially at the end of the month when the ration cards are all used up.

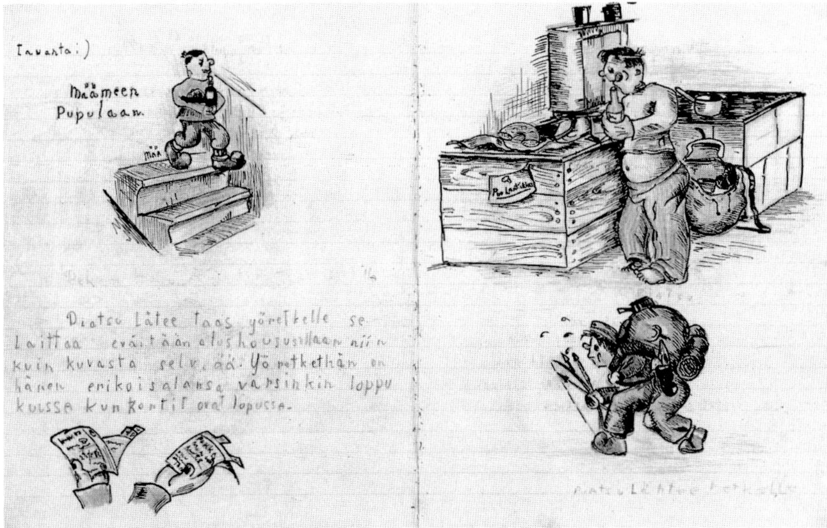

Figure. 15. Kaivanto's journal entry for June 30, 1946. Text (beginning on the previous page, not illustrated) reads:

Sunday 30.6.46 / [Cousin] Jukka was here yesterday. He went home for the night and returned in the morning. We went to the woods with my father, to look for a big rock that father had talked to me about. And we found it. It was the "Hirvisimuna" rock that I had heard so much about // Hirvisimuna // Main cave / A tunnel to another cave // An entrance to a cave. It is difficult to describe the Hirvisimuna cave in a drawing // KIPA [Kimmo], WHERE ARE YOU? / JUHUUUUU... WHERE ARE YOU? / A typical view from Hirvisimuna // Just found a duck's nest from which we removed four eggs. We tried to get the chickens to hatch them, but they did not do it and two of the eggs broke. I tried to hatch the other two eggs in the oven.

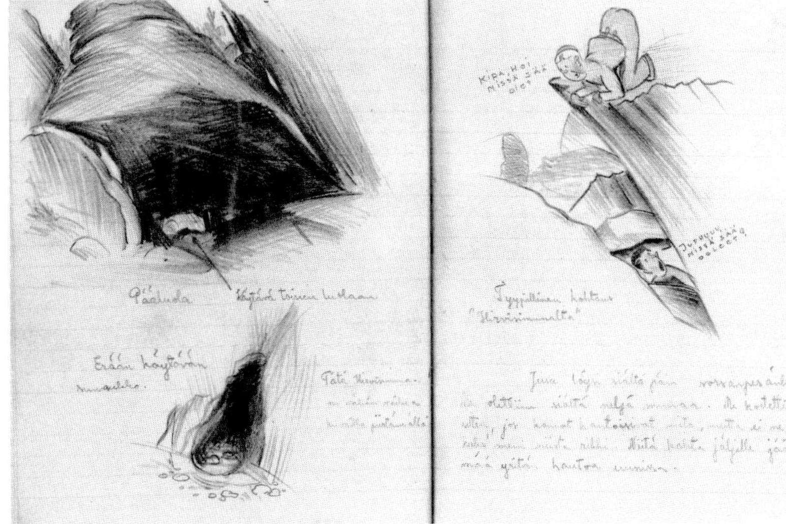

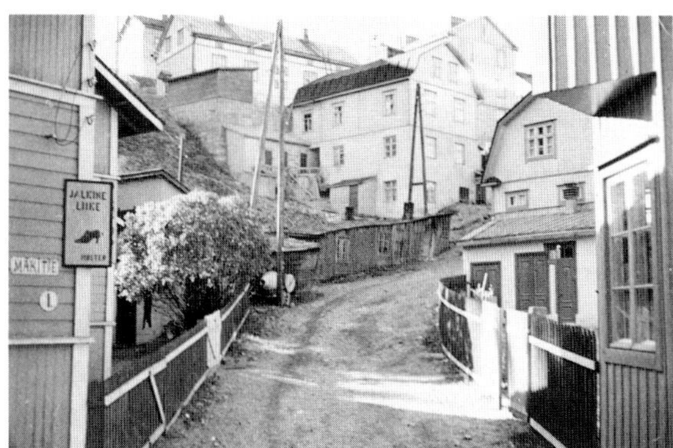

Figure. 18. A view of Pispala. Photo by V.O. Kanninen

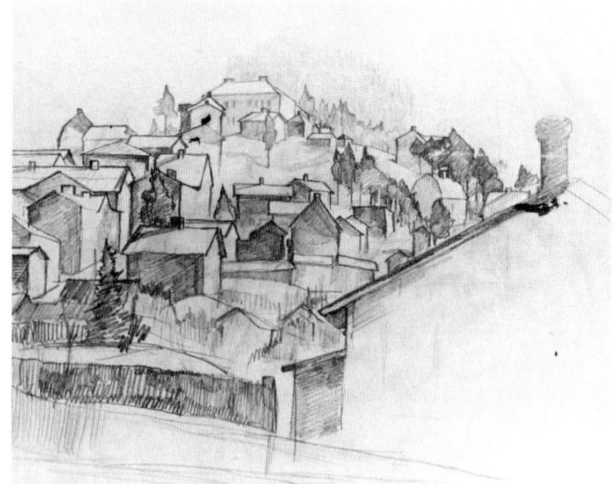

Figure. 19. Reino Viirilä. *From Pispala*, 1935, drawing. Collection Tampere Museum. Photo by Juhani Riekkolo

of a carpenter who also earned his living by the family trade, is one of the many celebrated authors to have lived and worked in Pispala. His classic 1950 novel, *Moreeni*, set in the period of the Finnish Civil War, drew the country's attention to the way ordinary working-class citizens perceived the world around them. Another Tampere author to rise to national prominence was Väinö Linna (b.1920). Linna's autobiographical novel, *The Unknown Soldier* (1954), is the story of a young factory worker who is conscripted into the senseless war and who bitterly questions the ideological abstractions which lead to mass death and destruction. Later, he expanded this theme into an ambitious historical trilogy, *Here, Under the Northern Star* (1959-1962), which has earned him an exalted place in Finnish literature. Linna broke ranks with the Romantic Nationalists by implying that the victory of the White faction in the Finnish Civil War had sacrificed the workers' aspirations to decadent bourgeois values. Viita and Linna represent the conscience of industrial workers in numerous towns like Tampere, and are credited with empowering the laboring classes at that crucial moment when Finland was in the throes of defining its national agenda.

But the local painters at the turn of the century did not quite achieve the renown of Linna and Viita. The appellation, "typical Tampere artist" almost always signified an inability to achieve national stature. Gabriel Engberg was one such native son who could never shake off the stigma of provincialism. Other artists of local fame in the 1930s, Allan Salo (1901-1978) and Reino Viirilä (b. 1901) also sought to depict the life of factory workers and common laborers at a time when Tampere lacked art schools,

exhibition spaces and official encouragement (fig. 20). But by the 1950s, efforts to impart rudimentary training in various fields of art were underway and an artists' colony had begun to emerge. Several new exhibition spaces and studios eventually materialized with the aid of public funding. The establishment of Tampere University, which took shape in slow stages during the 1950s and the 1960s, also helped bring about a greater awareness of and interest in culture. As the university became fully functional, it brought about a dramatic change in the intellectual and artistic climate of Tampere. The Tampere Museum of Modern Art (Tampereen nykytaiteen museo), first of its kind in Finland, was founded in 1966 and housed in a converted 1928 patrician villa which once belonged to the pharmacist and collector Oskar Severin Haapanen. But the city's first museum specifically built to house modern and contemporary art had to await the initiative of a remarkable businesswoman, entrepreneur and collector, Sara Hildén. She donated her collection to the city with the stipulation that it be housed in a specially designed building. After years of planning and negotiations, the museum, bearing her name, opened in 1979 and has since played an important role in art collecting and education in Finland (fig. 21).

A continuing rivalry between Tampere and Helsinki illustrates the Finnish debate over center and periphery. The capital is unmistakably the seat of power and thus a magnet for cultural activities. But the rugged individualism of industrial entrepreneurs who breathed life into small, prosperous industrial towns such as Pori and Tampere and Nokia is generally in greater evidence away from the capital. Tampere's innovative and adventurous

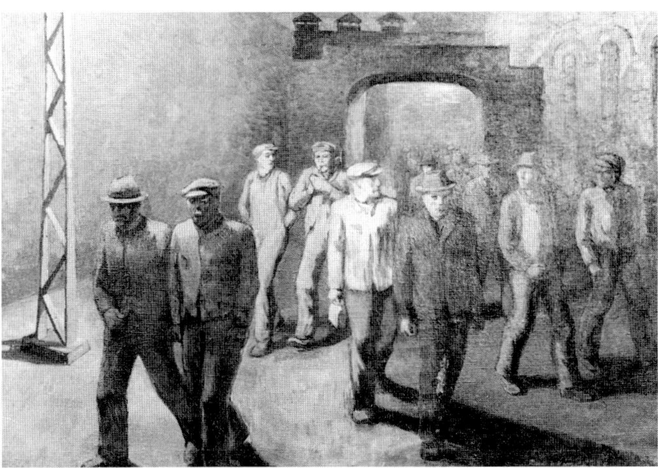

Figure. 20. Reino Viirilä. *Return from Work*, 1938, oil on canvas, 26-3/4 × 39-3/8" (68 × 100 cm). Collection Tampere Museum

Figure. 21. Installation view of one of the galleries in Sara Hildén Museum, Tampere, showing Alberto Giacometti's *Woman on a Chariot*, 1943. Photo by Timo Vuorikoski, 1985

citizens have taken it upon themselves to place their city on the cultural map. From the textile tycoon Finlayson to the footwear king Aaltonen, the trader Nikolas Tirkkonen and paper manufacturer Rafael Haarla to the enterprising goldsmith and patron of the arts, Kustaa Hiekka, each has bequeathed fine collections, public monuments and buildings to the city.

◆

In keeping with the tradition of unremitting hard work and self-improvement exemplified by Viita and Linna, Kaivanto enrolled in art classes while holding down a full-time job with Mainos Lehmus. There was no art academy in Tampere,[7] so he studied graphics and printmaking with Aukusti Tuhka (1895-1973) at evening workshops sponsored by the Tampere Artists' Association, and drew from live models at a studio run by the Tampere Art Society. By 1953, he had saved up enough to enroll in what was then the Institute of Industrial Arts (Taideteollinen oppilaitos) in Helsinki. Notwithstanding his respect and enthusiasm for the teachings of the famed industrial designer Tapio Wirkkala (1915-1985), and his newfound friendship with classmate Kain Tapper, Kaivanto had to bow to economic pressures and abandon his studies at the end of the school year in 1954. He had met and married Kirsti Anna-Liisa Saukkokoski earlier that year and the couple decided to return to Tampere, partly because Kimmo had a secure job there and the cost of living was considerably cheaper than in the capital. An equally important reason for the move back to Tampere was Kaivanto's impatience with academic training: it added lit-

tle to his already advanced skills and delayed the process of establishing himself as an independent artist. He surmised, correctly, that no amount of schooling can possibly equip anyone to make the leap to professional status. Far from accepting defeat, Kaivanto returned to Tampere with a steely determination to succeed as an artist on his own. He continued to work in advertising, first as a graphic designer and later as an art director, but also began to paint with purposeful vigor.

His debut as an artist came in 1956 when he participated in the 25th annual show of the Tampere Artists' Association.[8] He exhibited *The Tent Builders* (present whereabouts unknown), a figurative monotype made in a relatively free, simple style. Not even the local press paid attention to his work in the otherwise verbose reviews of the exhibition. Although this important event in the artist's career passed unnoticed by the media, the exposure exhilarated Kaivanto and convinced him that art was indeed his calling. Accepting this as a learning experience, he now devoted all his energy to his art and continued to experiment with a variety of styles and techniques. At the same time, he wisely held on to his job at the agency and performed to his employer's full satisfaction. He was even awarded first prize for the best Finnish poster of 1961, *Cotton Is Fashion*. Reconciled to his need to make a living to support his family, he instinctively made a prudent separation between what he needed and what he wanted to do. By this time Kaivanto had already made his breakthrough as an artist, and endeavored, perhaps a bit unnecessarily, to keep a clear distance from applied art. Advertising work had, however, given him an eye for the effective idiom that would prove extremely

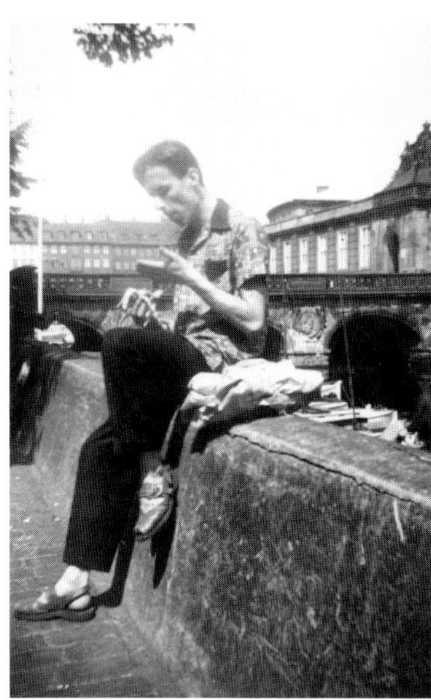

Figure. 22. Kaivanto in Copenhagen, 1957

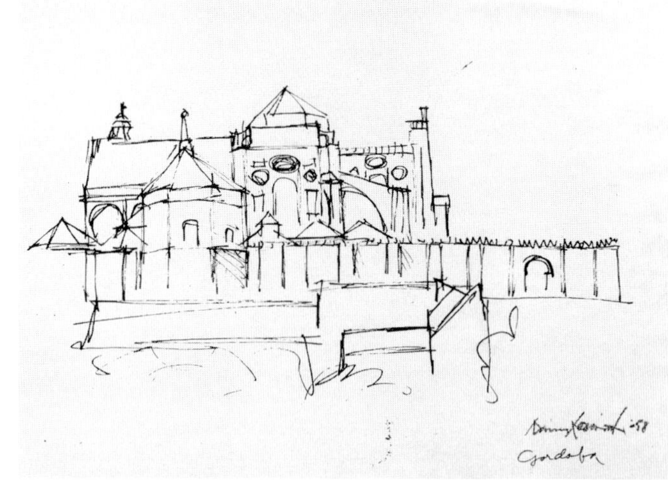

Figure. 23. Kimmo Kaivanto. *"Gordoba"*, 1958, ink on paper, 7-7/8 × 9-7/8"
(20 × 25 cm). Collection of the artist

useful in his future work as an artist.

He debuted in Helsinki in 1957, participating in the fifteenth Young Artists' Exhibition. From then on he showed on a regular basis in group exhibitions, the most important among these being the annual exhibition of Finnish Artists' Association and Young Artists' Exhibition, where his work generally elicited positive reviews. His style at this time can be best characterized as a stringently structured Expressionism with romantic undertones; he favored dark, intense colors frequently framed in thick black lines. He was significantly influenced by two study trips, to Copenhagen in 1954, and to Spain four years later. During the trip to Copenhagen, undertaken while he was a student at the Institute of Industrial Arts, the artist soaked up an enormous body of information from visits to Danish museums and monuments (fig. 22). The six-week trip to Spain, made under a grant from the city of Tampere, resulted in a vast number of sketches and studies (figs. 23, 24). Between these two trips, he had his first solo exhibition in 1959 at Gallery Pinx in Helsinki.

The work produced between 1956 and 1961 can be characterized as Kaivanto's youthful oeuvre, and shows him to be a gifted pupil of the modernist school. The critics spoke of influences from Rouault and Derain, and there is a degree of truth in those observations: his dark color-scale has a heavy intensity and his terse construction exhibits features of post-Cubist composition. Subjects were mainly taken from his trips abroad, a conspicuous exception being *The Onion-Domed Church*, 1957, based on Tampere's Eastern Orthodox Church built in 1899 (figs. 25, 26). Kaivanto has exhibited this work several times and I personally remember it from a group exhibition in 1968, where its mysterious tone and intense color scale attracted attention. Even though the subject was a familiar hometown church, it was the element of the exotic that attracted him. Everyday motifs in his own environment were not yet able to inspire the young painter to create major works.

Following his 1958 trip to Spain, Kaivanto's style became more non-figurative, bordering on the abstract. As is the case with so much other non-figurative art, however, Kaivanto's pictures always have a transparently representational motif behind them, openly declared in their titles, e.g. *Alcázar*, 1960 (Plate 2), an undisguised Spanish townscape and *Gallop*, 1960 (Plate 3), which endeavors to capture the dynamic motion of a galloping horse.

During these early years Kaivanto also executed his first public projects. In 1959, he won first prize in a mural competition for the Saukonpuisto elementary school. *Our Friends*, completed in 1960, is painted in a playful, Miró-like style, in a considerable departure from his usual approach (fig. 27). Again in 1961, he won a commission to do a mural for a retirement home in Koukkuniemi, which was painted in 1962. The high, narrow panel, *As to the Good So Also to the Evil*, executed in oil on canvas, is in the lyrical abstract mode characteristic of the time. He went on to win two more competitions to decorate school buildings, in 1966 and 1967 respectively (fig. 28).

These more-or-less abstract works coincided quite well with new developments underway in the country. In the late 1950s, Finland was emerging from a sustained period of cultural isolation which had begun in the 1930s and continued through the years of post-war reconstruc-

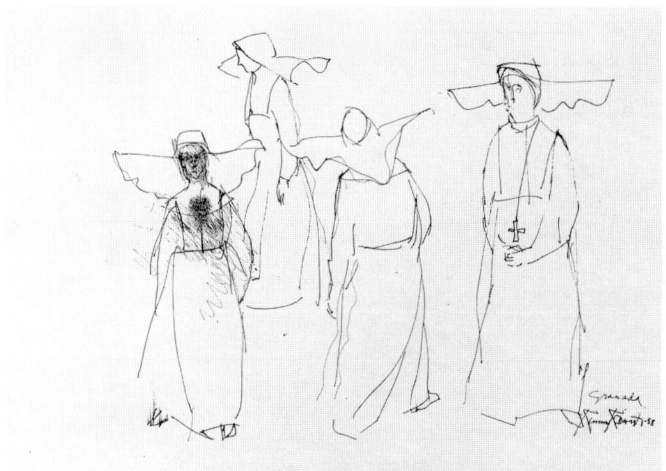

Figure. 24. Kimmo Kaivanto. *Granada*, 1958, ink on paper, 7-7/8 × 9-7/8" (20 × 25 cm). Collection of the artist

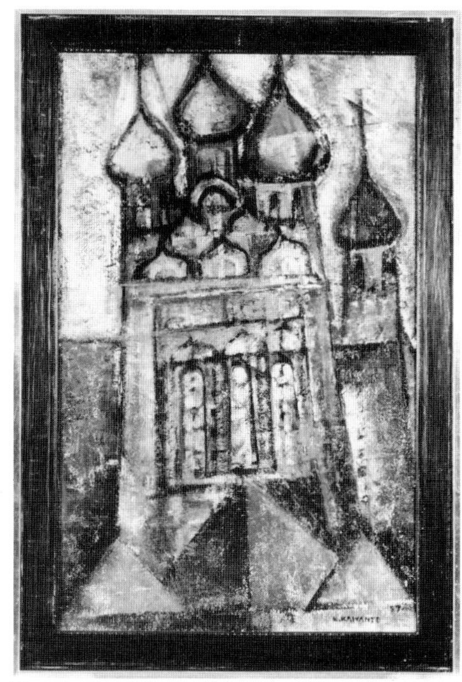

Figure. 25. Kimmo Kaivanto. *The Onion-Domed Church*, 1957, oil on composition board, 49-3/4 × 34-7/8" (126.5 × 88.5 cm). Private collection

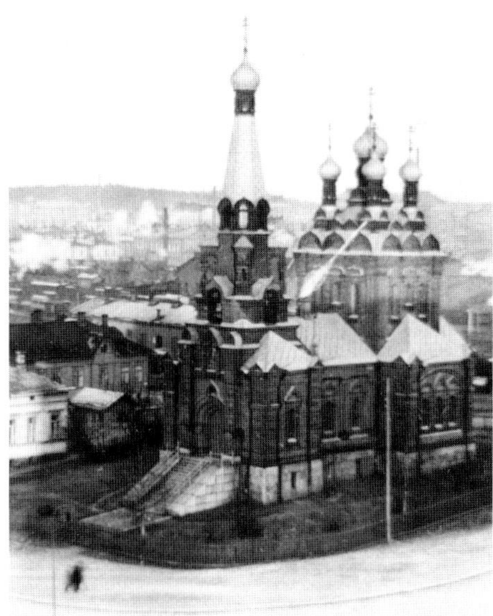

Figure. 26. Eastern Orthodox Church, Tampere, 1932. Photo courtesy of Tampere City Museum

tion. Once the nation had achieved a measure of economic security, isolation had naturally given way to a tremendous hunger for greater international contacts. The younger generation now freely indulged their long suppressed desire to try modern forms of expression which they had only heard about or experienced second-hand in reproductions. With the easing of travel restrictions, many artists were able to go abroad to study and to gain firsthand familiarity with the most recent developments. Several large exhibitions of art from France in the early 1950s also proved an important source of inspiration for Finnish artists.[9]

In a conservative society, such sudden and overwhelming exposure to modern ideas did not also mean immediate acceptance. In fact, the primary public reaction to imported modernism was one of dismay and rejection. The polemics of the time, as recorded in the popular press throughout the 1950s, reflect an incessant furor over "new-fangled ideas." At the very least, these exhibitions sparked a necessary debate between the small band of would-be reformers and the powerful conservative forces within the Finnish cultural establishment.

Although the general public regarded abstract art as alien and "incomprehensible," and resented its alarmingly radical approach, the young were attracted precisely to its liberating, radical quality. By the mid-1950s abstract entries had begun to dominate all the Salon exhibitions in Finland, nowhere more conspicuously than at the Young Artists' annual shows.[10]

♦

Like most of his contemporaries, Kaivanto watched the international art trends of the 1950s with great interest. With few opportunities to participate in the international arena, Finnish artists embraced the predominant ideas from other shores more enthusiastically, if somewhat uncritically. As we have seen, Kaivanto had already experimented with non-figurative elements, and one might say that for a while he was even swept up by the fashionable abstract styles. But as we shall see, his deep emotional commitment to physical reality would never quite permit him to make a complete break with figurative content. This ultimately proved to be his liberation from the tyranny of prevailing and changing fashions which enmeshed so may Finnish artists.

◆

If Finland was unreceptive to abstract trends in painting during the 1950s, there was a sea change in attitude by the early 1960s. Finnish scholars consider this a time when Finnish art "caught up" with art movements abroad. Considering Finland's long cultural isolation mentioned earlier, this urge to measure up to the rest of the world was understandable enough. But this attitudinal shift was not as abrupt and arbitrary as it might appear. The philosophical underpinnings of abstract painting as articulated in Europe under the rubric of Art Informel (referred to as "Informalism" in Finland) during the late 1950s and the early 1960s, had found a resonance in the Finnish temperament. This explanation may seem obvious to the Finns and somewhat simplistic to outsiders, but it has been a subject of intense discussion and debate in the Finnish art world. Although we should be wary of generalizations, it is nonetheless important to take into account what was in the air at that time. Having participated in numerous panel discussions about this issue, the author can testify to a prevailing general consensus among Finnish artists and historians that the national temperament, or collective psyche, often determines why certain influences take root in a culture while others fall by the wayside. Soili Sinisalo's observations in this regard are particularly acute:

In Finland, Informalism's attraction was perhaps based on the need for liberation and the movement's seductive radiation of primitive force. Informalism represented some mystical and lyrical tendencies that a Finn could identify with on the basis of earlier periods of Expressionism or even much older, historical movements. So it was quite natural to join the new movement through which one also hoped to move from isolation to international interaction.[11]

The indisputable fact is that this new trend swept over Finland with a numbing force in 1961 and 1962. The first sign that something new was afoot came in reports on Informalism filed from the Venice Biennale in 1960. For

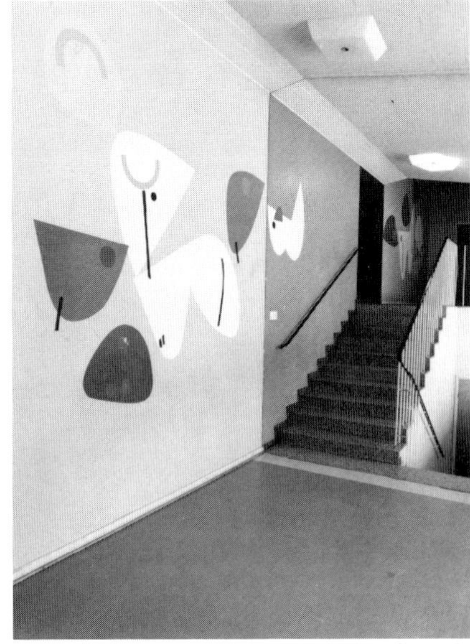

Figure. 27. Kimmo Kaivanto. *Our Friends*, 1960, alkyd paint on plaster, 110-1/4 × 472-1/2" (280 × 1200 cm). Saukonpuisto Elementary School, Tampere

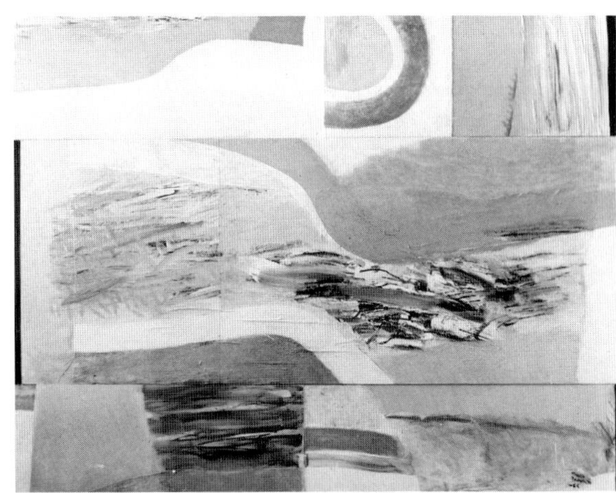

Figure. 28. Kimmo Kaivanto. *Summer Pictures*, 1966, oil on canvas, 98-1/2 × 118-1/8" (250 × 300 cm). Pellervo School, Tampere

a time, the Venice Biennale was the only forum where Finnish art was shown regularly alongside work by leading figures in international contemporary art.[12] It was one of the few events frequented by Finnish artists and copiously covered by the Finnish press. At home, Finland's first real exposure to international contemporary art came through the exhibition *Ars 61*, where foreign Informalists were well represented, while the Finnish participants were chosen from among less radical groups.[13] The 1962 triennial of the Finnish Academy of Fine Arts, however, was completely dominated by the Informalists.[14] That same year, Finnish Informalism could also be seen at many gallery exhibitions, and the Informalist boom had arrived in full force.

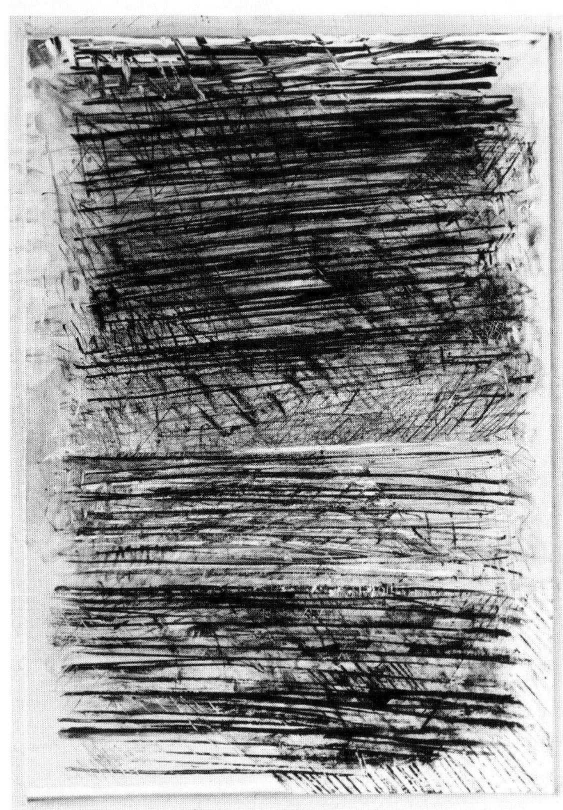

Figure. 29. Kimmo Kaivanto. *Maritime Incidents*, 1967, oil on canvas, 68-1/8 × 49-5/8" (173 × 126 cm). Collection Sara Hildén Art Museum, Tampere

Kaivanto was among the leading Finnish painters to make a serious contribution to this trend, although, as he said in a 1982 interview, he never accepted the Informalist label:

I'm regarded as a typical Informalist of the sixties, but I don't see myself as one at all. [To me] the whole idea of Informalism was to start painting without knowing its outcome. I always knew from the beginning what I wanted to achieve.[15]

Kaivanto's definition is perhaps more applicable to the offshoots of Informalism, namely Spontanism and Tachism. It is nonetheless debatable how many Finnish Informalists (or others for that matter) followed the ideology articulated by Kaivanto. For most Finnish artists working in the Informalist mode, the picture-making process was a planned and goal-oriented activity, in the course of which they utilized free-association techniques to achieve pictorial effects that were often linked to experiences of nature.[16]

Kaivanto's "Informalism" was, nonetheless, a decisive step towards an idiom that was to prove useful in many other connections. Through the use of free, almost automatic brush strokes, he created pictures that were substantially different from his earlier paintings, yet just as effectively conveyed his impression of nature in Finland. In 1962, Kaivanto, an inveterate city dweller, acquired a summer house on Arkkusaari Island in Ruovesi at the northern edge of Lake Näsijärvi: his experience of nature here, in what is perhaps the most romantic part of Finland, began to take on an increasing importance in his painting.

◆

Landscape has been an enduring subject matter in art, but it is questionable whether its importance has been matched anywhere outside the Nordic countries. Finland's vast wilderness, dramatized by the changing seasons, is certainly an important reason why landscape figures so prominently in Finnish art. Few people outside Scandinavia appreciate that during the "white nights" of high summer, it is possible to sit by the window and read a book by natural light the whole night long. Or that during the dark, icy days of our sunless winter, only the ubiquitous blanket of snow provides a semblance of light. Even though many Finnish artists studied and traveled abroad as far back as the 19th century, first in Germany and later in Italy and France, it was always their work based on nature in Finland that had earned them their most important success. In recent years, Mediterranean France, Italy, and Spain have also attracted many Finnish painters and significantly influenced their art. But very rarely have they been successful at home with work based on foreign themes. It was precisely this visual formulation of their unique concept of nature that inspired national pride in a country which did not think of itself as a nation until the mid-nineteenth century, and did not become a nation-state until 1917. During the nationalist period of the 1930s and 1940s, many Finns considered all foreign–particularly French–influences on Finnish art to be fundamentally undesirable, and strove, sometimes successfully, to combat international trends.[17]

When abstract movements began to make inroads into Finnish art, it was natural for many artists to turn to themes from nature for their abstractions. Their work now stressed color and light rather than form, since nature in Finland posed different problems from the more struc-

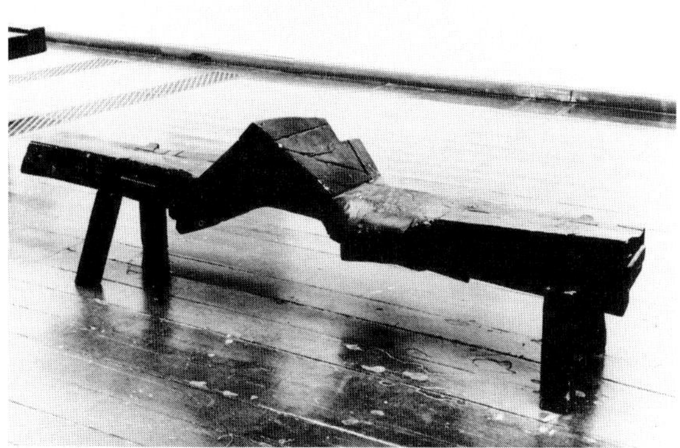

Figure. 30. Mauno Hartman. *The Bench*, 1965, wood, 19-5/8 × 78-3/4 × 15-3/4" (50 × 200 × 40 cm). Collection of The Museum of Contemporary Art, Helsinki

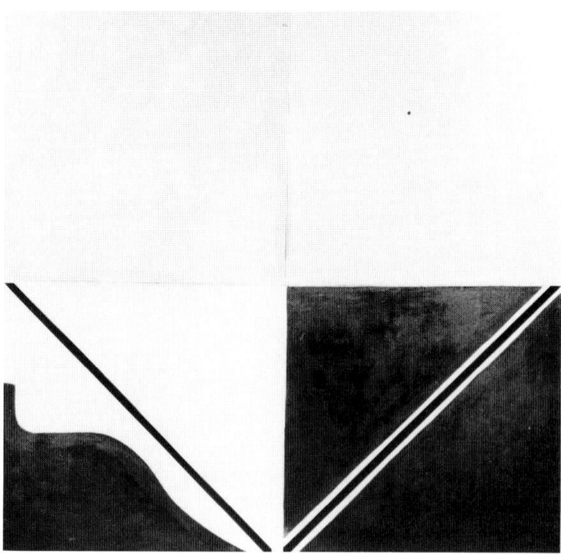

Figure. 31. Ahti Lavonen. *Red Square with Diagonal*, oil on canvas, 1968, 74-3/4 × 74-3/4" (190 × 190 cm)

tured landscape of southern and central Europe. The emphasis was no longer on nature itself, with trees and mountains and watercourses, but rather on nature's more abstract–and thus perhaps more universal–characteristics. This approach seems to have particularly suited Kaivanto's temperament, and the spontaneous abstract idiom remained an important element in his work for more than half a decade.

In paintings done between 1962 and 1967 the artist described his intense experiences of nature with great precision: the light over a bay in summer; a gathering thunderstorm; the sun's reflection on snow under a willow scrub; a cloud that touches the surface of the lake in the distance; stones seen through clear water.[18] In one instance, *Afternoon in Viale Trieste*, 1966, there was even a foreign theme: a view of Venice, showing the way light strikes when one emerges from the shadows of the greenery around the Biennale park (Plate 15). But the exotic element, barely decipherable from a few details, is not particularly conspicuous. Actually, the painting could also be interpreted as a Nordic color vision on an unusually bright summer day.

Maritime Incidents, 1967 demonstrates the dualistic character of Kaivanto's work (fig. 29). On the one hand he is an Expressionist striving to convey a powerful emotional experience; on the other, a classicist aspiring to a painstakingly-rendered and richly finished painting.[19] The two approaches are obviously irreconcilable, and at first glance the Expressionist seems to gain the upper hand. The whole is a cascade of marks made by the spontaneous and chance movements of the artist's brush. Not until the eye registers the representational aspect and

deciphers the sea as a reflecting surface under a sky covered with rain clouds, with a strip of sunlight far off on the horizon, does one note the deliberate composition. The experience is further intensified by the fact that the canvas is laid down on a larger board, and the painting's linear structure extends beyond the canvas. Kaivanto later used this relief method to create a number of works which straddle the boundary between painting and sculpture. It is such conscious pre-visualization of a painting that leads Kaivanto to dissociate himself from the Informalist ideology. The response that *Maritime Incidents* gradually evokes in the viewer corresponds precisely with the experience of nature Kaivanto intended to convey.

Just as some of his works originate in his observation of nature, the process and the medium also serve as sources of inspiration. In a note about his painting during the 1960s, he wrote:

When I progress on the surface of the picture line by line into the distance, I experience them [the pictures] as "expeditions" of a kind, sailing trips into the infinite. They often look like seascapes, but I am not sure whether in the final analysis nature is always the point of departure.[20]

This methodology, of course, seems to echo that of the Informalists. But perhaps it is just a question of a shift in emphasis. Each artist works in a continual dialogue with his medium. From Kaivanto's more-or-less spontaneously drawn lines a vision of the sea suddenly appears. And then, at this stage of the work, the concrete memory-picture of his experience of nature emerges: this is just how the sea looked at that time and at that place. And then the rest of the work becomes a realization of the par-

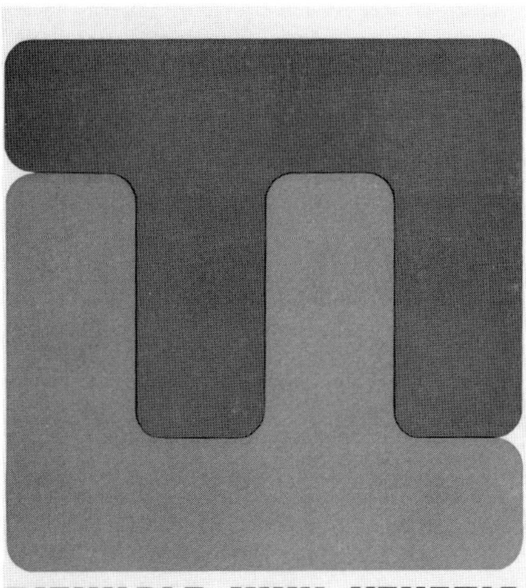

Figure. 32. Back cover, Finland's 1968 Venice Biennale catalogue designed by Kaivanto (A.67)

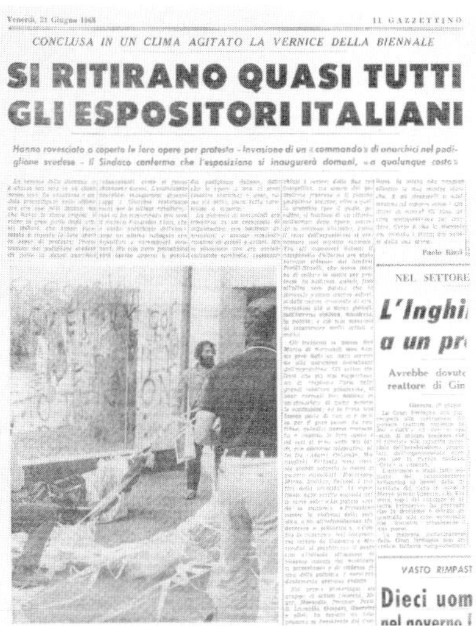

Figure. 33. Italian newspaper report on the opening of Venice Biennale. Headline reads: The Biennale's opening ends in agitation: Almost all the Italian participants withdraw, *Il Gazzettino*, 21 June 1968

ticular visual impression that the picture itself coaxes out from the memory's recesses.

◆

As early as 1962, Kaivanto had made his first sculpture, a relatively simple, helmet-like form resembling the upper half of a human skull. The artist later developed this helmet-skull theme in a series of objects of biting political satire. Among the simplest, and perhaps the most ironic, is *Smiling Killer*, 1965-68 (Plate 25), made from two helmets stuck together, the opening between them creating the impression of a satanic smile. Conceived in 1965, it was not completed until 1968, the year of a profound upheaval in attitude for the artist.

Until then, Kaivanto had worked the way most artists do: keeping abreast of the art world, imbibing impressions and influences from teachers and colleagues, looking at other artists' work, and generally groping his way to a personal idiom. And he had succeeded fairly well: in many ways he was able to consider himself an established painter, and the critical and commercial success he enjoyed was not insignificant. He had also received and executed a number of public commissions, thereby acquiring a feel for both the monumental scale, and a work's ability to reach out and affect the viewer in a context outside of the museum, art gallery or salon. He had, in fact, honed these communicative skills through years of working as a successful graphic designer and an advertising artist. His art had taken on a new energy, combined with a technical perfection that was viewed as characteristic of "ad art" in some quarters. But even those who derided his background in commercial art could not help being envious of his ability to reach the public through accessible idioms and images.

Kaivanto belongs to the generation of Finns whose childhood was spent amidst the privations and political uncertainties of World War II and its aftermath, but who were too young to assume an active role in the events that affected their lives. By the 1960s, this generation was entering what would normally be the most productive period in a person's life. Many of the prominent leaders of the student revolt of the sixties belonged to his generation, although the crowds they led mostly consisted of the post-war generation. It is not inconceivable that the anti-bourgeois and anti-establishment sentiments that led to widespread student unrest around the world in the 1960s were fueled by their bitter childhood memories.

Finland's political insularity and geographic isolation has always made the country slow to react to world events. While the 1968 Czech uprising, the so-called Prague Spring, with all its implications, was widely discussed in Finland, it was uncommon for Finnish artists to respond to such a world event through their art. Kaivanto, however, found himself in the midst of it ahead of most of his colleagues. For 1968 was also the year of the Venice Biennale where he was one of three artists chosen to represent Finland along with the sculptor Mauno Hartman (b. 1930) and the painter Ahti Lavonen (1928-1970) (figs. 30, 31). By the time the exhibition opened in June, the student revolts had spread, first to Paris and Milan, where violent clashes with the police had already made headlines, and finally to Venice. For Kaivanto, the experience was like waking up from a deep sleep. View-

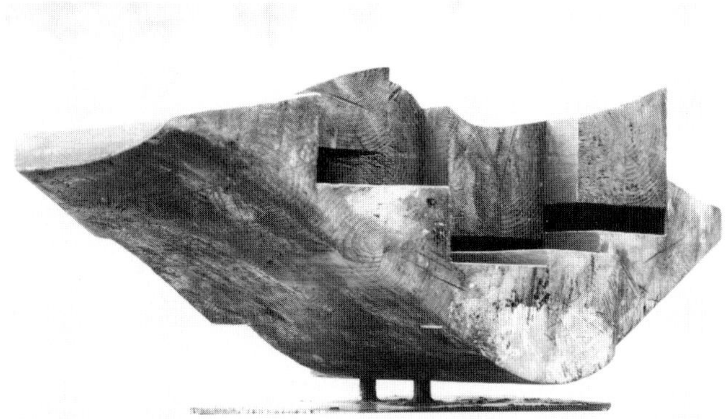

Figure. 34. Kimmo Kaivanto. *Underground Town*, 1964, wood, 10-1/4 × 26-3/8 × 17-3/8" (26 × 67 × 44 cm). Collection of Tampere University

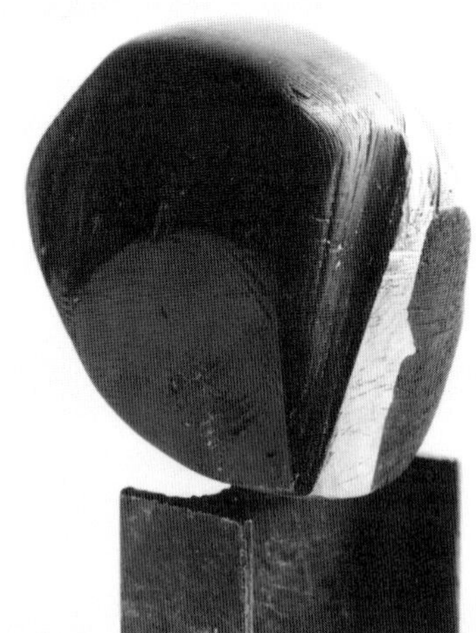

Figure. 35. Kimmo Kaivanto. *Heretic*, 1964, tin and wood, 13-7/8 × 5-7/8 × 7-1/8" (35.5 × 15 × 18 cm). Collection of Sara Hildén Art Museum, Tampere

ing his own work in this atmosphere of heated exchange between demonstrating youths and police armed to the teeth, in a time when ruthlessness and brutality were pitted against exalted commitment, left him feeling that he had been "building castles in the air." As he later described the experience, "It felt quite ridiculous to be showing my aesthetic and lyrical paintings when people were carrying hand grenades in the streets."[21]

The work he had taken to show in Venice represented his "Informalist" period and its extension, a combination of free forms and carefully delineated surfaces with which he had begun to experiment around the mid-1960s. He represented a country where pictorial art had lived in intense proximity to international developments for at least the past decade, and he felt confident that he was working in an international idiom. Here, in Venice, where art people from all corners of the world met, he had nothing to be ashamed of. He had also designed an effective cover for the exhibition catalogue which the Finnish committee for the Venice Biennale had published for its three represented artists (fig. 32).[22] The cover design was based on two entwined forms representing the letter "F," one as green as a Nordic summer meadow or a spring birch forest, the other blue, like the sky high up in the zenith on a sunny Nordic day. But in Venice, where the exhibition pavilions were closed in protest, and where artists and students chanted and yelled and demonstrated everywhere in this numbingly beautiful city, this exercise in aesthetics and art based on meditative communion with nature unfortunately struck a false note (fig. 33). This discordance was further sharpened by the fact that Kaivanto's two Finnish colleagues likewise represented the same internationally correct but slightly passé aestheticism: Hartman with his lofty constructions of beautifully patinated pine logs, and Lavonen with abstract pictorial creations that were a kind of wintery parallel to Kaivanto's summery visions.

This was a decisive turning point in Kimmo Kaivanto's artistic career. It forced him to reconsider his own work in a different light, and he knew he had to respond to the human condition, to the larger world he inhabited, a different world whose hitherto unknown dimensions were revealed to him that year in Venice.

The work he produced in the uneasy months after his return still had that old lyrical tone, but it was fighting a difficult battle. One can view these paintings as fish floundering on dry land. At the same time, these last "castles-in-the-air" paintings strike a pathetic• note, showing that the dreamy and subjectively lyrical elements were too deeply imbedded in Kaivanto's Finnish soul. The transformation which was now to take place pushed these characteristics aside, though only temporarily.

But soon his painting took on the style which has been recognized as typically "Kaivantoan": symbol-charged, technically impeccable, stylistically representational yet often Surrealistic in content. For the first time he was able to combine all his skills to produce works of great insight and beauty. From an eclectic seeker, as most artists are during their formative years, he now became an innovative picture-maker who had attained a pictorial idiom at once personal and universal. He had stopped seeking: he had found.

Kaivanto's work after returning from Venice was not as radical or divorced from his earlier quests as it might

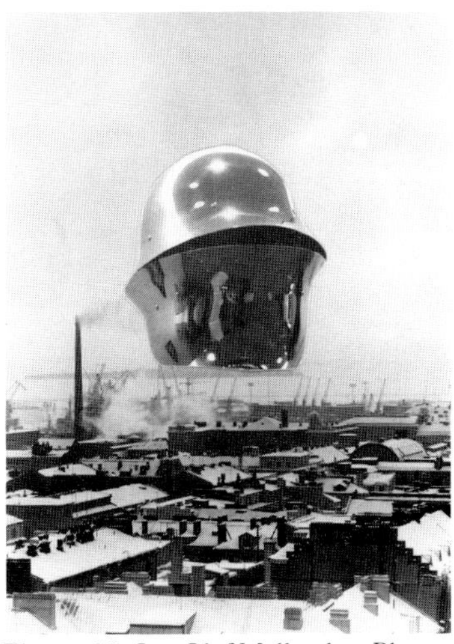

Figure. 36. Jan-Olof Mallander. Photomontage, 1969, 8-1/2 × 6-1/4" (21.8 × 15.9 cm). Collection of Kimmo Kaivanto

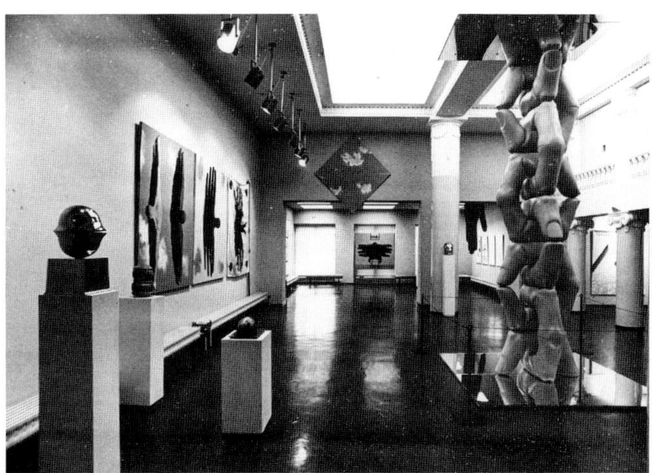

Figure. 37. Installation view of Kaivanto's exhibition, *Fingers at Play*, Amos Anderson Art Museum, Helsinki, 1971

appear. As early as 1962, he had made his first sculpture, *Militarist*, 1962 (Plate 11), employing a theme to which he would return after witnessing the violent clashes of 1968. During the next few years, two others works with a similar theme followed: *Underground Town*, 1964 and *Heretic*, 1964 (figs. 34, 35). Created in response to the Cuban missile crisis of 1962 and the subsequent escalation of the Cold War, they bear witness to Kaivanto's sensitive reactions to world events. The same sensitivity forced him to turn his back on his earlier production and come to grips with an idiom which, when first shown in the winter of 1969, proved admirably suited to the course on which he had now embarked.

If Kaivanto the Expressionist had dominated his Informalist period, it was now the technical perfectionist who rose to the fore. Kaivanto claims that he actually enjoyed the rigors of this precisionist style, which he viewed as a kind of protest against the prevailing predilection for "painterly qualities."[23] But the Expressionist still lurked in the background, for an uncontrollable urge to cry out with horror lies behind these impeccably conceived and well crafted pictures. However, Kaivanto also understood that the unarticulated scream is not an effective mode of communication. More sophisticated means were obviously needed, and they were provided by his long experience in the advertising world. When it comes to satire, there is hardly anything in Nordic art that can match Kaivanto's work of the late 1960s and early 1970s. The symbols of seductive beauty found in militarism and the destructive forces of nature, juxtaposed against the humanism and gentleness of nature as Kaivanto sees it, serve as archetypal symbols for our time.

In February 1969, Kaivanto opened a small show of thirty-six serigraphs and objects at Galerie Artek in Helsinki. At the Finnish Artists' Association's annual exhibition, simultaneously in progress at the Helsinki Art Hall, the artist was showing his more familiar works: large, simple abstracts with atmospheric interpretations of nature in an Informalist style. The Artek exhibit, titled *Other Pictures and Objects* presented something completely different. The unorthodox artist-critic, Jan-Olof Mallander's penetrating review of the show was illustrated with one of Mallander's own photomontages which spoke of the power of Kaivanto's new work in a way no words could express (fig. 36).[24] The collage was a kind of visual proposal for public monuments to be scattered around Helsinki. There on a skerry, beyond the city's snow-covered roofs and construction cranes, Mallander had Kaivanto's menacingly magnificent *Smiling Killer* dominating the landscape.

The late sixties were a time of great upheaval not only for Kaivanto, but for the Finnish art scene as a whole. Typically, for a country which has always been slow to react to the outside world, Informalism had been succeeded by many different trends, although belatedly. Super-realism and Pop Art were mixed with new European influences including Realitées Nouvelles from France and the British version of Pop art, which was then viewed as a variation of American Pop. Little, if any, of the work in these styles could be seen in the original in Finland. Although Stockholm's Moderna Museet had mounted a few influential exhibitions, information came mostly from art journals.[25] Other voices were also beginning to be heard in the art world: Happenings were all the rage, and

Conceptual art was gaining acceptance. There was the hippie movement with its flower power, accompanied by a renaissance of Oriental philosophies of various persuasions. The influential Cheap Thrills Gallery, which would later become a major vehicle for these new international trends, did not come into existence until 1971.[26]

Kaivanto's little show at Artek was followed two years later by a major retrospective, *Fingers at Play*, at Helsinki's Amos Anderson Art Museum (fig. 37). In his catalogue text, the artist announced a clear change of course, but also added that "perhaps tomorrow I will once again embark on my sea of canvas in order to seek new horizons towards which to sail."[27] This was Kaivanto's characteristic way of protecting himself: no matter how accusingly his finger points, he also leaves a way open for forgiveness. Despite everything, he cannot give up hope for mankind.

The exhibition received an overwhelming response. It could not have come at a more opportune moment: Finnish cultural circles were ready to receive and to applaud his impressively executed pictures and to refute their accusations. And that is precisely what the critics did: they applauded Kaivanto's excellent technique, his brilliantly expressed opinion, but they did not by any means accept any guilt. The Left cried out that Kaivanto did accuse someone, but did not openly identify the guilty party. The Right saw his social commitment as proof that the Finnish cultural world was dominated by left-wing radicals. Here again, they said, is an artist who has been subverted by political propaganda. Mallander also made an attempt to find cracks in Kaivanto's position. Although still almost unreservedly supportive, he came to the conclusion that Kaivanto's success derived from an open acknowledgment of his conflict. In a review headlined "Goldfinger's Forefinger: The Anatomy of a Conflict," he described the exhibition as "certainly one of the most important in Finland in the past five years."[28] He characterized Kaivanto's new style as "realism with a sense of guilt," but was evidently impressed by the artist's struggle with his conscience. His production is "true, beautiful, and cruel in its hopeless vulnerability," Mallander wrote, and provided his own theses about conflict as a driving force in art:

Kaivanto experiences his situation as full of conflicts. He can no longer paint blueness and seas of light. The colors themselves remain, as does the soberness of the composition, but now they are only contained as elements of his concept, which is transformed towards figurativeness and an active struggle with his conflicts...For although making art purely by definition means

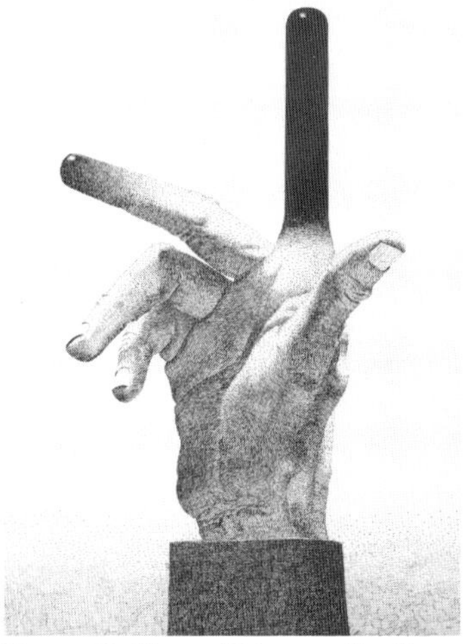

Figure. 38. Kimmo Kaivanto. *Forefinger*, 1969, serigraph, 34-5/8 × 24-3/4" (88 × 63 cm)

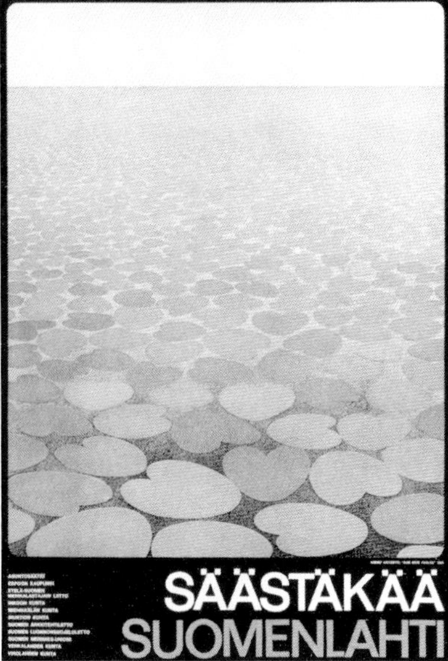

Figure. 39. Poster for the book, *Säästäkää Suomenlahti* (Save the Gulf of Finland), 1972, reproducing Kaivanto's painting, *When the Sea Dies*

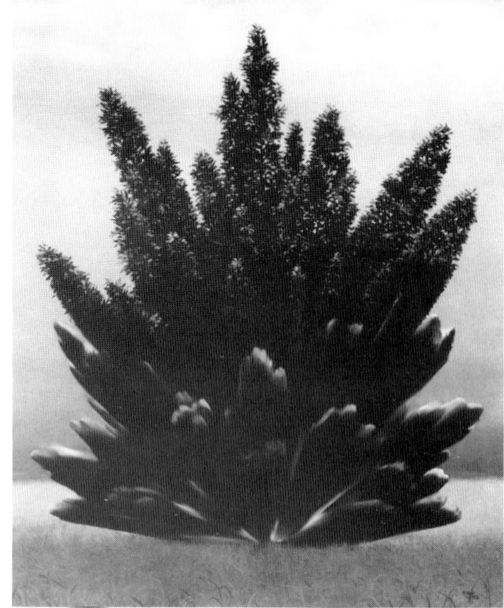

Figure. 40. Kimmo Kaivanto. *Silence*, 1973, oil on canvas, 76-3/4 × 63-3/4" (195 × 162 cm). Collection of Sara Hildén Art Museum

conflict with the absolute, that which is present in everything, then art is still the unique medium for solving this conflict. Art is still the best instrument man has for coming to grips with himself, making the invisible visible, making the subconscious conscious, and transforming it in practice in society in a more total and a truer way than any other activity.[29]

The very fact that this exhibition moved Mallander and others to lengthy discussions about the state and the function of art, and the artist's role in society, is an eloquent testament to Kaivanto's creativity. Markku Valkonen, another widely respected critic, began his review of the exhibition with an unusual general introduction:

Man's development began when he found that he was able to use nature, and since then everything has gone to hell. Man is a curious but destructive animal. He has a finger in the game everywhere. There are big and little fingers. The big fingers are aggressive, [and] prod nature, hav[ing] at the same time given it their little finger. Nature bites back. Now the whole hand is going, but the message of pain does not seem to have reached the brain.[30]

The finger theme attracted the most attention and caused reviewers to engage in verbal gymnastics. Kaivanto had also exploited his theme to the full. There were marching fingers, fingers as rolling swastikas and victory monuments. There were hands with outstretched fingers transformed into threatening birds or military uniforms with flapping sleeves hung over the backs of chairs. The fingers were often a symbol of power—as in the image where an erect forefinger is transformed into a billy club (fig. 38). But there were also fingers linked in hope-inspiring chains of cooperation. This chain of fingers reached its most monumental form in a sculpture Kaivanto was commissioned to make for the lobby of Helsinki's newly renovated City Hall. This work, unveiled in situ in January, 1972, was first exhibited here in 1971, when it was considered by many to be his most important work. And then there was perhaps the most concentrated but also the least tendentious of the finger ideograms: the *Blue Thinker* series exploring different media–gouache, serigraphy, and sculpture. Kaivanto rarely alludes to art history, but he does so here, so directly that the sculpture was given the title *Blue Thinker (Rodin Theme)*, 1971 (Plate 35).

If fingers were Kaivanto's metaphor for man's messy handling of world events,[31] a number of his other pictures became symbols of man-made ecological disasters. *When the Sea Dies I*, 1969 and its subsequent variations unequivocally deal with this theme. Eutrophication of small watercourses and shallow lakes was a burning ecological

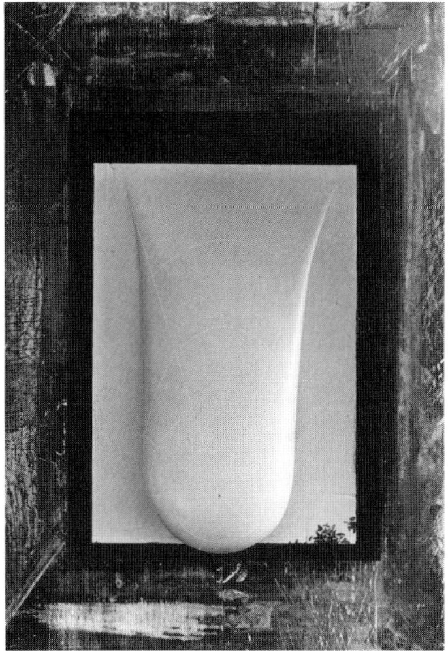

Figure. 42. Kimmo Kaivanto. *I Love Private Mornings*, 1968, painted wood relief, 20-1/2 × 14-7/8 × 1-7/8" (52 × 38 × 5 cm). Collection of Kaija Junnila

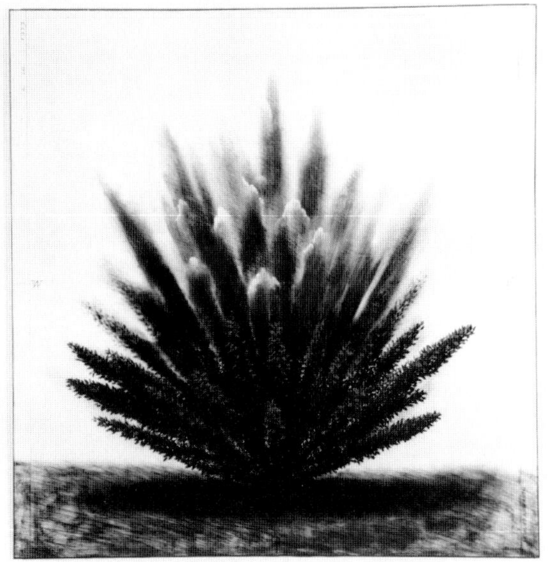

Figure. 41. Kimmo Kaivanto. *Supergrowth*, 1973, oil on canvas, 76-3/4 × 76-3/4" (195 × 195 cm). Private collection

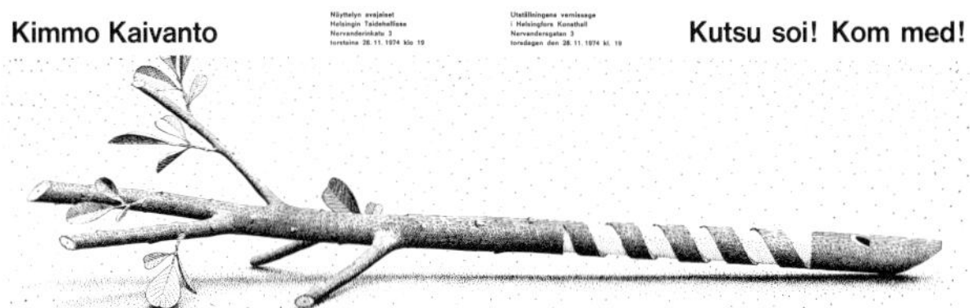

Figure. 43. Invitation to the opening of Kaivanto's one-person exhibition at the Helsinki Art Hall, 28 Nov. 1974

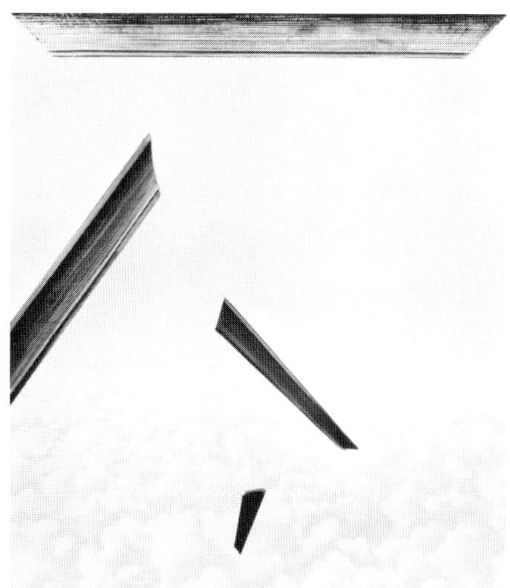

Figure. 44. Kimmo Kaivanto. *Immoral Landscape*, 1970, oil on canvas, 63-3/4 × 55-1/8" (162 × 140 cm). Collection of the artist

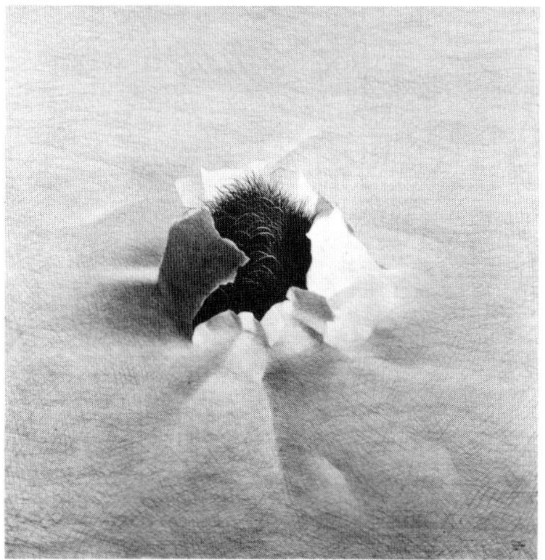

Figure. 45. Kimmo Kaivanto. *Optimistic Mistake*, 1974, oil on canvas, 63-3/4 × 63-3/4" (162 × 162 cm). Collection of Sara Hildén Art Museum, Tampere

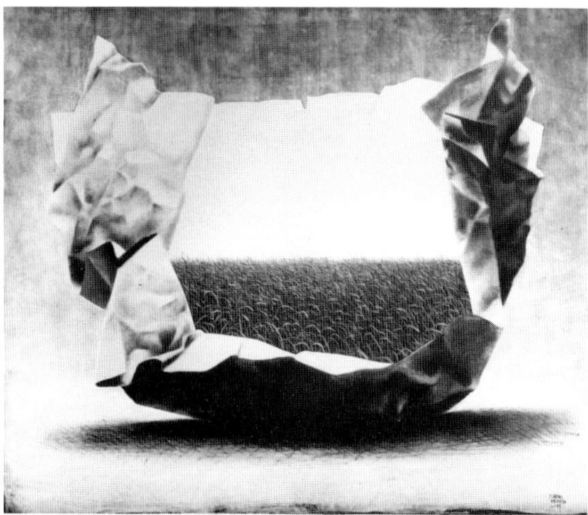

Figure. 46. Kimmo Kaivanto. *Parcel on Ice*, 1973, oil on canvas, 63-3/4 × 76-3/4" (162 × 195 cm). Collection of Sara Hildén Art Museum, Tampere

issue in Finland during the late 1960s. Kaivanto elevated the theme to an apocalyptic level by extending it to a much larger body of water, the sea. To a Finn, the "sea" means the Baltic Sea, that brackish body of water whose only release into the great oceans of the world is through the Danish Straits. The ecological balance of this sea is extremely delicate, and major changes were beginning to be registered at this time in several shallow bays whose gradual overgrowth was attributed to the constant rising of the land along the Baltic coast. *When the Sea Dies* thus became an icon for many environmental protests throughout Scandinavia, and was reproduced in millions of copies (fig. 39).[32]

Kaivanto returned to the theme of environmental conservation in a major 1974 exhibition at the Helsinki Art Hall. Now the negative forces were counterbalanced by positive ones, demonstrating that the artist had recovered from the shock of 1968, and that the old nature-lover, humanist, and optimist-lyricist had regained the upper hand. But the means were still the same: effective pictorial ideas executed with superb technical control, and terse, finely honed, aphoristic form.

But depicting the anatomy of destruction still played an important role, for example in *Silence*, wherein a mushroom cloud takes the form of a verdant bush (fig. 40). Origins of this motif have been noted in a war game with paper figures Kaivanto had made at the age of nine.[33] Between paper soldiers and paper tanks he placed explosions made of crumpled paper, giving the scenery an authentic look. The nine-year-old was, after all, living in a country in conflict, and war was the primary topic of discussion. War games have interested children in peace time, so why shouldn't they in times of war? Many drawings with war motifs have also been found among the papers preserved from Kaivanto's childhood. Strangely enough, there was even one that seems to incorporate a dream of peace, where verdant trees grow out of cannons and the smokestacks of warships. This sketch thus appears to have been the early seed of the visions of the forty-year-old artist: the mushroom cloud transformed into a bush with living, green leaves. But war is not the only evil that destroys the world and its inhabitants; in peace, the world is confronted by a new threat from mankind. In what might be described as a reverse version of the same theme, *Supergrowth* depicts a bush that becomes a mushroom cloud (fig. 41).

His two major exhibitions of 1971 and 1974—versions of each traveled to other venues throughout Finland—also contained images of optimism. *I Love Private Mornings*, first shown in his 1969 Artek show, embraced two themes which the artist had developed in numerous paintings and objects: the female breast and the globe (fig. 42). The globe was depicted in many tragic roles, at times tied up and suffocating, at times growing into a grotesque figure with wildly gesticulating or truncated limbs. (One of these pieces from 1968 bears the title *Globulus Hystericus*–a play on the medical term, *globus hystericus*, for the hysterical sensation of a lump in the throat). It was sometimes realized as a pear-shaped punching bag, or compressed into a sharp-edged cube. Female breasts, by contrast, are shown growing out of flowering poppy fields, as in *Morning*, 1972 (Plate 43). In another highly captivating and simultaneously thought-provoking work, *Touch*, 1969 (Plate 26), Kaivanto contrasts the soft sensuality of breasts with the hardness of stone, creating a sculpture which appeals directly to emotions deeply rooted in the psyche.

Another theme with positive connotations was the willow whistle, a humble wind instrument children fashion themselves out of willow twigs in the spring. Since the willow is known for its ability to put out roots and begin to grow again, Kaivanto's simple flute also embodies a firm belief in the power of survival. This picture of the twig, cut and worked with its green shoots intact, has an everyday credibility not found in the surrealistic greenery growing out of warships, and even less in the exploding bushes of its adult nightmare version (fig. 43).

Several authors have pointed to Kaivanto's links to Surrealism in the spirit of René Magritte.[34] The kinship might at times seem conspicuous, as in *Immoral Landscape*, where the painting's own frame seems to implode into a cloud-covered sky (fig. 44). For Kaivanto, such play on the tools of his trade has long provided a vocabulary with which he layers and heightens his pictorial metaphors. Paper, the most basic of artists' materials, provides the symbolic basis for his picture-games in works dating from 1974. Now it stands as a space shuttle ready for countdown, there it crashes ingloriously with its wings charred. Here it lands softly and is transformed into a verdant meadow, or again sails out over blue infinities until it becomes blueness itself. But the paper is also an artificial skull which is shattered by the mighty force of grass growing out from the earth. And paper is the container for such precious things as warmth, love, and unfettered nature (figs. 45, 46).

Other tools of the trade–the brush, masking tape–also become motifs and metaphors. A letter with text is transformed into a mirror-smooth evening sea. At times the painted blue line itself becomes both the symbol for a wound or a chasm, and the motif itself: what is being depicted is precisely a blue line, as in *Pathetic Mirror Picture*, 1972 (Plate 41).

◆

The period from autumn, 1968 to the exhibition at the Helsinki Art Hall at the end of 1974 was among the most productive in Kaivanto's life. It is as if pictures were born in a kind of storm of creation. One idea after another was developed and tested, not only in oil, but in gouache, prints, and even in three-dimensional form, all preceded by a seemingly endless pile of drawings and sketches.

Another characteristic of Kaivanto's work is his independence from artistic heroes or models, Finnish or foreign. To the extent that Kaivanto did find kindred spirits in art, they came later in life, and were always acknowledged with a shock of recognition.[35] His strongest driving force has come from his commitment and desire to participate in world events. But the same commitment which earned him critical accolades and public adulation at his exhibitions in 1969 and 1972, targeted him for attacks by the late 1970s when Finnish political life had became increasingly polarized. Political involvement, primarily left-wing, increased within Finnish cultural circles of the 1970. Interest was fixed on world events, dominated by the Vietnam War. But such one-dimensional political commitment did not suit Kaivanto's temperament; his protest was universal rather than issue-specific. And that brought an onslaught of criticism and negative appraisal of his work. Much later, he himself articulated his position:

I usually depicted these aspects as masks, gloves, boots, without personal features and individual characteristics. With my stereotypes I tried to protect man, so that the message would not be aimed at private individuals but rather at the system of violence created by man.[36]

The seventies were not a time for lyrical introspection in Finland. Kaivanto was accused of nostalgic subjectivism and romantic dreaming. Some people were especially affronted that he had chosen to place a battered wooden rowboat in the middle of an exhibition room at the Helsinki Art Hall in 1974 (fig. 47).[37] At a time when Finland's ancient craft of boat-building was in danger of dying out with the advent of metal, plastic, and fiberglass boats, the artist wanted to draw attention to the timeless qualities embodied in this lowly object: its organic construction material, the tradition of craftsmanship and an utterly functional design. But the sales pitch of the modern leisure-boat industry was based on freedom from the bothersome maintenance and care demanded by the traditional wooden boats. For Kaivanto, however, the boat also symbolized something else: the thoughtless junking of an entire culture. In an interview back in 1967, he had compared the artist's work to the construction of a boat:

The boat builder succeeds when the board does not split, and the completed boat exisits in a state of functioning equilibrium. A successful work of art also is in a state of equilibrium in which the external forms must be made to correspond to internal pictures.[38]

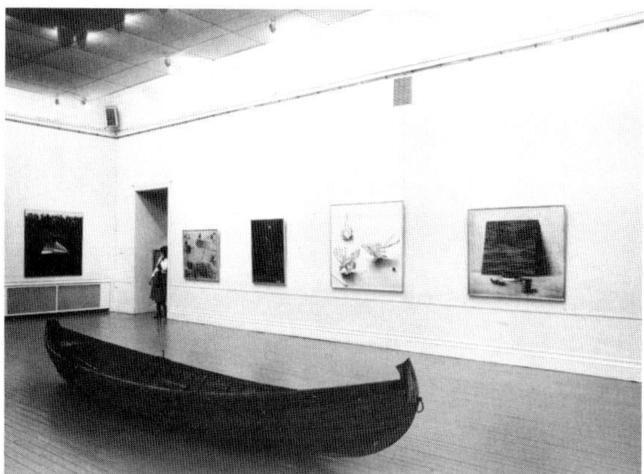

Figure. 47. Installation view of Kaivanto's one-person exhibition at the Helsinki Art Hall, 1974

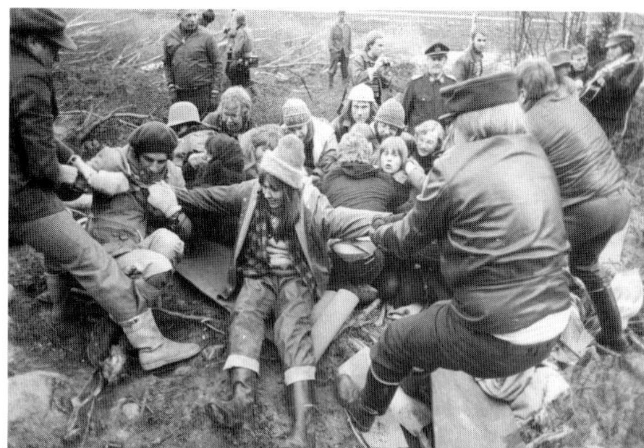

Figure. 48. Environmental protest at Koijärvi, 1979. Photo courtesy of Pressfoto, Helsinki

In 1974, Finnish public opinion was not yet mature enough for this kind of thinking. It would take until the end of the decade before the Green Movement got a proper foothold. The first major conservation protest in Finland was organized in 1979, when a group of young people chained themselves together in an attempt to prevent the dredging of Lake Koijärvi, an area in southern Finland known for its wildlife (fig. 48). A number of protesters were arrested and fined, but by 1983 "The Greens" had gained their first representation in the Finnish parliament, five years ahead of the official founding of the Green Party. The world for which Kaivanto wanted to win a hearing coincides in many respects with this Green ideology. It is characteristic, however, that Kaivanto refuses to join any specific interest group. His art is not in the service of any ideology; it just seeks to attract attention to dangerous trends. Perhaps Mallander was not far off the mark in his review of the 1974 exhibition when he called Kaivanto "the bad conscience of Finnish art."[39]

♦

Most observers would have expected Kaivanto to withdraw into a protective shell after such severe chastisement. Indeed, given Finland's small cultural circle, the criticism he endured must have hit particularly hard. And it is true that even though he remained active and participated in many exhibitions at home and abroad, including the 1976 Venice Biennale, his production seemed to shrink and the echo of his appearances through the first half of the decade gradually died out. But this was an illusion, for in reality his studio was seething with activity. Kaivanto was engaged in two major commissions that would have a decisive influence on his future development as an artist. One was a mural for the Tampere City Hall, commissioned to commemorate the city's bicentennial, and unveiled on October 3, 1976. The second was the stage design for *The Red Line*, an opera by Aulis Sallinen (b.1936), which premiered at Finland's National Opera in November 1978.[40]

In commissioning the City Hall mural from Tampere's native son, who had achieved unprecedented national and international recognition, the authorities had given the artist complete freedom to choose his own subject, style and medium. Kaivanto opted for a historical theme and depicted it with passion and professionalism. In the mid-1970s, one would have hardly expected a socially committed modern artist to create a historical panorama that left nothing to be desired when it came to concrete references to important events in the city's past. Despite its realistic style and figurative approach, which the artist had consciously chosen in order to make the work accessible to the public, the thirteen-part mural should be counted as one of the high points of the artist's achievements.

To create the mural, Kaivanto had moved in the spring of 1975 into a studio on the top floor of a turn-of-the-century building in Tampere's central square, as close as one can get to the absolute heart of the city. His windows overlooked the square which was the stage of numerous dramatic episodes in the history of the city, and he chose to call his mural *The Square* (fig. 49). Despite, or perhaps because of, its simple and sober compositional

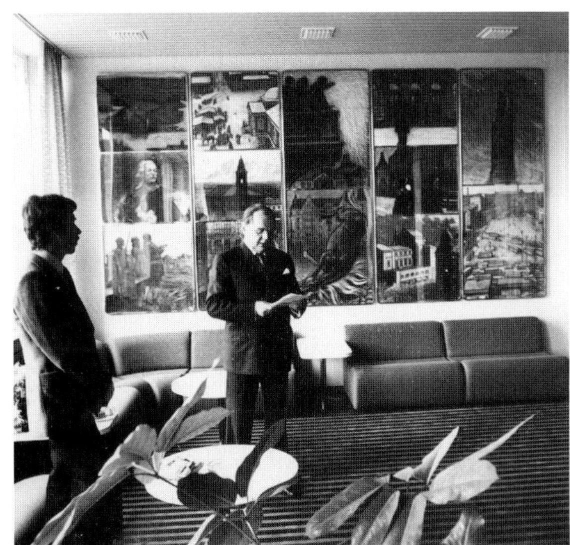

Figure. 49. Dedication ceremony for Kimmo Kaivanto's mural, *The Square*, Tampere City Council Chamber, 3 Oct. 1976. Kaivanto with City Council Chairman Vilho Halme

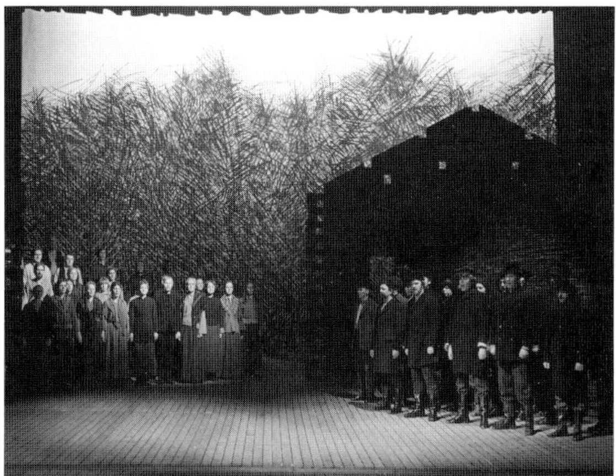

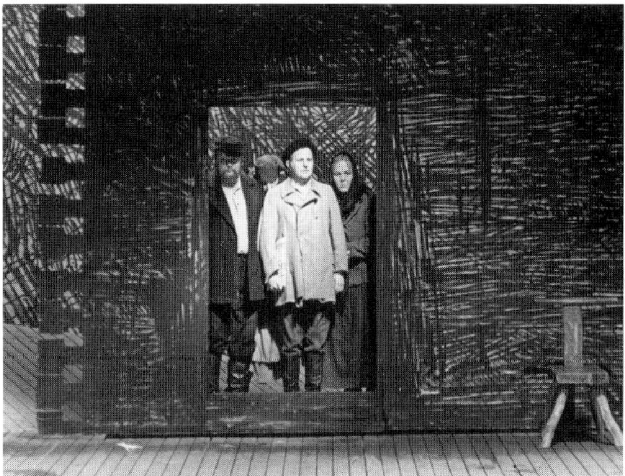

Figures. 50, 51. Premiere performance of *The Red Line* at the Finnish National Opera, Helsinki, 30 Nov. 1978

structure, each section is imbued with a grave intensity. The most poignant of them all is the central panel depicting a falling horse, clearly one of the innocent victims of the Civil War of 1918. The drama of this panel is intensified by the fact that the twelve other depictions are relatively static; not even the bustle of modern day traffic on the square, clearly sketched from his studio window, upstages its dynamism. But the deliberate and lingering quality of other panels conveys the full weight of historic events. The whole can best be described as a painterly equivalent of a monumental bronze.

The other major project during this period was the stage design for the opera *The Red Line*. Here, too, Kaivanto was forced to take into account important events in Finnish history. The opera, based on a novel by Ilmari Kianto (1874-1970), revolves around the first general parliamentary election in Finland in 1907, when socialism also won its first victory.[41] The impoverished people of Kianto's depiction were still a reality in many parts of the country right up to World War II, and the urban migration of poor peasants had a profound effect on the country's social structure in the 1950s and 1960s. Kaivanto was obliged to find an artistic idiom to suit the somber mood and the mammoth scale of the opera stage. Once again, he fell back on the drawn line. The graphic effect he achieved with his method proved highly suited to this purpose, even if there were certain problems in carrying out the work in practice, forcing him to attach brushes to the end of long sticks which, in a kind of weird ballet, he swung back and forth over the backdrops rolled out on the floor. Even though opera set designers are rarely accorded any special mention, it is clear that Kaivanto's black-and-

white set decorations contributed greatly to the success of this performance, not just on its home stage in Helsinki, but also at numerous performances abroad (figs. 50, 51).

These two commissions forced the artist out into unfamiliar territory and provided important stimulus to "sail towards new horizons," as he would have said. History painting–a genre thought to be anachronistic if not extinct–and stage design offered new challenges to a painter accustomed to an easel painting format. But these commissions did not offer any solutions by themselves. The artist had to find them on his own. And when he did, they provided him with pictures in a style which can be described as meditative realism. This stage in Kaivanto's development can be seen as one of thoughtful recreation, a pause before a new wave of activity around 1980 returned him to a period of dynamic easel painting.

Once again it was the Finnish landscape on his island of Arkkusaari in Ruovesi which provided both a rejuvenating private happiness and the inspiration and strength to

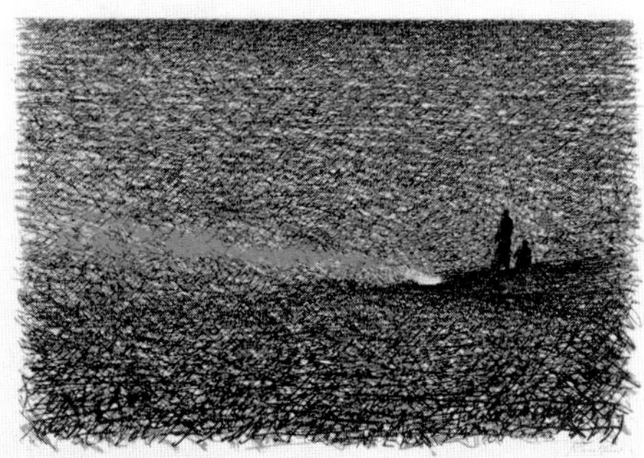

Figure. 52. Kimmo Kaivanto. *Eino Leino*, 1979, serigraph, 17-3/4 × 24-3/4" (45 × 63 cm)

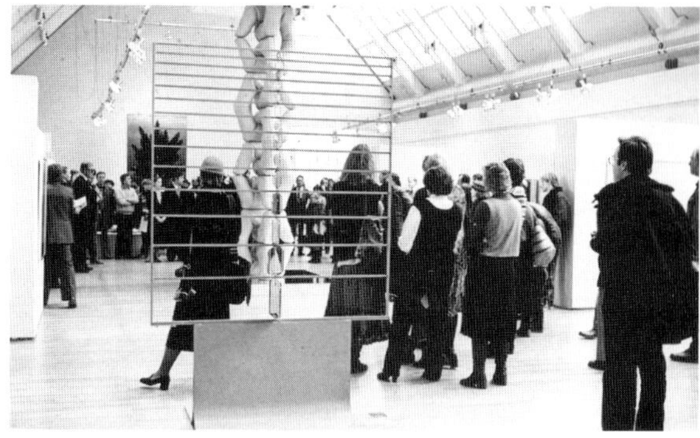

Figure. 54. At the opening of Kaivanto's retrospective exhibition at Södertälje konsthall, Sweden, 1981

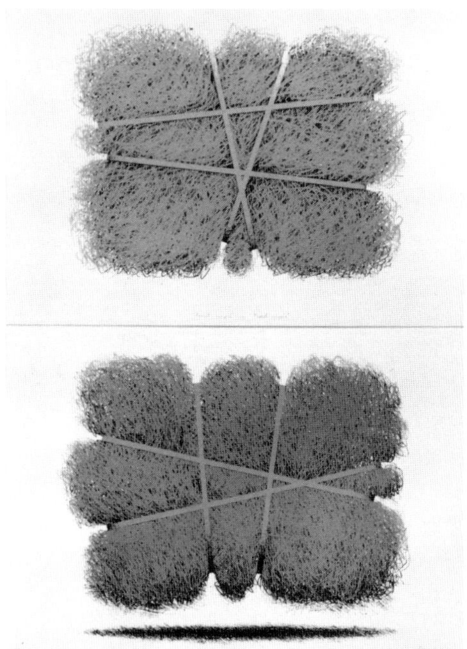

Figure. 53. Kimmo Kaivanto. *A Package of Love–A Package of Warmth*, 1981, serigraph, 55-1/8 × 39-3/8" (140 × 100 cm)

find new paths. His journal entry for August 6, 1977 reads: "Great things do not occupy my mind. It is just my prosaic loneliness which seeks security in the nearby trees and rocks. I want to decorate nature with flowing silken ribbons as a sign of mankind and love."[42] And once again he returned to the landscape. But now it was not the color and light that engaged him as they had in his Informalist years of the 1960s, but the relationship between man and nature. He had given much thought to this relationship while working on the stage sets for the opera, when he was forced to think about an interpretive approach unlike any he had encountered in easel painting. Towards the end of the 1970s, he settled on simplified realism, consciously shunning the exactitude of the photo-realist school. His

brush-strokes revived the graphic lightness that characterized his landscapes of the 1960s, and most of these works were conceived as serigraphs. They are often simple pictures of open water with a little islands here and there, at times with a couple of figures on the shore, at others with light shining from an opening between dark trees, a bonfire on the shore, or a bolt of lightning striking the highest point on one of the islands (fig. 52). They are conspicuously literary, his point of departure being a poem entitled "Nocturne" by Finland's most beloved lyricist, Eino Leino (1878-1926).[43] Parts of the text can be glimpsed in the dark waters of the picture, whose surface shimmers with criss-crossing lines from this poem. In a series of gouaches from the same time, the theme is the lonely, windswept island, doubtlessly a symbol of the artist's soul shaken and tossed by the storms of life. But the artist remains standing on its shore, and it is clear that he has found new peace after the stormy seventies. A large diptych entitled *A Package of Love–A Package of Warmth*, is a light play on words in Finnish (fig. 53).[44] Everything positive is put in a package, gently tied with knots that seem inviting and easy to untie. It seems to proclaim that even though the shell may be brittle, our inner peace gives it strength. Now things are under control: Kaivanto is once again ready to step out of his meditation chamber and get involved with the world around him, where all is not so gentle and beautiful.

◆

The decade of the 1980s began with a hectic schedule of exhibitions. In 1981 he was honored with a major retro-

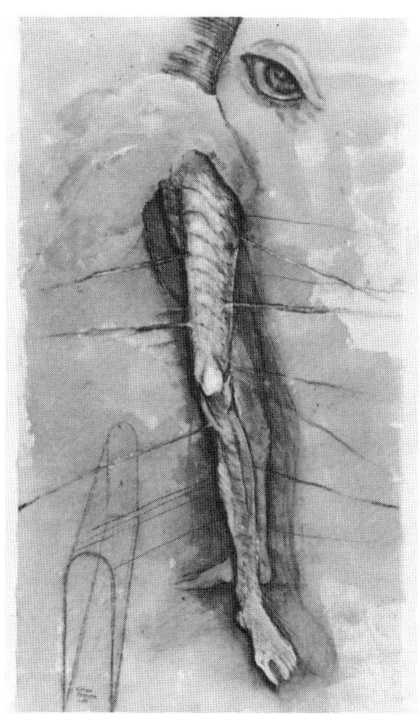

Figure. 55. Kimmo Kaivanto. *Saint Sebastian II*, 1988, acrylic on canvas, 76-3/8 × 47-1/4" (194 × 120 cm). Collection of Sara Hildén Art Museum, Tampere

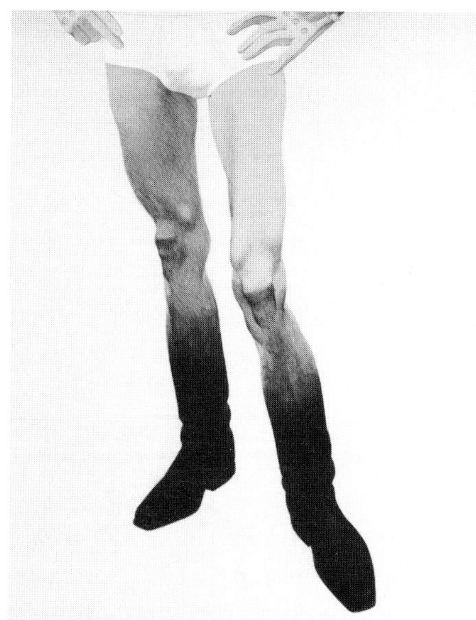

Figure. 56. Kimmo Kaivanto. *Grandson*, 1969, oil on canvas, 63-3/4 × 55-1/8" (162 × 140 cm). Collection of the artist

spective in the municipal art hall of Södertälje, a town thirty miles south of Stockholm (fig. 54). Here Kaivanto showed a number of new figurative works, mostly portraits of youths with lost facial expressions and starkly accented clothing. He had also explored the female nude, a classical theme in art in which he had hitherto shown no interest. As evidenced by notices in the Swedish press, the exhibition was exceptionally well received. This was particularly gratifying for Kaivanto; the usual Swedish reaction to Finnish art had always been friendly but condescending–the critical attitude of those who saw themselves as closer to the cultural power centers toward artists from small nations. Thus this exhibition ushered in the decade on a positive note, reminding Kaivanto of a previous occasion when Swedish art circles had also received him generously. Reviewing the large 1967 biennial of Nordic art at Stockholm's Liljevalch Art Gallery, the influential critic, Lars-Erik Åström, had singled out Kaivanto's work as "a very fine experience."[45] For Kaivanto, it was a much needed positive counterbalance to the vacillating critical attitudes at home.

The tempo of exposure quickened the following year: Kaivanto was chosen "Artist of the Year," invited to show at the 1982 Helsinki Festival; and the Sara Hildén Art Museum in his home town of Tampere was planning a major retrospective of his work. In addition, he also undertook to redesign the stage sets for *The Red Line* for its performance at the prestigious Savonlinna Opera Festival. As if that were not enough, a substantial monograph on the artist was also being published that year, and with customary care, Kaivanto himself helped produce it, assisting the authors, Soili Sinisalo and Jaakko Lintinen

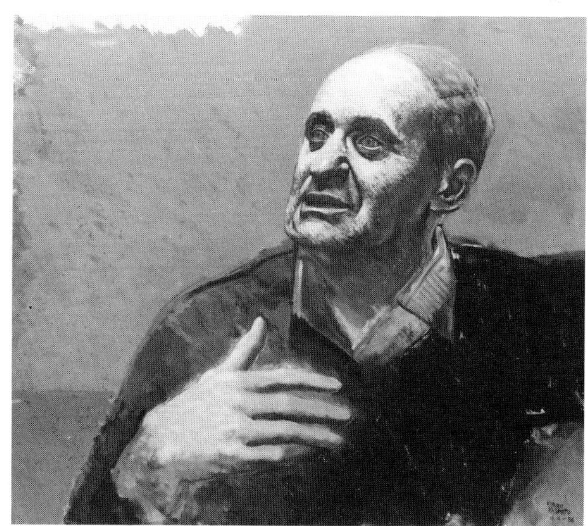

Figure. 57. Kimmo Kaivanto. *Portrait of Väino Linna*, 1986, Oil on canvas, 47-1/4 × 55-1/8" (120 × 140 cm). Collection of Tampere City

with research, selecting the illustrations, and designing the jacket and layout.[46]

Even as his two major exhibitions of 1981 and 1982 were providing a retrospective look at his career, Kaivanto was planning a change of course. This was particularly obvious in a new suite of paintings entitled *The Eyewitness of the Case* (Plate 46).[47] Arne Törnqvist provides an apt description of this enigmatic series:

The faces are naked, bewildered, without a history... already disillusioned and with incipient hardness. The padded jackets swell at the shoulders like puffed sleeves seen on depictions of the hopeful youths of the early Renaissance.[48]

That they are members of some youth gang is clear enough, but they are represented singly, as individuals, and just like individuals they are frightened, bewildered, defeated. In a moment of drama, their gang solidarity seems to have failed them; each has only himself to trust, and each suddenly realizes how little that is. Kaivanto has said that the idea for the series was born when he witnessed a street fight late one night in Tampere.[49] The idea took concrete shape when he saw subsequent confrontations between rival youth gangs and met vagrant Finns at Stockholm's main railway station. In spite of all the talk of social solidarity, it is still the individual that counts. Let the sea die; let battalions of oppressors march on. The situation does not become real to us until the artist lets us experience it through an individual. What the figure sees is not what is essential: it is how he experiences it. When I saw these pictures for the first time my thoughts went to a passage in the epic poem of space, *Aniara* by the Swedish poet Harry Martinson (1904-1978) in which a deaf man and a blind man recount their experience of the catastrophe which preceded their flight out into space.[50] The deaf man speaks of the worst sound he ever heard: it was not heard. The blind man talks of the horrible light which blinded him, and which he could not see. But, as the blind man adds in a chilling detail, he saw it with the back of his neck. Arne Törnqvist's final comment on the series is perhaps most fitting: "What kind of case is it we are witnessing? Perhaps only the future will give us the answer."[51]

In the final analysis, these images deal with man's innermost being. The quest seems to have shifted from dealing with the relationship between man and nature to man's relationship with himself. But here, too, is the duality so characteristic of Kaivanto's work. At times he observes the surface, the physical form, the landscape of the skin, as intensely as one experiences one's own body. At other times he penetrates profounder feelings in a synthesis of his earlier work and his current preoccupation. This ambivalence is perhaps best demonstrated in *Saint Sebastian II*, 1988 (fig. 55; Plate 55): the graceful stretch of long legs with arrows thrust into the flesh also remind us of the pair of shiny booted legs in his paintings from the 1970 (fig. 56). But are they arrows, or barbs aimed at us? Kaivanto himself said in a catalogue, "The philosophies of exposure, martyrdom, hypocrisy have always fascinated me. Are the arrows piercing the flesh of Saint Sebastian, or pushing out towards the viewer?"[52]

Perhaps it was this newfound interest in transcending the physical appearance to plumb the psychic depths that led Kaivanto to accept a commissioned portrait during this period. Although an accomplished draftsman, the artist had shown no interest in portraiture, just as he had not explored the nude as a subject until 1981. But in 1979,

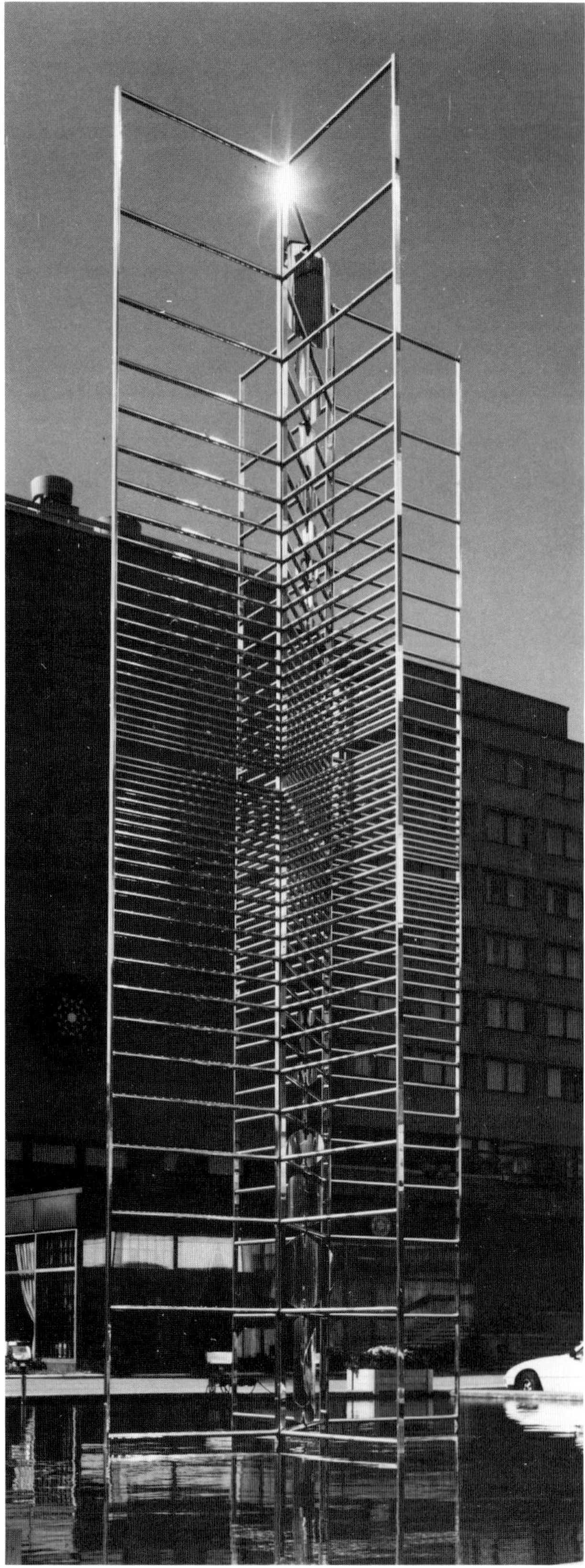

Figure. 58. Kimmo Kaivanto. *Ode to 60,000 Lakes*, 1972, stainless steel, h. 393-3/4" (h. 10 m). Hotel Hesperia, Helsinki

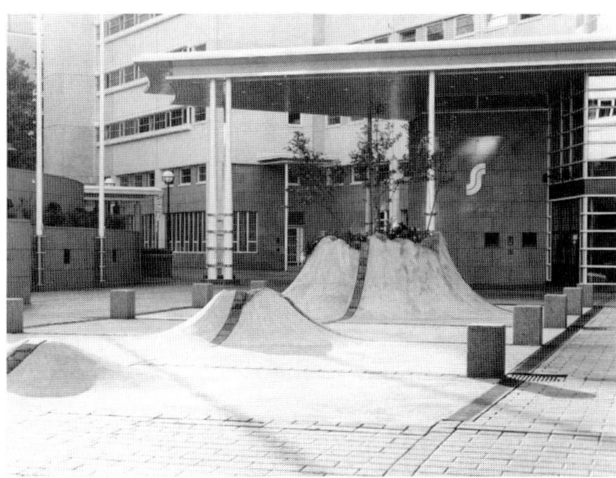

Figure. 59. Kimmo Kaivanto. *Natura Non Facit Saltus*, 1991, concrete and plants, 688-7/8 × 279-1/2 × 62-1/8" (17.5 × 7.1 × 1.6 m), Ässäkeskus, Helsinki

when he agreed to paint the portrait of a Tampere businessman as a friendly obligation, he was intrigued by the challenge. In an interview at that time he had spoken of the intellectual rather than technical demands of portraiture, stating that for him, "most of the work is done outside the sitting, when the realism of the model is not present."[53] Soon he got a model who provided a far greater challenge. When the legendary Tampere author Väinö Linna turned fifty in 1970, his publishers wanted to honor him with a public portrait, but Linna would not hear of it. In 1986, the writer, then sixty-six and ailing, was persuaded to permit his portrait to be painted. Kaivanto, having grown up in the same town, was an old acquaintance of Linna, and knew that the author could not possibly endure the ordeal of posing for a formal portrait. Accepting the commission, the artist announced that he would visit Linna a few times, on each occasion for no longer than a quarter of an hour to study his most characteristic traits. The resultant portraits, for they were executed in two variant versions, should be considered among the most important within Kaivanto's suite of figurative paintings (fig. 57). Handing over the work to the city authorities, Kaivanto said "I hope my picture will convey the intelligent restlessness" that distinguishes all creative artists.[54]

Although Kaivanto is one of the Finnish artists most consistently mentioned in the art columns of newspapers and periodicals, and a much sought-after subject of popular articles in weekly magazines, he remains an intensely private person.[55] Since the mural commissions of his youthful years, he has not participated in any public competitions, the exceptions being those for the Tampere

City Hall and decorations for the Finnjet ferry in 1977. On the other hand, he has been asked to do numerous sculptures for public sites. In addition to his *Chain of Fingers* for the Helsinki City Hall, these include *Ode to 60,000 Lakes*, 1972 (fig. 58), installed outside the Hesperea Hotel in Helsinki. The latter holds a special position in Kaivanto's oeuvre, more for the unique approach that guided its conception, than for the impression it now makes on the viewer. Like another monumental construction of 1985, *Silver Bridges*, also known as "The Blue Tower" in the Forum building in Helsinki, this work is currently obscured by its restless surroundings. But *Ode to 60,000 Lakes*, as its title implies, is not only a homage to preservationist sentiments but also incorporates ecologically correct technology. When Kinetic art came to Finland along with many other fashionable trends in the 1970s, numerous Finnish sculptors worked with kinetic constructions driven by electric motors. Kaivanto, however, felt that ecological themes must be handled with a demonstrable concern for the environment and thus pioneered the use of wind power to drive his kinetic sculpture. He also innovated the use of metallic surfaces of varying reflectivity to enhance the kinetic effects. Unfortunately, the work which was intended to celebrate the beauty of Finnish nature is now almost drowned in dust, fallen victim to the unwise changes in the planning of its surroundings.

But Kaivanto's optimism has remained undiminished by such misfortunes, just as it had stayed the course in the face of intense public criticism and incomprehension of the seventies. Nowhere is this more evident than in his 1991 public work, *Natura Non Facit Saltus*, at the entrance to Ässäkeskus, a Helsinki office and residential complex (fig. 59). Again, it is an ode to nature, spiced with mild irony: three concrete mounds, each larger than the other symbolize the inexorable forces of growth which are continually working to reclaim the territory encroached upon by man, in this case an asphalt driveway. The first mound, a barely perceptible tumor, indicates that the forces within are active; the second has cracked open in the middle, making way for growth; and finally the knoll with a crater in which a shadbush sapling is planted. One is reminded of James Thurber's fable, "The Last Flower," which affirms that life will win out in the end, no matter what the prophets of doom say. And Kaivanto has provided for the forces of life as they would no doubt manifest themselves over time. The shadbush will grow into a lofty tree bearing bright red serviceberries.[56] It will be a while before "art" will attain its fullness, with nature's help.

◆

After the untimely death of his wife, Kaivanto moved to

Helsinki in 1989 to start a new life. He recently renovated a spacious duplex apartment in a historic building on Kapteeninkatu. Here he lives and works, drawing strength from his new family: his present wife, Sari Roiha, an architect, her daughter, Mira, and his own two daughters, Kirsi and Kati, with whom he stays in almost daily contact.

Last summer, when the air had grown transparent, and the sky was blazing with a blue intensity, I sat in Kaivanto's comfortable new studio-workshop. The beautiful weather should have tempted me outdoors, but I was captivated by documents of a prodigiously creative life in art spread out before me: folder after neat folder of photographs and clippings and notes carefully organized by an assistant at the Sara Hildén Art Museum. Two large paintings hung above the work table, and although I had never visited the place they depicted, I felt I recognized it. They were two views of the artist's summer studio on Arkkusaari Island, one of its interior and another of the studio window seen from the outside. Then I realized that the latter view had been reproduced so many times in so many publications that one had the sense of actually having been there. A window like that under a roof like that had to be that studio.

During the long hours I spent there, my eye returned again and again to the view depicting the studio interior. It served as a relaxing place to rest my eyes, somewhat in the manner of Swiss watch-factory workers who take their eyes off their precision work to gaze at the magnificent mountain ranges rising just outside their factory windows. But the studio interior was no distant horizon: it radiated warmth and closeness. I could not remember having seen it in any of his exhibitions; it seemed far too intimate, far too personal for that. Obviously made by the hands of a skilled draftsman, the painting radiates the love for the tools and the surroundings that nurture the creative act: there stands the easel, there the draftsman's work table; there the newly stretched canvases hung up to dry. Everything is neat and clean, but cozy and inviting to work. And outside the large, floor-length window, one can see the summer foliage: inviting, but slightly vague and distant, stimulating without being disturbing, yet assuring that life will go on. And in the midst of the greenery is a simple woodshed with a sizable pile of chopped wood stacked neatly against the wall.

The other view is clearly painted from the vantage point of the woodshed, since the same shed and wood pile are seen reflected in the window panes. The interior is bathed in a mild, soft, misty, warm light, with rafters pitched high like the mighty shingled roofs of Finland's medieval granite churches. This interior reminds me of another famous studio, Akseli Gallen-Kallela's *Kalela*, also located in the wilderness of Ruovesi.[57] But *Kalela*, built at the turn of the century, is a majestic structure of heavy

pine logs, almost a miniature castle perched on a hill, half hidden among the pines of a rocky lake shore. Kaivanto's summer hideout, on less rolling, tamer terrain is on a much more modest scale, and constructed of such humble materials that it almost appears fragile. But the interior has some of the same atmosphere of gentle coziness; a good place for an artist to live and work.

A few months later I once again sit at the work table in Kaivanto's Helsinki studio. Now the autumn rain is pounding the asphalt courtyard, and the gray daylight struggles to reach the ground. As I switch on the lamp above the work table, the boxes of clippings and photographs stacked around the room recede in the warm darkness. Before me lies a bundle of pictures from Kaivanto's archives from which illustrations for the catalogue will be chosen. Contemplating a photograph of Kaivanto with his father in military uniform, I decide that there is no reason to go into his private life in more depth. An artist is always private, in the creative act, in the way he works. For Kaivanto, too, creativity is often a dialogue with what is very close to him–the family, the home, natural surroundings–on the one hand, and the outer world, the society, "his fellow man" on the other. The radical changes that Kaivanto's art has undergone over the course of forty years of intense creativity also reveal this duality. Yet there is a clear, consistent line–what is generally referred to as a "red thread" in Scandinavia. In Kaivanto's case this thread is blue. He has said of this characteristic blue color, "Blue for me is not a color–it is a state, a state of mind, a good state of mind."[58] But in order to be able to see beauty, to be able to achieve this good state of mind, one must also dare to see ugliness and evil. The black mushroom cloud grows against an ultramarine blue sky into a verdant bush. Kaivanto has certainly seen Nemesis, but each year he has also seen the promise of budding trees against the blue spring sky. The depressing darkness of the Nordic winter is followed by the joy of summer's lingering light. Art is actually "the best instrument that man has for coming to grips with himself."[59] Let it rain outside the window; here inside shines the ultramarine blue. The canvas is transformed into a sea; we hoist our sail and boldly embark on our journey. No one knows what lies beyond the horizon.

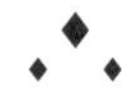

Notes: (See bibliography for published material referenced with alphanumeric codes, e.g., B.82, G.115, etc.).

1. Under Swedish colonial rule, certain towns were exempt from export duties to encourage trade, industry and investments.
2. See Bhupendra Karia, "Introduction" in [Exhibition catalogue] *Juhani Harri* (New York: Center for International Contemporary Arts, 1991): 5, 12.

3. Consecrated as St. John's Evangelical Church in 1907, it was renamed St. John's Cathedral in 1923 when the bishopric was transferred from Porvoo. It is now known as the Tampere Cathedral.

4. The administrative province in which Tampere is located is known as Tavastland in Swedish and Häme in Finnish. It is also referred to by its ancient name, Pirkanmaa.

5. Karia, *Juhani Harri*: 7.

6. Lambert Hjalmar Kaivanto (1887-1934) was an assistant to the master carver Nikolai Andreev, employed by Tampere Bentwood Company (Tampereen höyrypuuseppä yhtiö) responsible for the massive oak doors and interior wooden details after designs by Valter Jung.

7. The Tampere Academy for Art and Media Studies was established in 1991.

8. For further information on exhibitions cited in the text, please refer to bibliography.

9. The most memorable among these were *Pariisin nykytaidetta*, the Denise Renée collection of French contemporary art, mainly abstract paintings shown at the Helsinki Art Hall (Taidehalli) in 1954; *Paul Cézanne* at the Ateneum, 1954-55; *Salon de Mai: Pariisilaisten kuvanveistäjien teoksia* (Salon de Mai: Works by Parisian sculptors) also at the Helsinki Art Hall in 1955; and *Ranskan taidetta Ragnar Moltzaun kokoelmasta* (French art from the collection of the Norwegian collector Ragnar Moltzau) at the Ateneum in 1956. The last exhibition included works by Braque, Chagall, Estève, Kandinsky, Léger, Picasso, Roualt, Singier, da Silva, Villon and others, which many Finnish artists saw for the first time.

10. *Nuorten näyttely*, or the Young Artists' Exhibition, was first held in 1939, initiated by Bertel Hintze (1901-1969), who headed the Helsinki Art Hall for four decades. Its primary purpose was to provide less-established artists an opportunity to show their work at a modest cost through a juried annual show. However, unlike other juried exhibitions, here the participating artists nominated their own candidates for the jury. Two other elements have made this an indispensable and coveted vehicle for young artists to break into the art establishment: first, the frequency of submission and acceptance in these exhibitions counts towards membership in the powerful artists' unions; second, the best entry qualifies for the prestigious Ducat Prize–an award which has come to signify an honor quite disproportionate to its cash value. Since its founding and initial success, this annual show has served as an efficient forum for numerous young Finnish artists seeking peer acceptance and popular prestige.

11. Soili Sinisalo, "Kuvataide 60-luvulla" (Art in the 60s) in *Ars Suomen Taide 6* (B.82): 182. *Ars Suomen Taide* (Finnish Art) published in six volumes (1987-90), is a standard reference work on Finnish art.

12. Finland has been represented in the Venice Biennale since 1954. A Finnish pavilion, designed by Alvar Aalto in 1956, was used until 1960. Since 1962, Finland has exhibited with Sweden and Norway in a new Scandinavian pavilion jointly constructed by the three countries.

13. This was followed by *Ars 65*, *Ars 69*, *Ars 74*, and *Ars 83*. The exhibitions were arranged by the Fine Arts Academy of Finland and held at the Art Museum of Ateneum in Helsinki.

14. "Informalism's breakthrough is a reality," was the title of *Nya Pressen's* review of the 1962 triennial (G.115), while *Kauppalehti's* review of the same exhibition was headlined "Informalists are big" (G.112).

15. Quoted in Hertta Coogan, F.56: 20.

16. Good examples include Ahti Lavonen's structure paintings, reminiscent of fields of ice; the atmospheric light effects in the work of Jaakko Sievänen (b.1932); and the dramatic cloud visions in Informalist compositions by Esko Tirronen (b.1934).

17. I have touched upon this question in "Sodanjälkeinen kuvataide vuoteen 1960" (Post-war pictorial art through 1960) in B.82: 76-111.

18. Timo Vuorikoski, Director of the Sara Hildén Art Museum in Tampere, has discussed how Kaivanto had conceived many of his paintings in A.148.

19. Vuorikoski, A.148: 20.

20. Kaivanto, B.50: 208.

21. Coogan, F.56: 20.

22. A.68.

23. Kaivanto, conversation with the author.

24. Jan-Olof Mallander, G.344.

25. During the sixties, when there were few opportunities to see international art in Finland, major exhibitions in nearby Stockholm routinely attracted Finnish artists and critics in large numbers. Some of the most memorable shows of that era include: *Rörelse i konstent* (Movement in Art), 16 May-10 Sept. 1961; *Fyra amerikanare* (Four Americans), 17 Mar.-16 May 1962; and *Amerikansk pop-konst* (American Pop Art), 29 Feb.-12 Apr. 1964.

26. Karia, *Juhani Harri*: 9.

27. A.83: 2.

28. Mallander, G.471.

29. Mallander, G.471.

30. Markku Valkonen, G.465.

31. See for example, Jaakko Lintinen, B.50: 98, 140.

32. The painting was reproduced on the book jacket and post for *Säästäkää Suomenlahti* (Save the Gulf of Finland), ed. by Tapani Eskola (Helsinki: Arkkitehtiliitto, 1972). 20 million postcards and stationery sets reproducing this image were issued by UNICEF in 1991.

33. [Gallery handout] Per Drougge, *Kimmos lekar–Kaivanto's konst* (Kimmo's games–Kaivanto's art), (Södertälje: Konsthall, 24 Jan.-5 Mar. 1981).

34. See for example Lintinen, B.50: 138; or Vuorikoski, A.148: 34.

35. On several occasions, Kaivanto has mentioned how he has been struck by parallels to certain parts of Francis Ford Coppola's film *Apocalypse Now* (see Coogan, F.56: 22). In a conversation with the author, he mentioned how upon seeing Cy Twombly's work in Madrid in 1987, he immediately recognized a kinship: *Victory*, one of Twombly's paintings in that exhibition, depicting a crashed paper airplane, reminded Kaivanto of the charred paper airplanes in his own 1973 painting, *Winners*.

36. Quoted in Lintinen, B.50: 129.

37. For example, Markku Valkonen called this element "a romantic but rather weird idea" in G.602.

38. Quoted in Karin Elimäki, F.8: 18.

39. Mallander, G.599.

40. Finnish composer Aulis Sallinen, in addition to *The Red Line* (1976-78), has written the operas *The Horseman* (1974, premiered in 1975), *The King Goes Forth to France* (1983, premiered in 1984), and *Kullervo* (1986-88, premiered in Los Angeles in February 1992).

41. Ilmari Kianto is best known for his humorous depictions of rural life in Finland.

42. Kaivanto, B.50: 208.

43. Eino Leino was an innovative Finnish lyricist who drew inspiration from Finland folk tales and epics.

44. The Finnish title is *Paketti Lempeä–Paketti Lämpöä*. Lempi is an archaic word for love (now replaced by its modern usage, Rakkaus); Lämpö means warmth.

45. Lars Erik Åström, G.290. Kaivanto was one of eight Finnish artists represented in *Nordisk konst* (see A.59), a biennial organized by the Nordic Art Association (Pohjoismainen Taideliitto). Kaivanto confirmed the importance of this criticism in a conversation with the author in August 1991.

46. B.50.

47. Although only the first six works realized between 1979 and 1980 share this series title, subsequent paintings entitled, *Youth*, *Shadow*, *Gang*, *Face*, and *In the Terminal* are also part of Kaivanto's fascination with Finnish youth gangs and the social alienation they represent.

48. Arne Törnqvist, G.770.

49. Quoted in Annika Winther, F.66: 31.

50. Harry Martinson, *Aniara: En revy om människan i tid och rum* (Aniara: A song about man in time and space), (Stockholm: Bonniers, 1956): 52-53.

51. Törnqvist, G.770.

52. Kaivanto, A.161.

53. Quoted in G.721.

54. Quoted in G.915.

55. See sections F. and G. in bibliography.

56. Tuomipihjala in Finnish, or the genus *Amelanchier canadensis*, is commonly known as June berry or serviceberry bush.

57. Akseli Gallen-Kallela (1865-1931), one of the leading Finnish painters at the turn of the century created a large number of pictures based on the *Kalevala* epic.

58. Quoted in Pirkko Hartiala, F.88: 76.

59. Mallander, G.471.

Plates

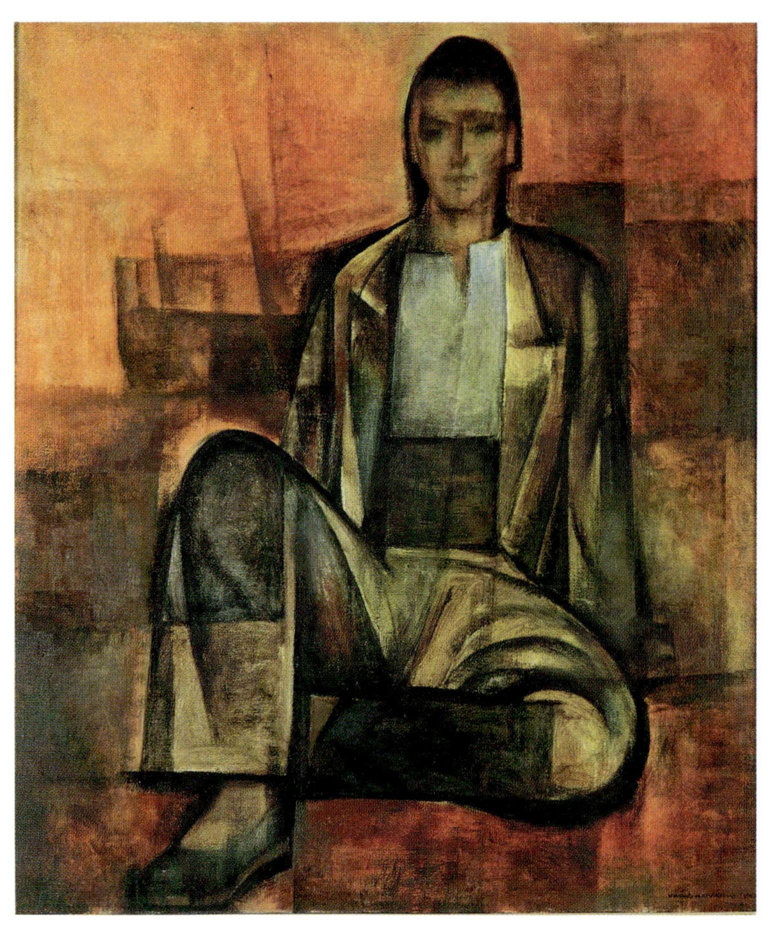

1. *Marochi*, 1958
Oil on canvas
44-1/8 × 38-5/8" (112 x 98 cm)
Collection of Tampere City

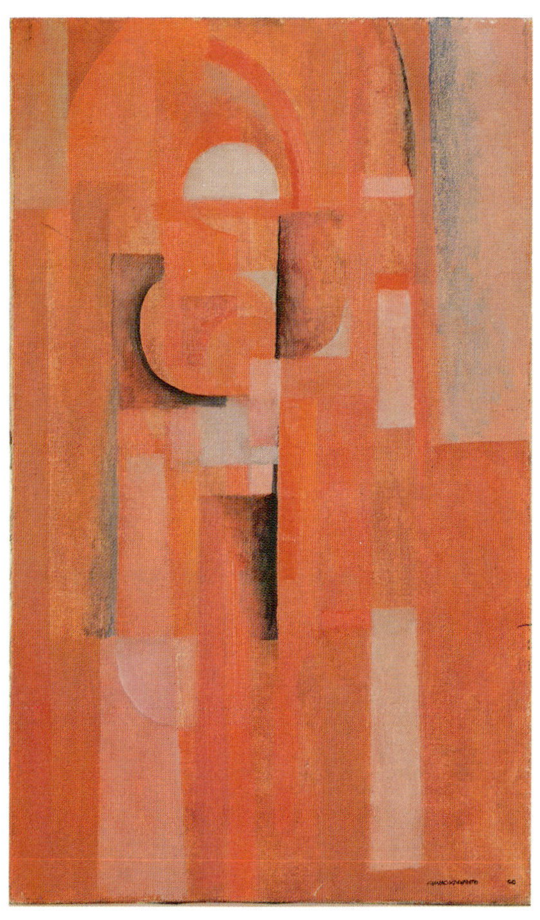

2. *Alcázar*, 1960
Oil on canvas
32-1/4 × 19-5/8" (82 × 50 cm)
Collection of Tampere City

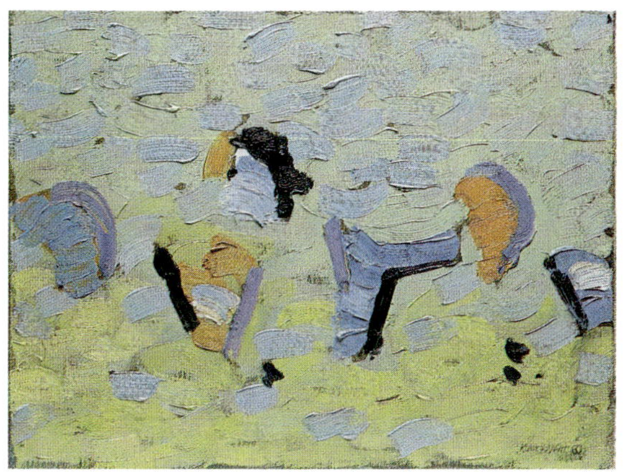

3. *Gallop*, 1960
Oil on canvas
14-5/8 × 19-5/8" (37 × 50 cm)
Collection of the artist

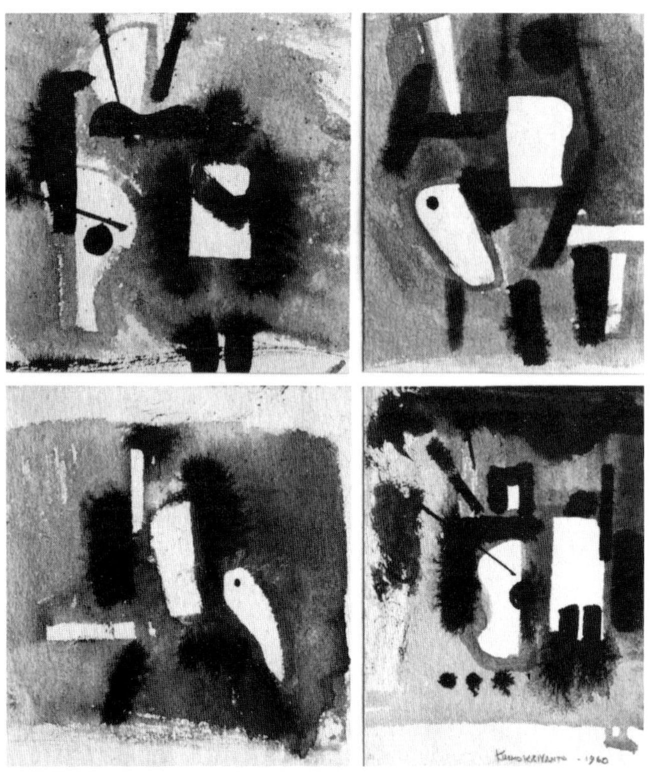

4. *Concert (II)*, 1960
Ink and wash on paper
8-1/4 × 7-1/4" (21 × 18.5 cm)
Collection of the artist

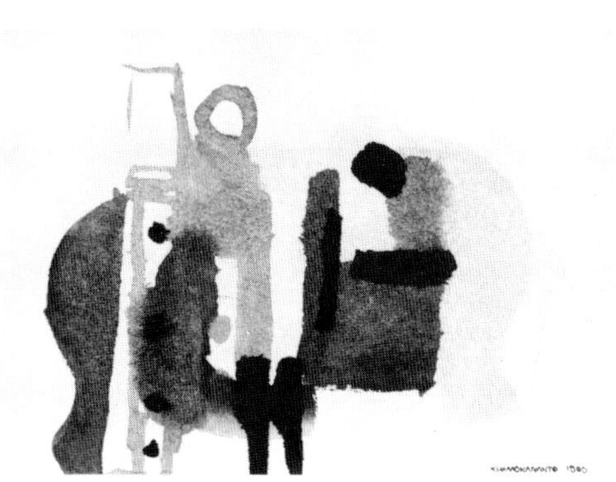

5. *Concert (I)*, 1960
Ink and wash on paper
4-1/2 × 6-3/4" (11.5 × 17) cm
Collection of the artist

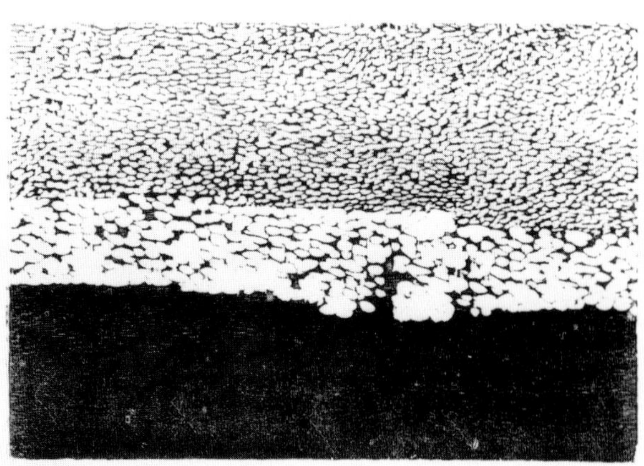

6. *On the Shore*, 1962
Woodcut
9 × 12-5/8" (23 × 32 cm)
Collection of the artist

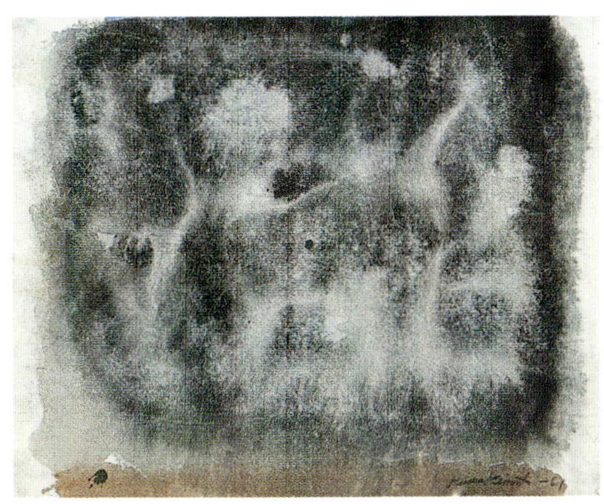

7. *Stone*, 1961
Gouache on paper
9-1/2 × 12-1/4" (24 × 31 cm)
Collection of the artist

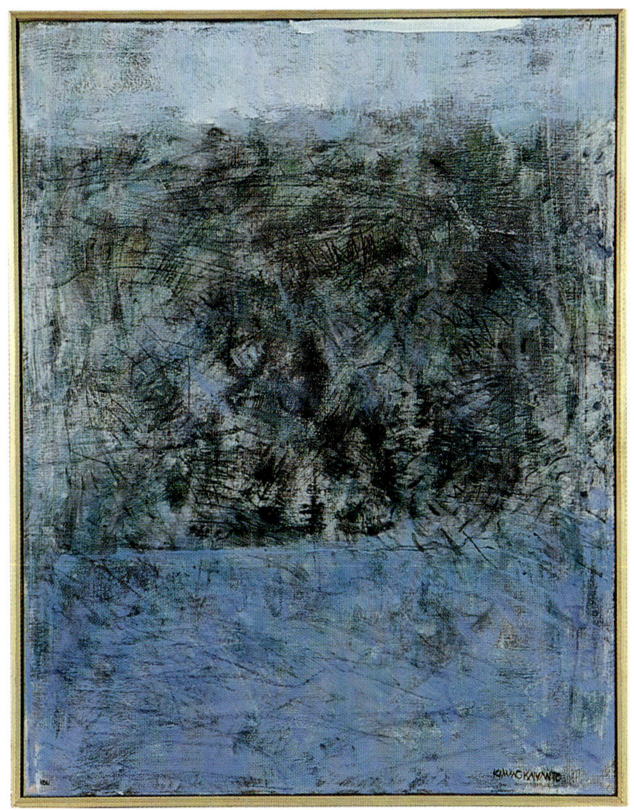

8. *Spring-Winter*, 1961
Oil on canvas
36-1/4 × 28-3/4" (92 × 73 cm)
Collection of Sara Hilden Art Museum, Tampere;
Collection Sara Hildén

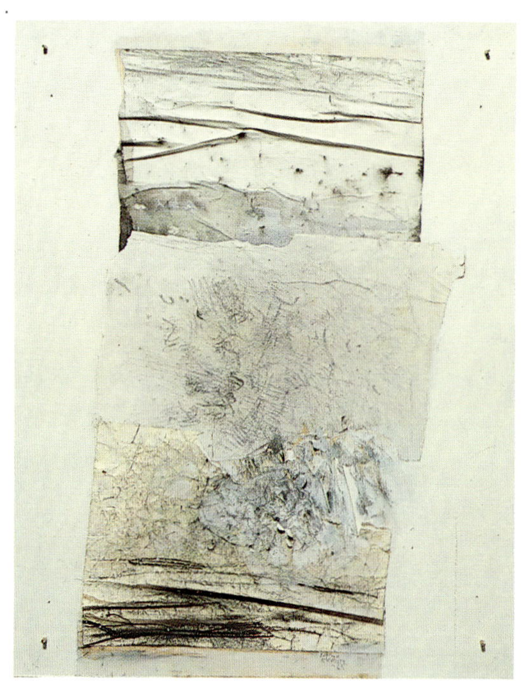

9. *Collage*, 1965
Gouache and colored chalk on paper laid on wood
34-5/8 × 27-1/2" (88 × 70 cm)
Collection of Sara Hilden Art Museum, Tampere;
Collection Sara Hildén

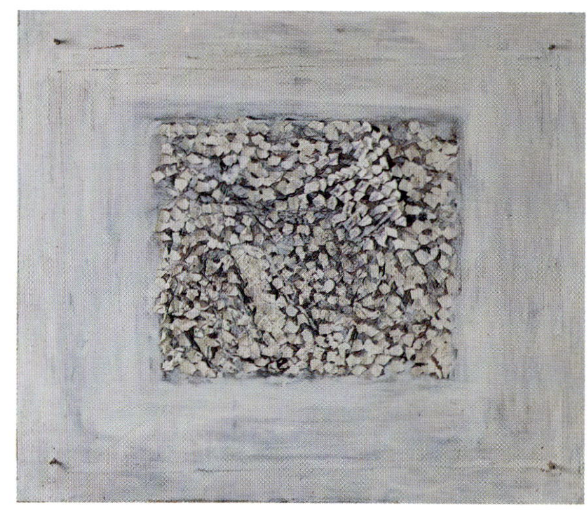

10. *Concrete*, 1965
Gouache on paper and composition board
24 × 28-3/4" (61 × 73 cm)
Collection of the artist

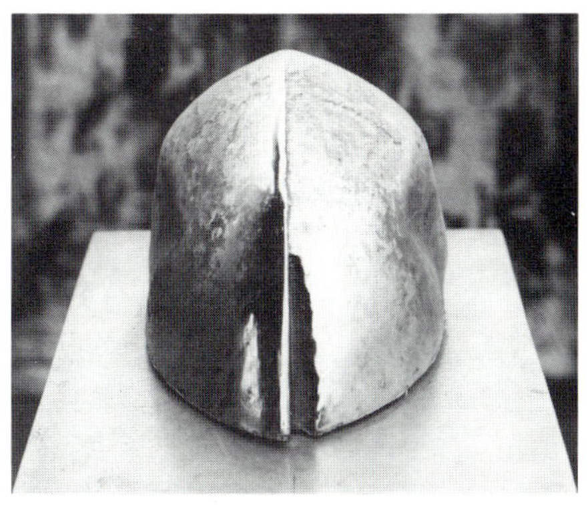

11. *Militarist*, 1962
Nickel-plated bronze
5-1/8 × 9-7/8 × 5-7/8" (13 × 25 × 15 cm)
Collection of the artist

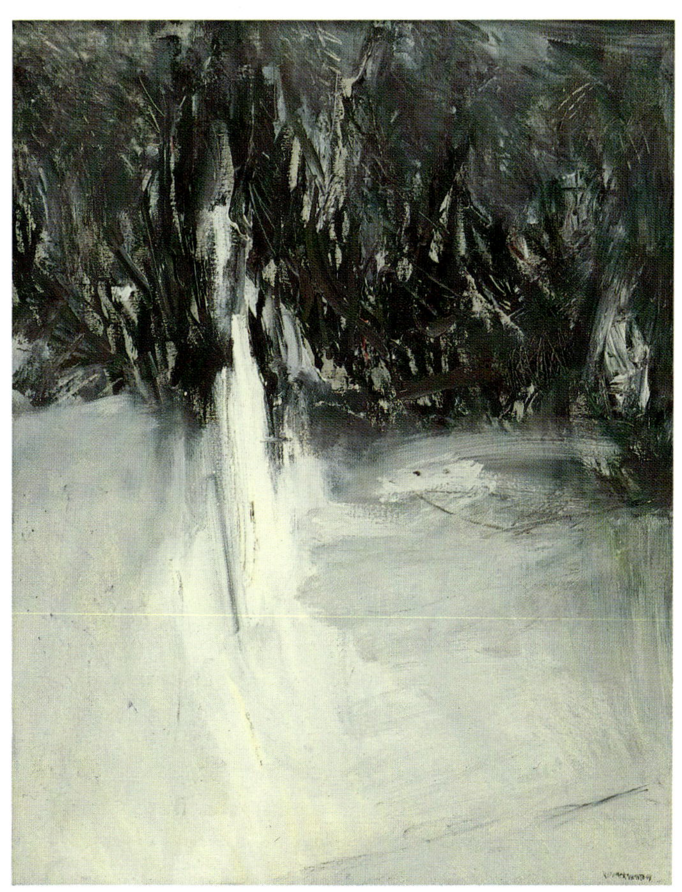

12. *Spring Light*, 1964
Oil on canvas
56-3/4 × 44-7/8" (144 × 114 cm)
Collection of Sara Hilden Art Museum, Tampere;
Collection Sara Hildén

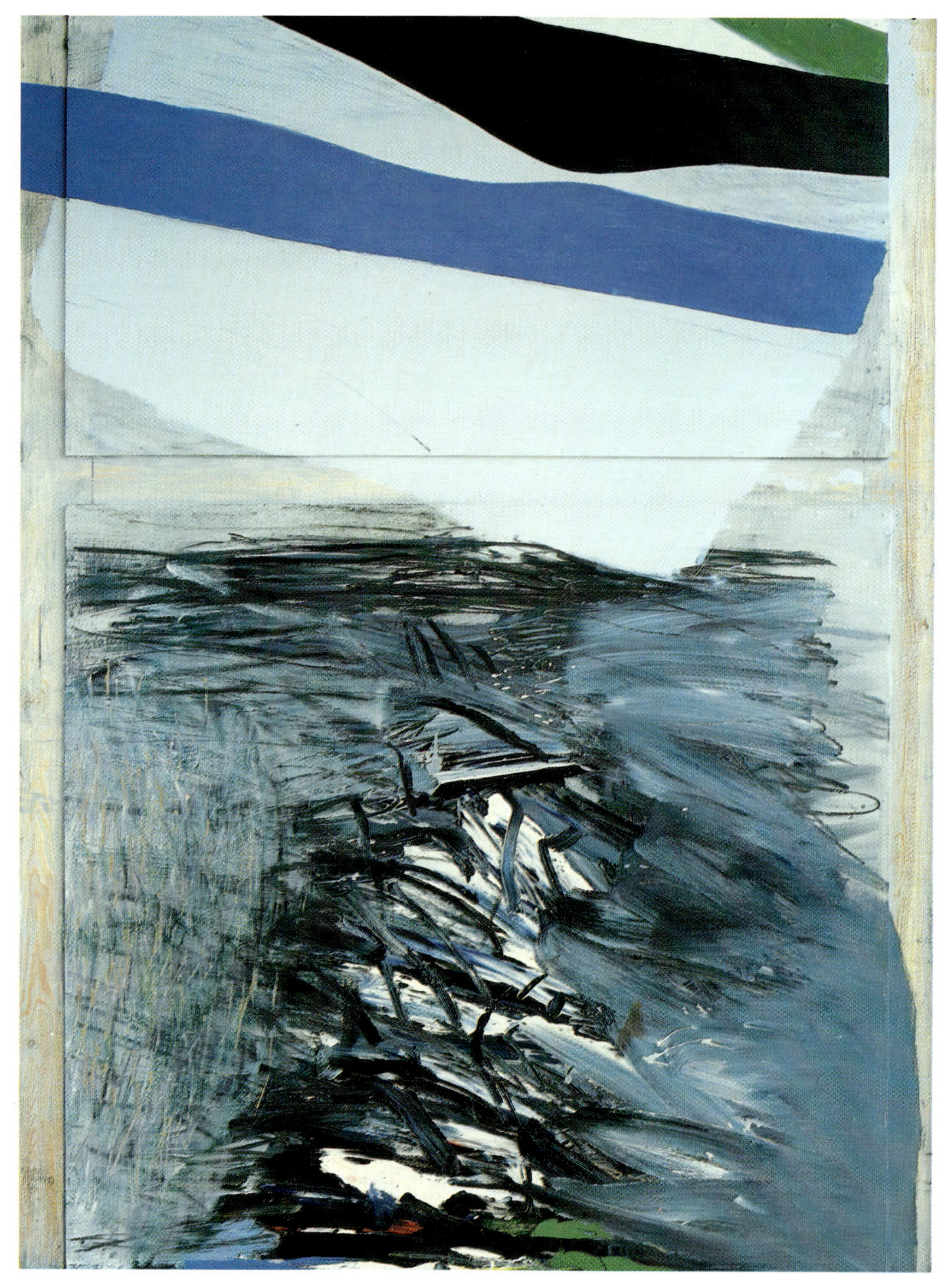

13. *Variation on the Blue-Green*, 1966
Oil on masonite
71-1/4 × 54-3/8" (181 × 138 cm)
Collection of Kansallis-Osake-Pankki, Helsinki

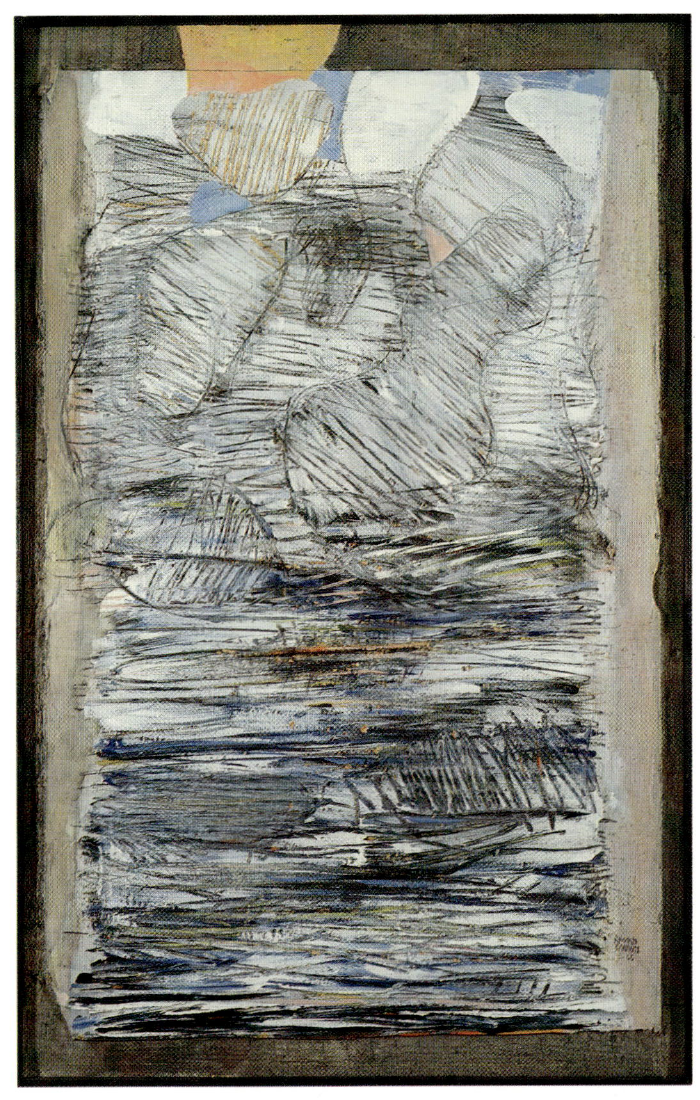

14. *Clouds Bathing,* 1966
Oil and graphite pencil on cardboard
58-5/8 × 38" (149 × 96.5 cm)
Collection of Sara Hilden Art Museum, Tampere;
Collection Sara Hildén

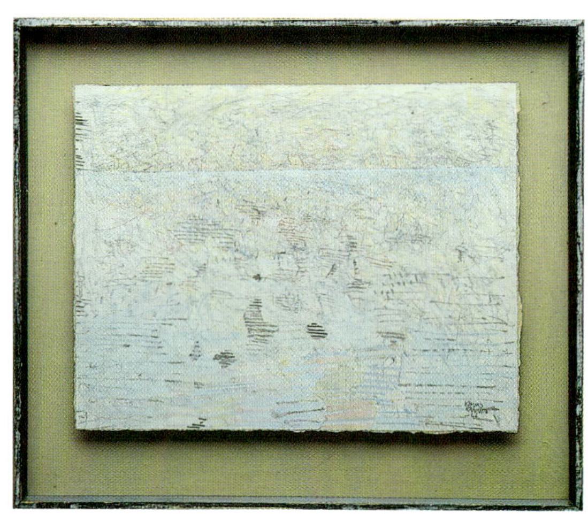

15. *Afternoon in Viale Trieste*, 1966
Gouache on paper
11 × 14-1/2" (28 × 37 cm)
Collection of Sara Hilden Art Museum, Tampere;
Collection Sara Hildén

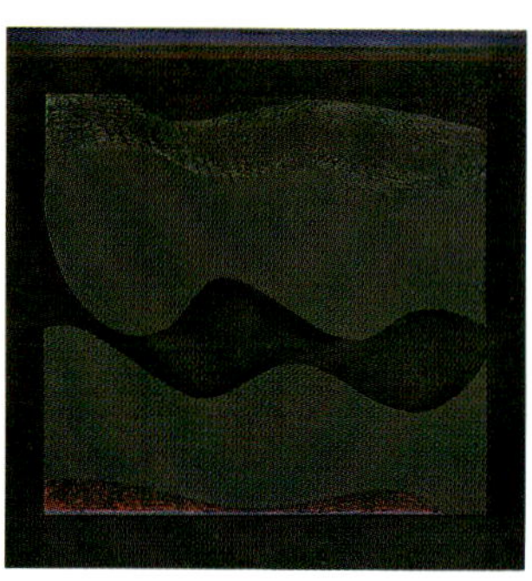

18. *Sunrise–Sunset*, 1967
Gouache and paper collage
13-3/8 × 13-3/8" (34 × 34 cm)
Collection of Sara Hilden Art Museum, Tampere
Collection Sara Hildén

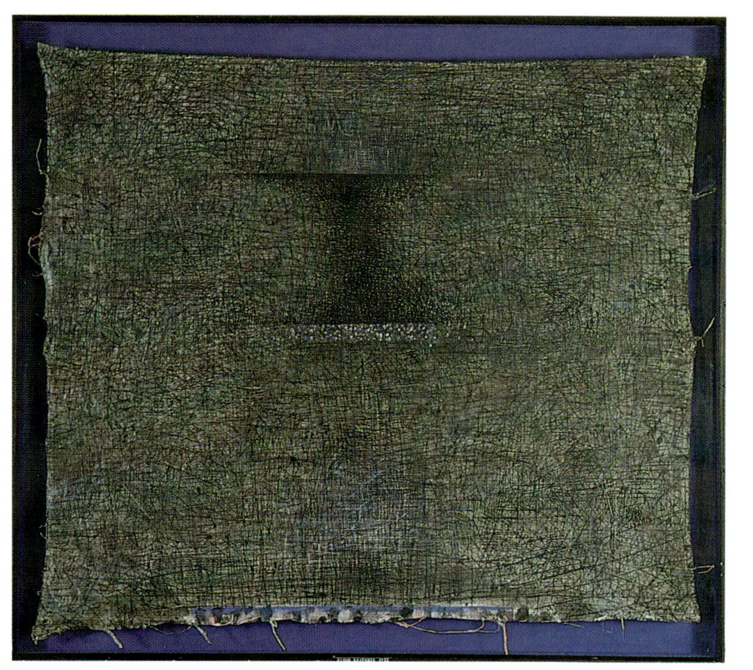

17. *Navark's Dream*, 1968
Oil and ink on canvas
37-3/8 × 42-7/8" (95 × 109 cm)
Collection of The Museum of Contemporary Art, Helsinki

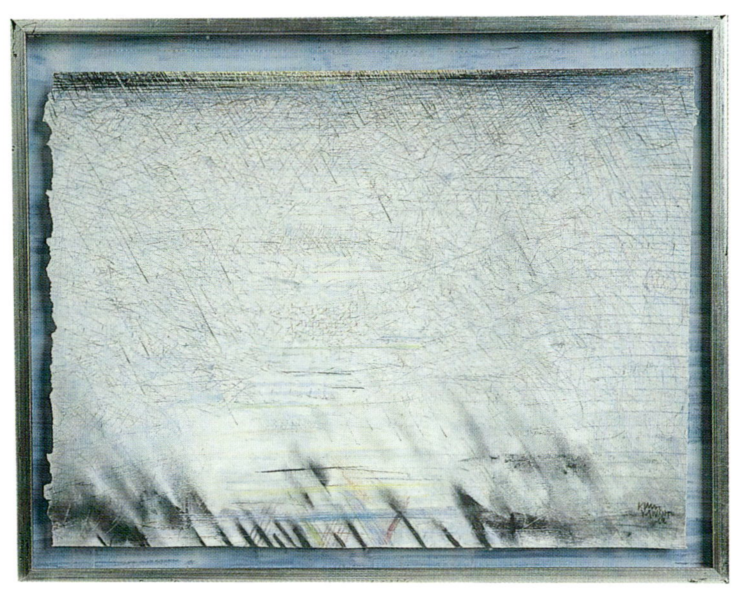

16. *Shore Picture*, 1968
Gouache on paper
23-5/8 × 31-1/8" (60 × 79 cm)
Collection of the artist

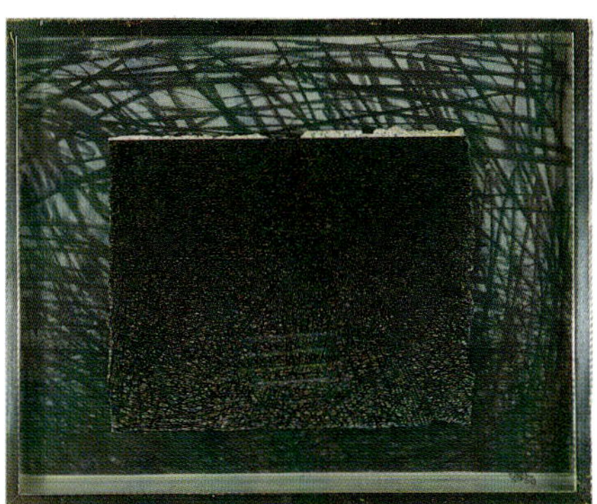

19. *Endlessly*, 1968
Gouache and ink on paper collage
19-5/8 × 25-1/4" (50 × 64 cm)
Collection of Sara Hilden Art Museum, Tampere;
Collection Sara Hildén

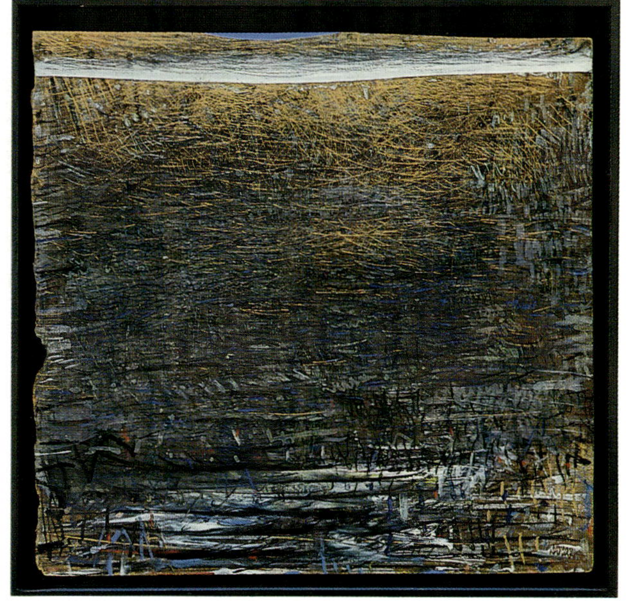

20. *Nocturne*, 1967
Oil and colored chalk on masonite
36-5/8 × 39-3/8" (93 × 100 cm)
Collection of Sara Hilden Art Museum, Tampere;
Collection Sara Hildén

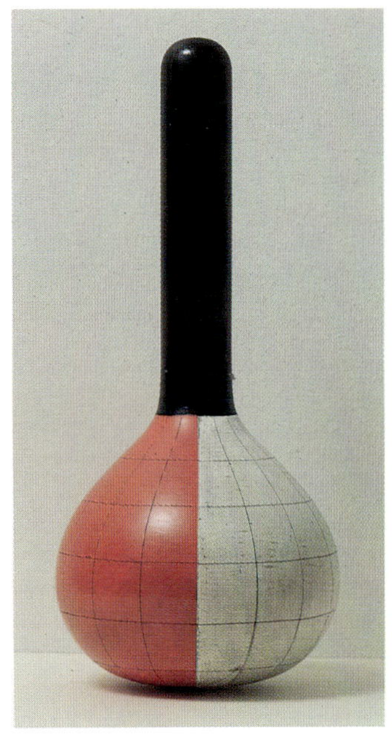

21. *Smooth Tower of Rubber*, 1968
Painted wood
h. 23-5/8" (h. 60 cm)
Collection of the artist

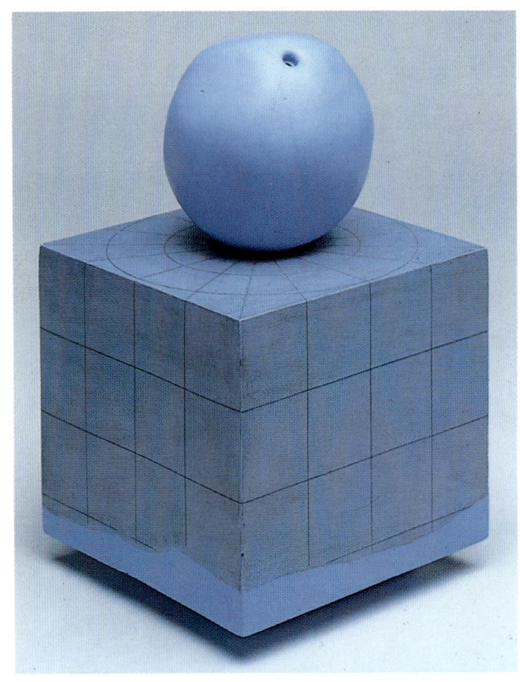

22. *Children are Round and Animals*, 1968
Painted wood
14-1/8 × 8-7/8 × 8-7/8" (36 × 22.5 × 22.5 cm)
Collection of the artist

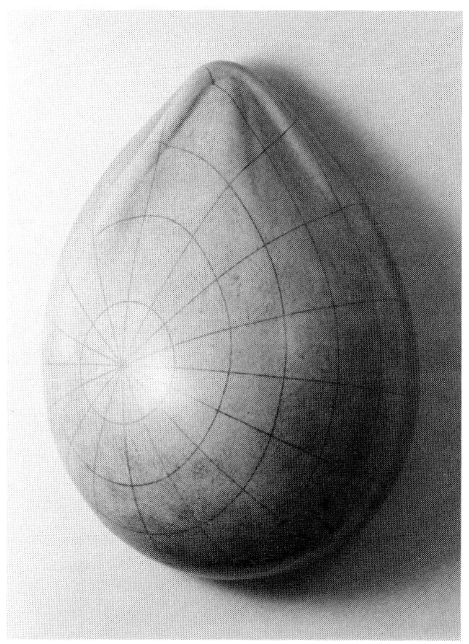

23. *The Globe*, 1967-68
Painted plaster
23-5/8 × 15-3/4 × 11-3/4" (60 × 40 × 30 cm)
Collection of the artist

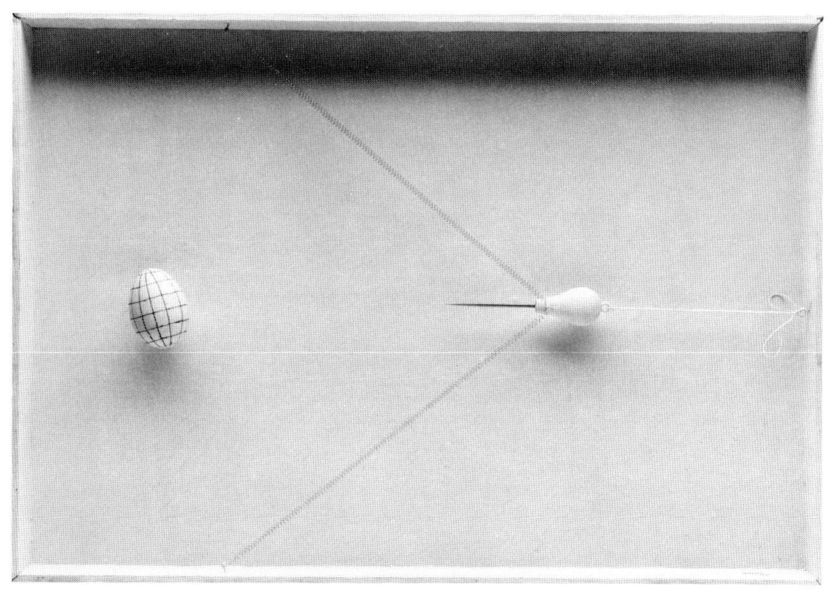

24. *Balance*, 1968
Assemblage
15-3/4 × 23-1/4 × 2" (40 × 59 × 5 cm)
Collection of the artist

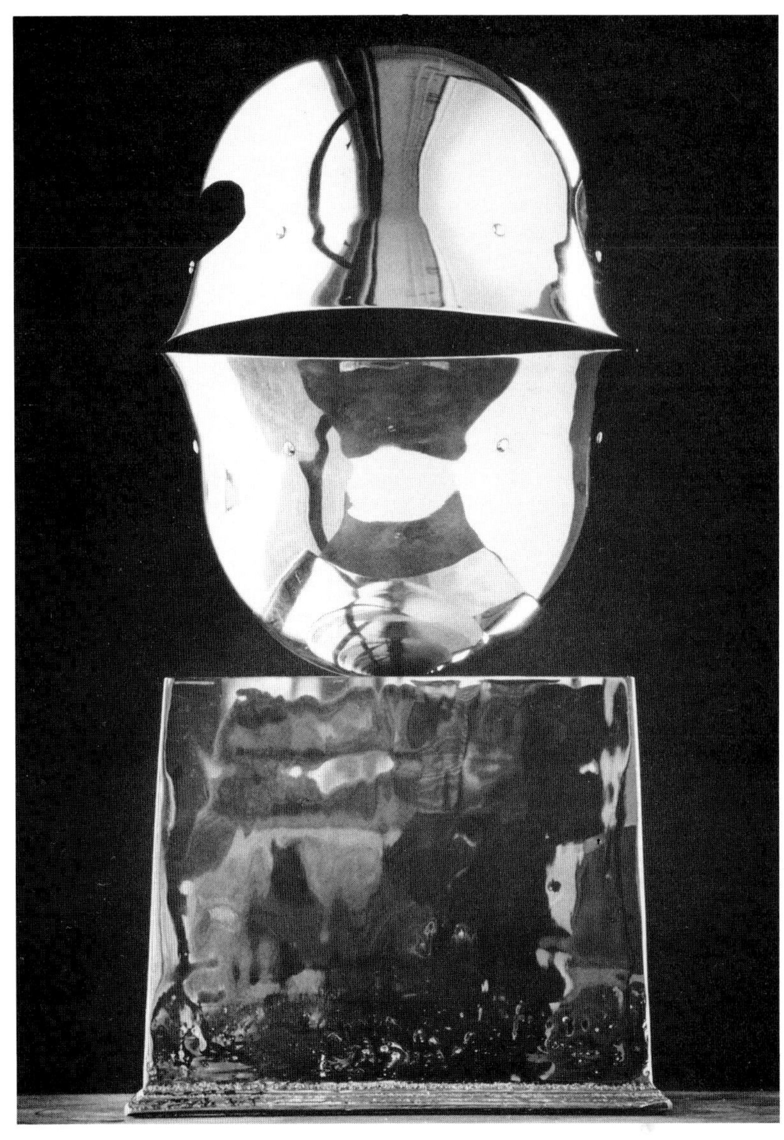

25. Smiling Killer, 1965-68
Nickel-plated bronze and steel
19-5/8 × 11-3/4 × 11-3/4" (50 × 30 × 30 cm)
Private collection

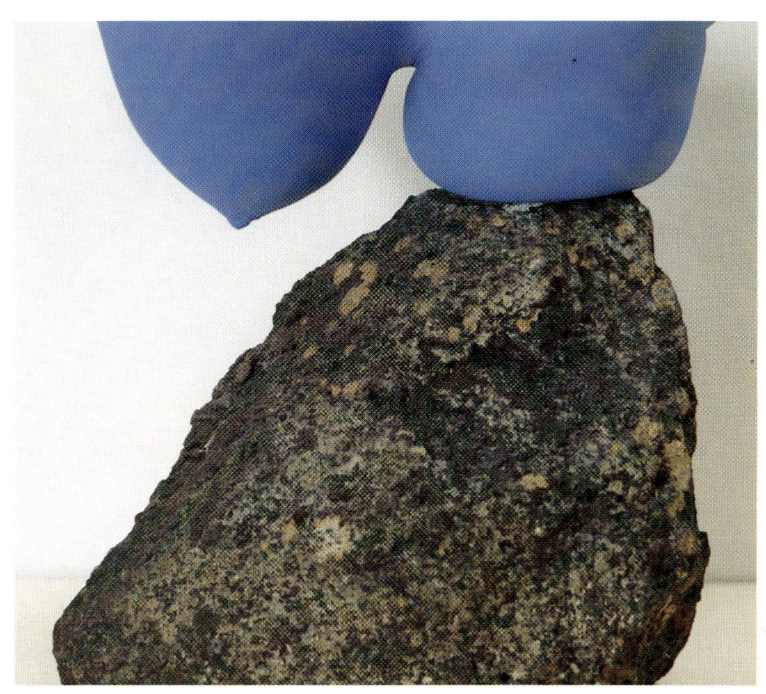

26. *Touch*, 1969
Plastic and stone
13-1/8 × 11-3/4 × 9-7/8" (33.5 × 30 × 25 cm)
Collection of the artist

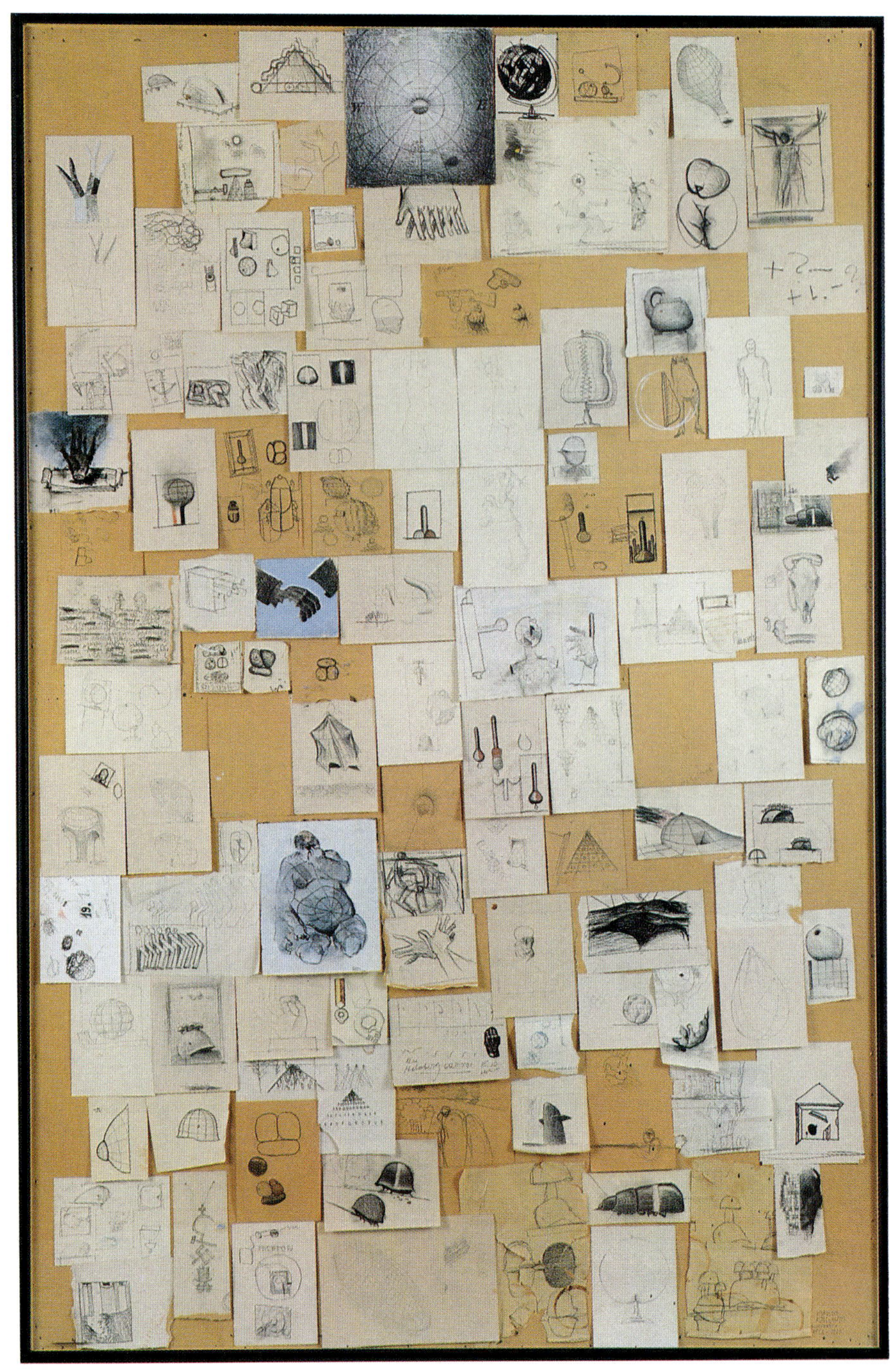

27. Sketches, 1962-69
Pencil, pen and gouache on paper
Over all: 65-3/4 × 44-1/8" (167 × 112 cm)
Collection of the artist

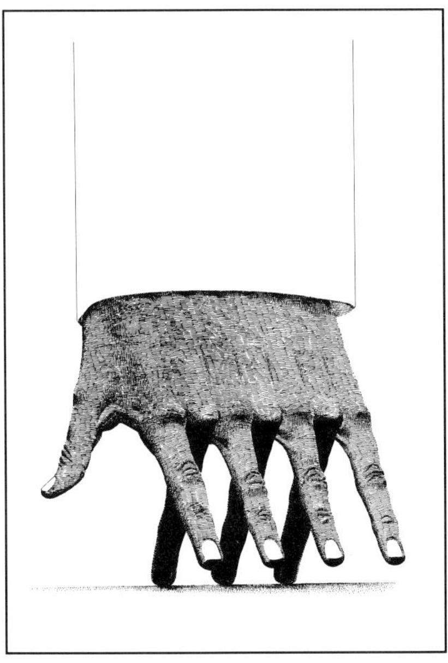

28. *The Hand*, 1969
Serigraph
34-5/8 × 24-3/4" (88 × 63 cm)
Collection of the artist

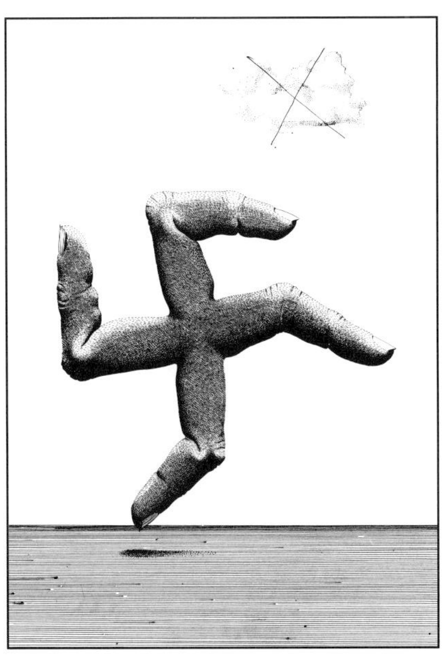

29. *A Question of Efficiency*, 1969
Serigraph
34-5/8 × 24-3/4" (88 × 63 cm)
Collection of the artist

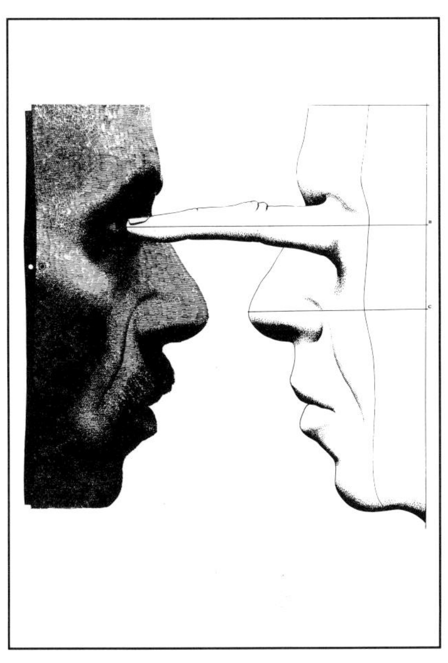

30. *Figure of Depth and Illusions, or I, I, I*, 1969
Serigraph
34-5/8 × 24-3/4" (88 × 63 cm)
Collection of the artist

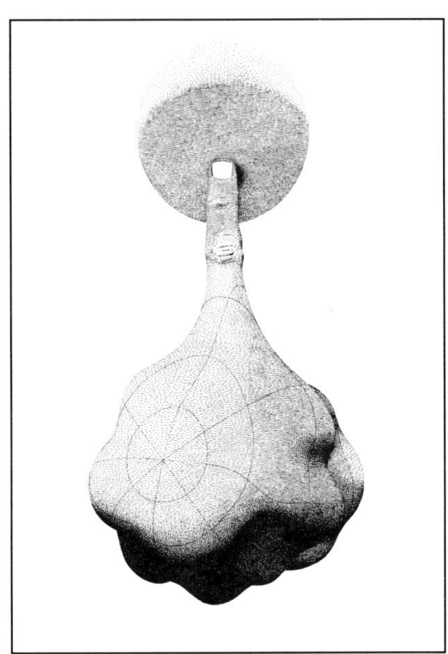

31. *Contact!*, 1969
Serigraph
34-5/8 × 24-3/4" (88 × 63 cm)
Collection of the artist

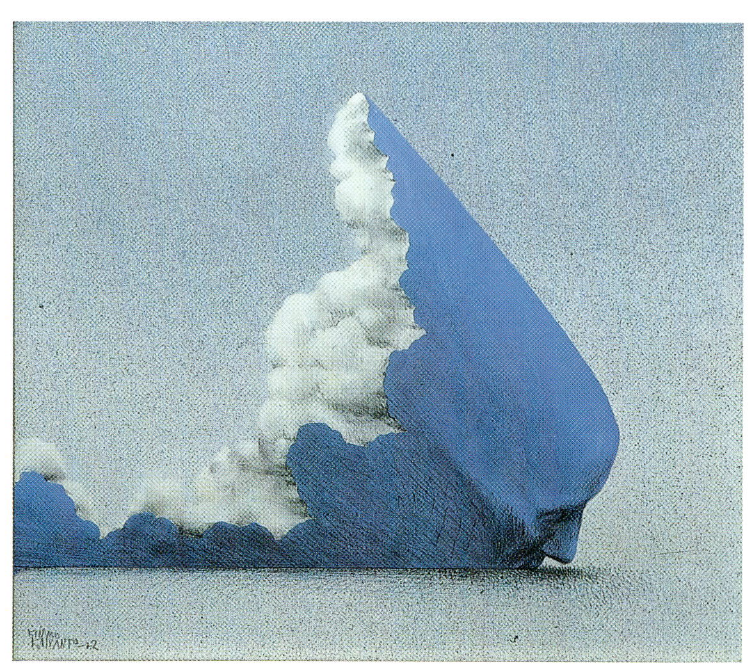

32. *Icarus*, 1972
Gouache on paper
13-3/4 × 16-1/8" (35 × 41 cm)
Collection of Leena Pelota

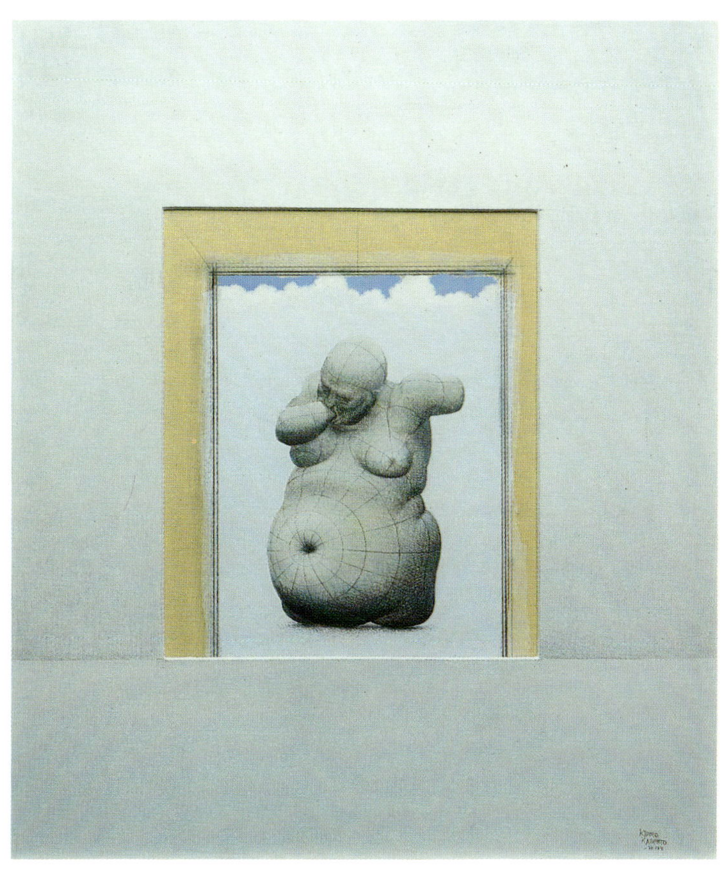

33. *View from the Main Steps of the Museum to the Town*, 1971-74
Gouache and colored pencil on paper
27-1/2 × 23-5/8" (70 × 60 cm)
Collection of the artist

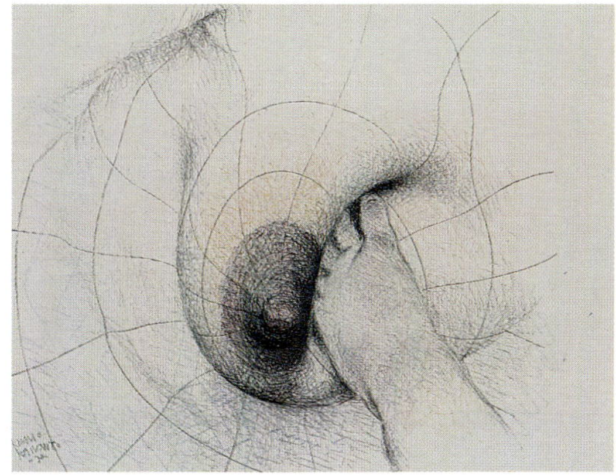

34. *Breast II (Natural Order)*, 1972
Pencil and colored chalk on paper
8-5/8 x 11-3/8" (22 × 29 cm)
Private collection

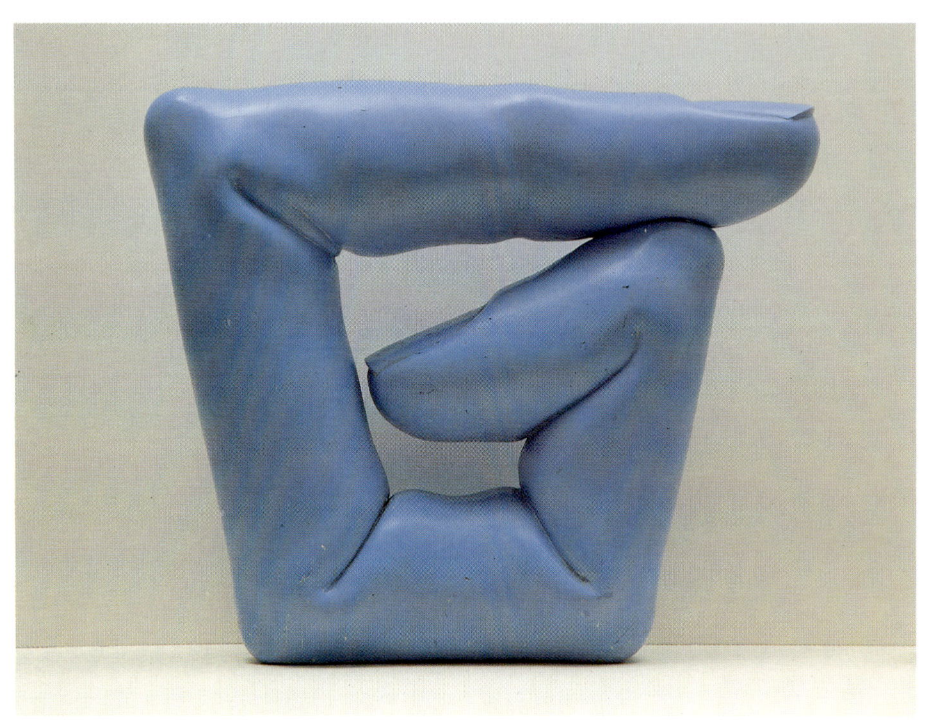

35. *Blue Thinker (Rodin Theme)*, 1971
Painted fiberglass
h. 16-1/2" (h. 42 cm)
Collection of the artist

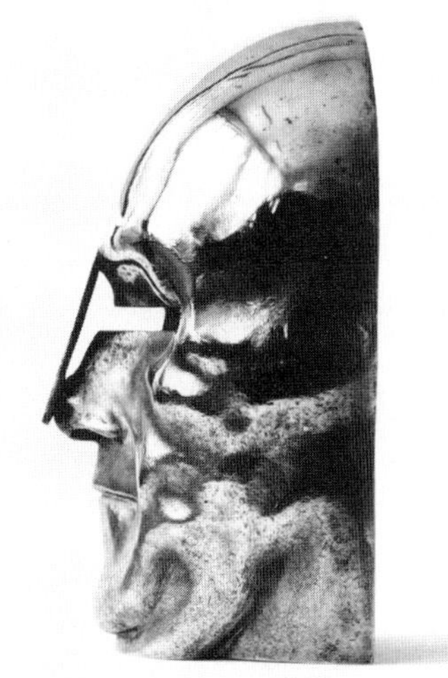

36. *Patakos*, 1970
Nickel-plated bronze and plastic
9-7/8 × 9-7/8 × 9-7/8" (25 × 25 × 25 cm)
Collection of the artist

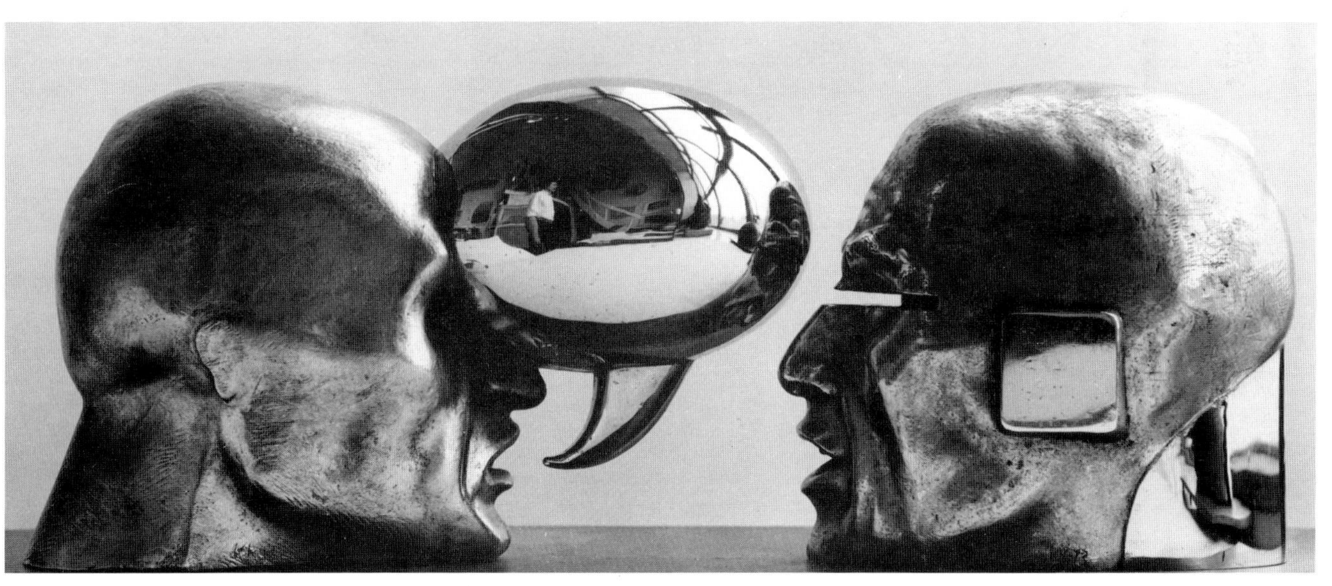

37. *Cold War*, 1973
Nickel-plated bronze
9-7/8 × 31-1/2 × 11-3/4" (25 × 80 × 30 cm)
Collection of the artist

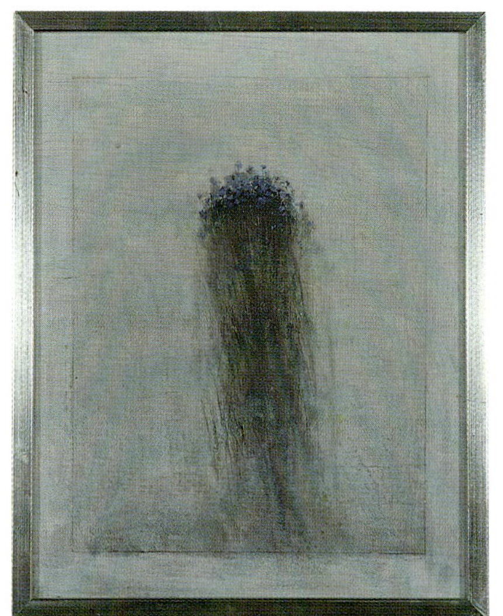

38. *Regards*
Gouache on paper
Collection of Kaija Junnila

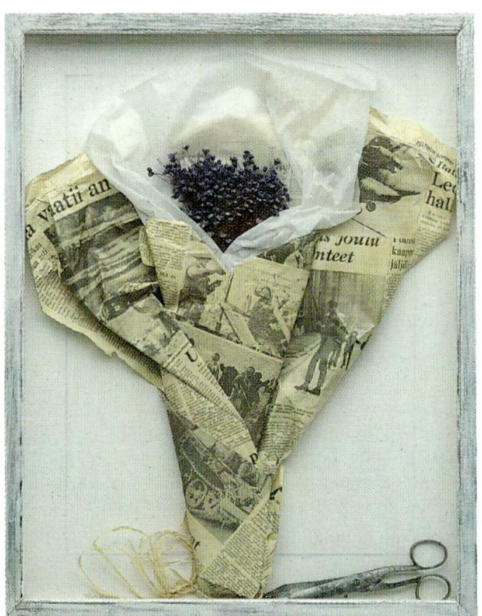

39. *To You*
Gouache and pencil on paper
Collection of Leena Pelota

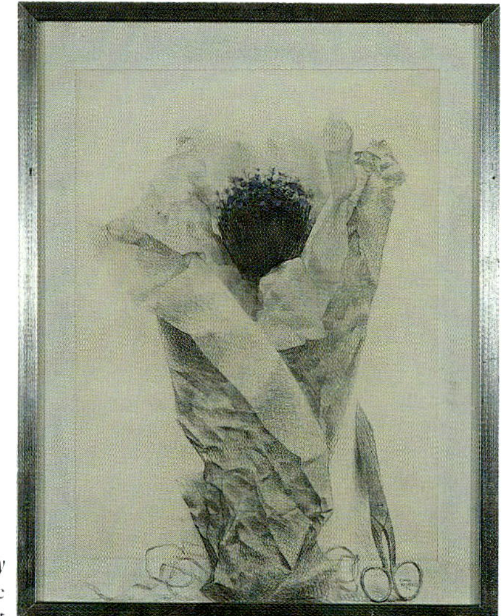

40. *Today*
Assemblage
Collection of the artist

Regards/To You/Today triptych, 1972
Each: 19-1/4 × 15-3/8" (49 × 39 cm)

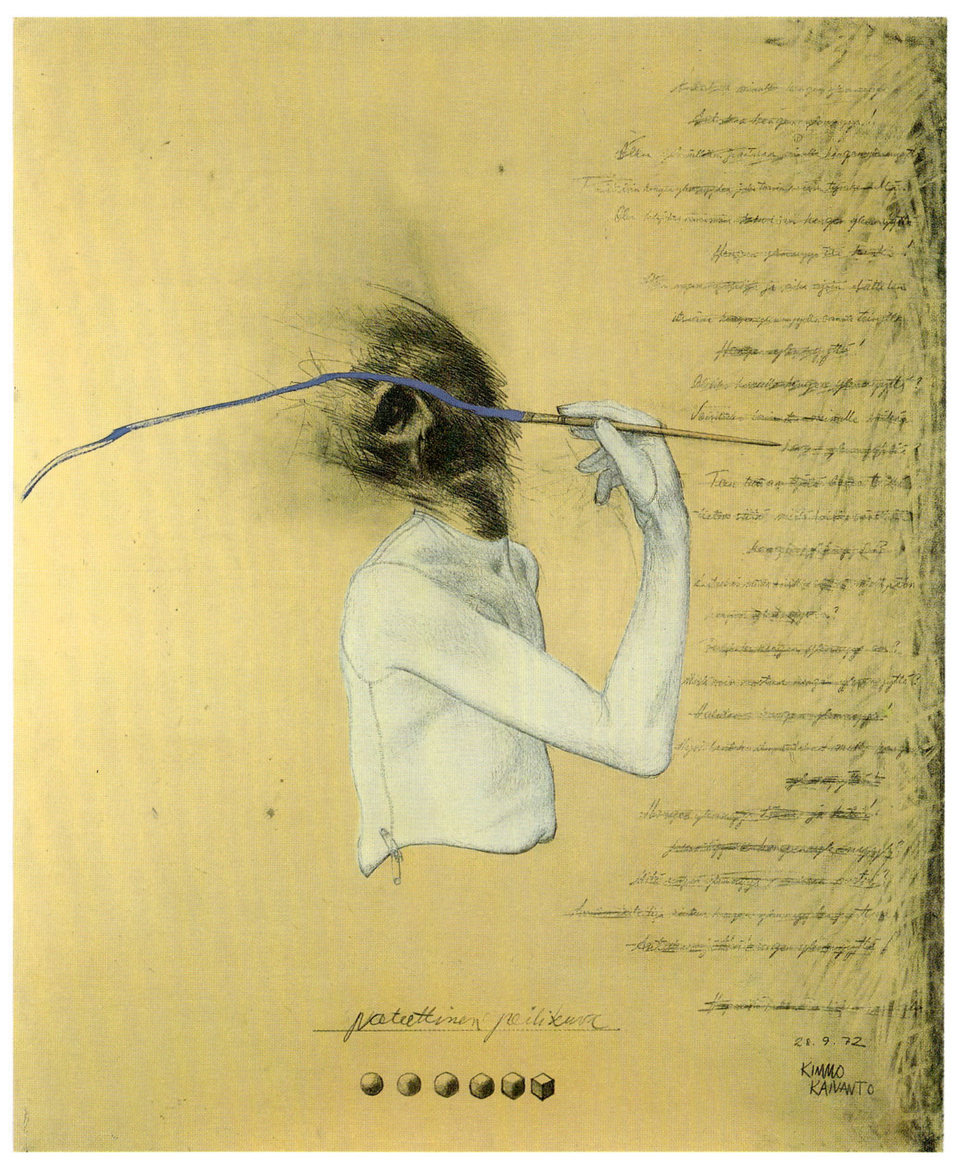

41. *Pathetic Mirror Picture*, 1972
Gouache and pencil on cardboard
55-1/8 × 46-7/8" (140 × 119 cm)
Collection of Sara Hilden Art Museum, Tampere;
Collection Sara Hildén

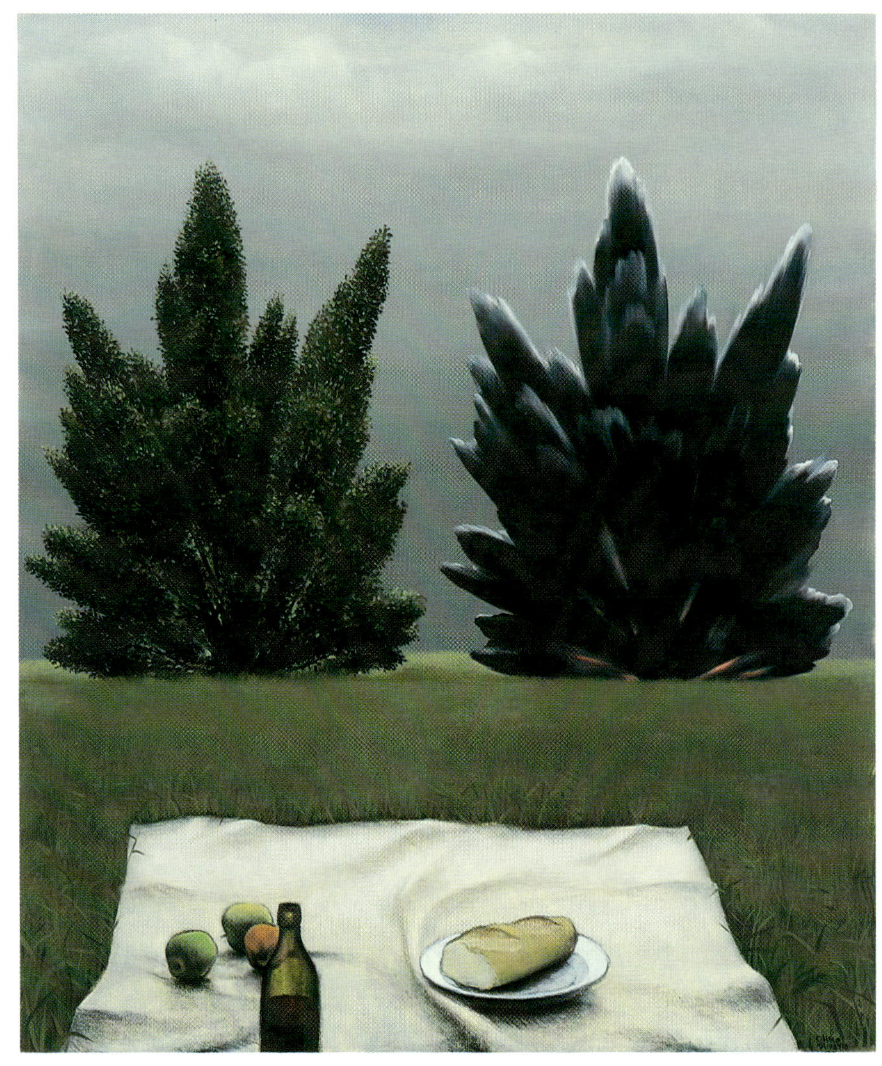

42. *Breakfast on the Lawn*, 1973
Oil on canvas
63-3/4 × 55-1/8" (162 x 140 cm)
Collection of Sara Hilden Art Museum, Tampere;
Collection Sara Hildén

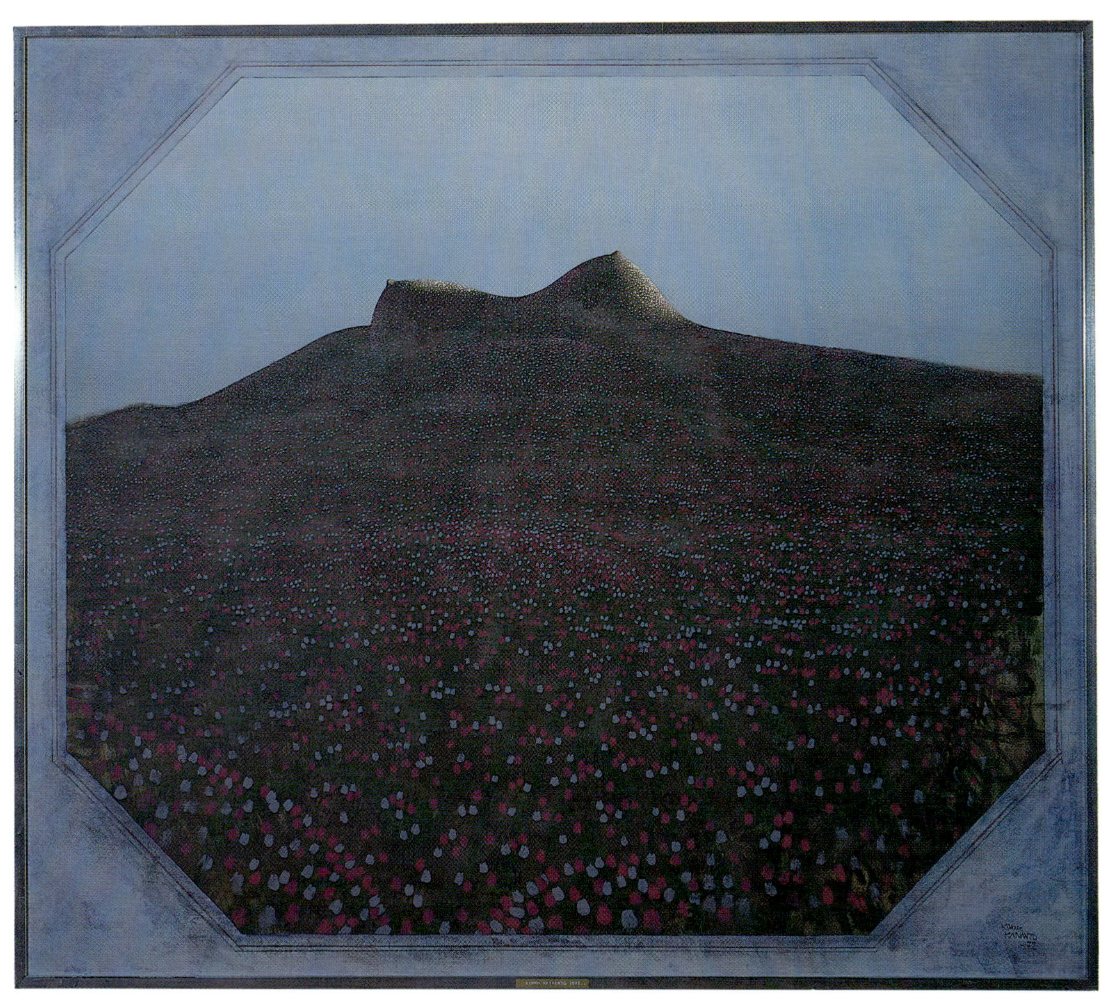

43. *Morning*, 1972
Oil on canvas
55-1/8 × 63-3/4" (140 × 162 cm)
Collection of The Museum of Contemporary Art, Helsinki

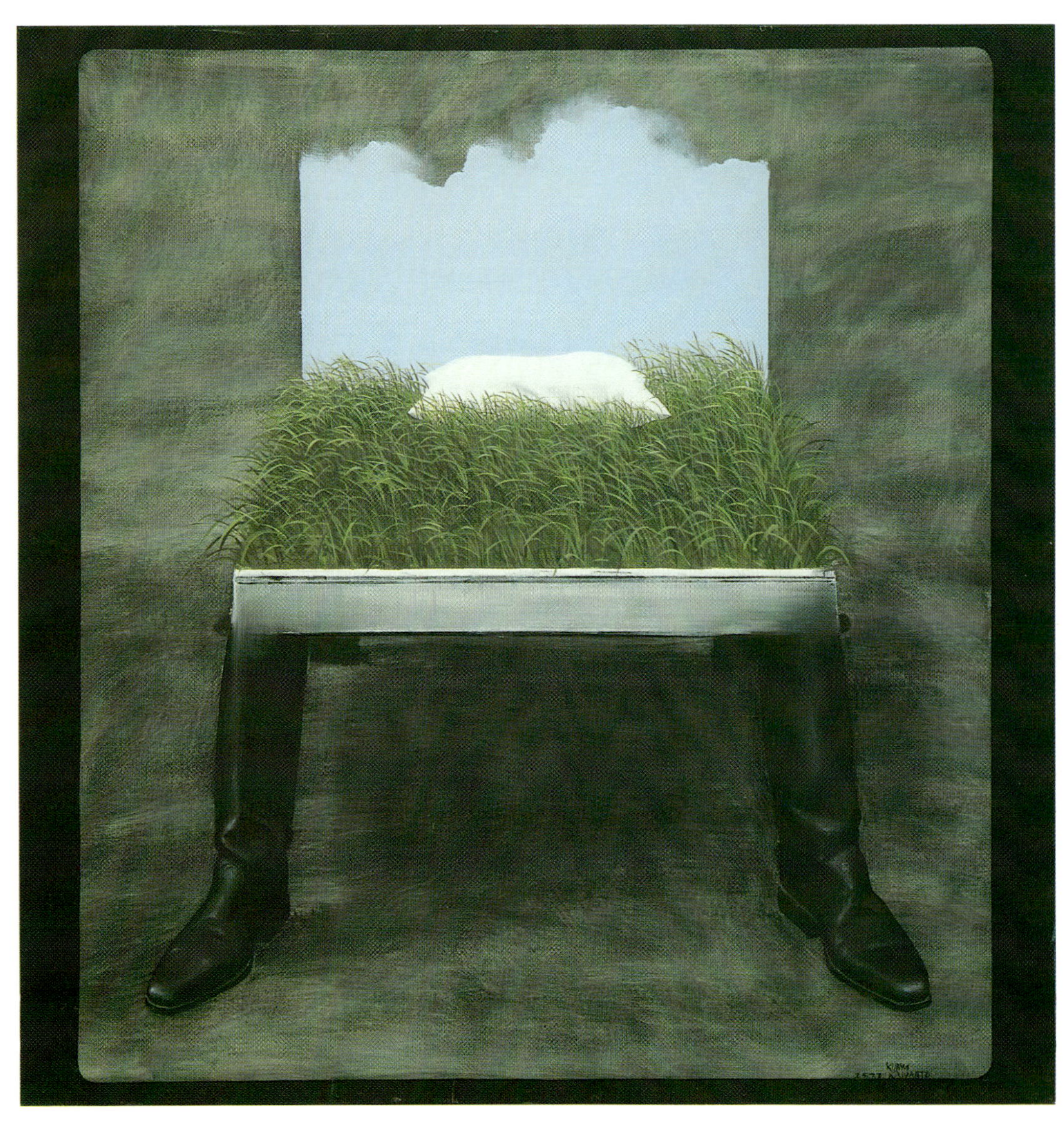

44. *Two Sides of the Medal*, 1973
Oil on canvas
63-3/4 × 63-3/4" (162 × 162 cm)
Collection of Sara Hilden Art Museum, Tampere;
Collection Sara Hildén

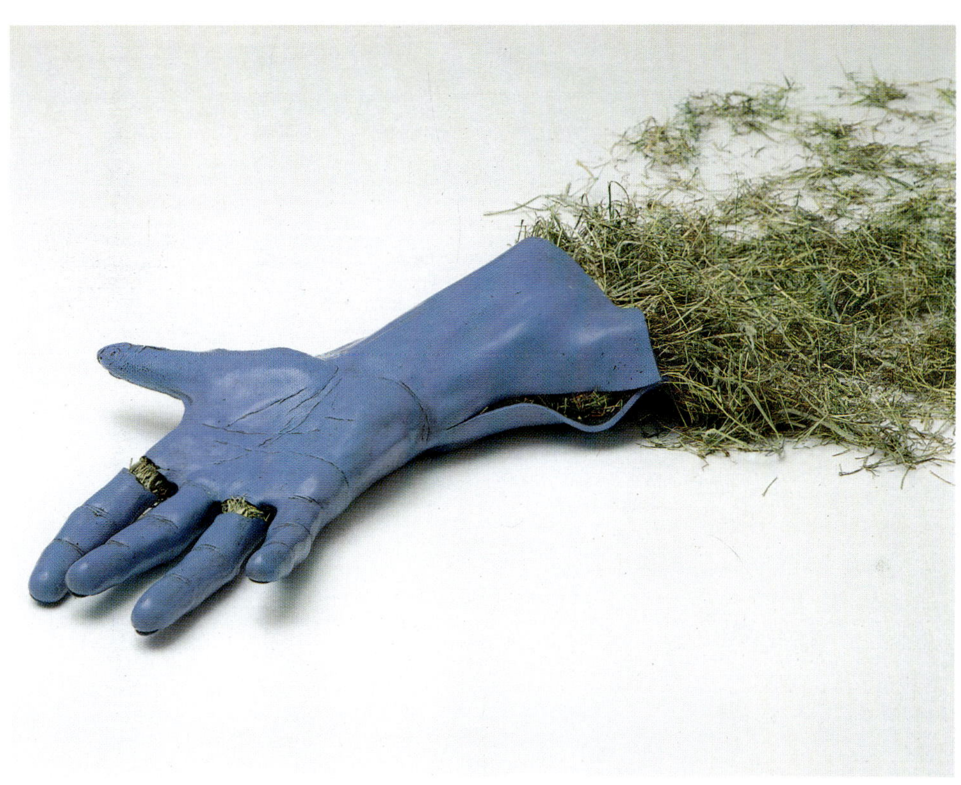

45. *Event in Nature*, 1973-80
Painted plastic and glass
11-3/4 × 47-1/4 × 27-1/2" (30 × 120 × 70 cm)
Collection of the artist

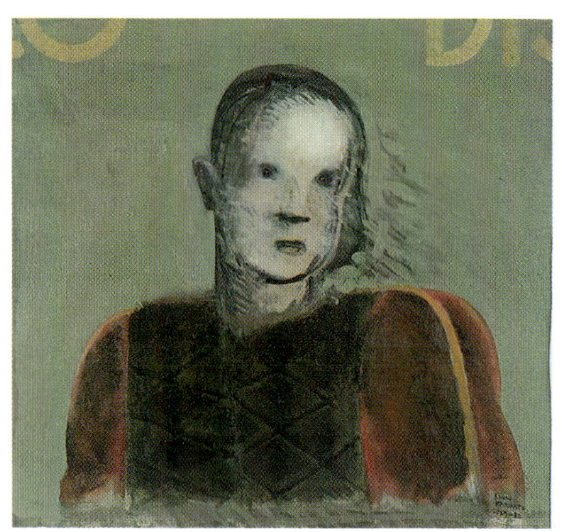

46. *The Eyewitness of the Case (A)*, 1979-80
Oil on canvas
22-1/4 × 24-5/8" (56.5 × 62.5 cm)
Collection of the artist

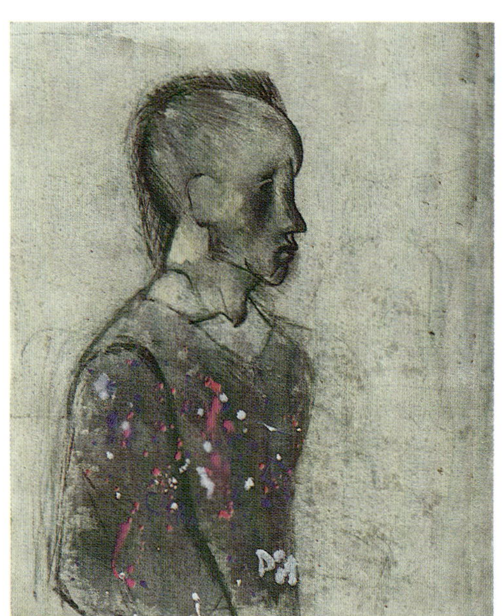

47. *Youth*, 1981
Gouache on paper
25-1/2 × 21-5/8" (65 × 55 cm)
Collection of Tampereen Alvesäästopankki/Tampere Regional
Savings Bank

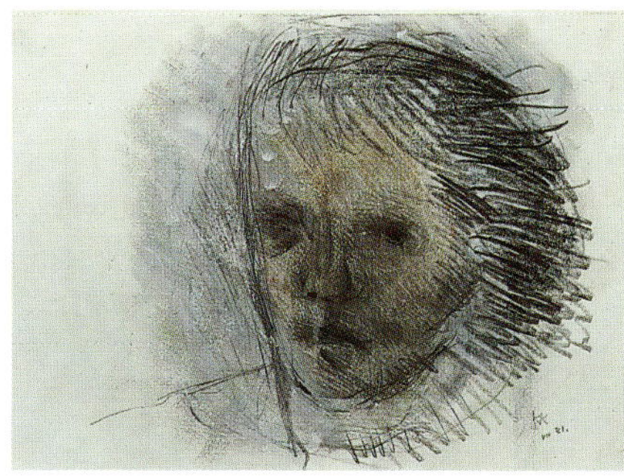

48. *Face*, 1981
Pencil and brown chalk on paper
8-1/4 × 11-3/4" (21 × 30 cm)
Collection of the artist

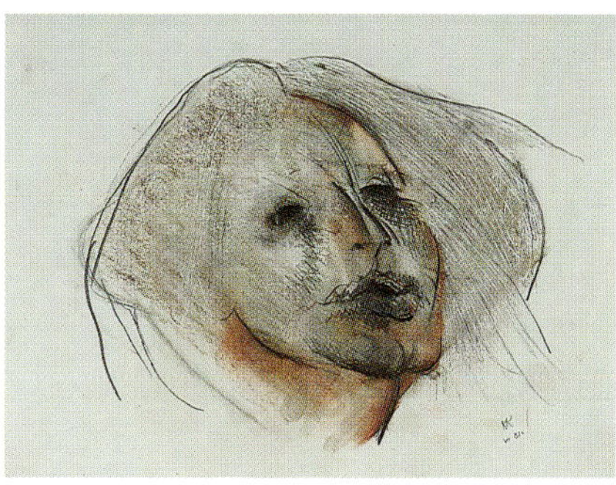

49. *Wounded Angel*, 1981
Pencil and chalk on paper
8-1/4 × 11-7/8" (21 × 30 cm)
Collection of the artist

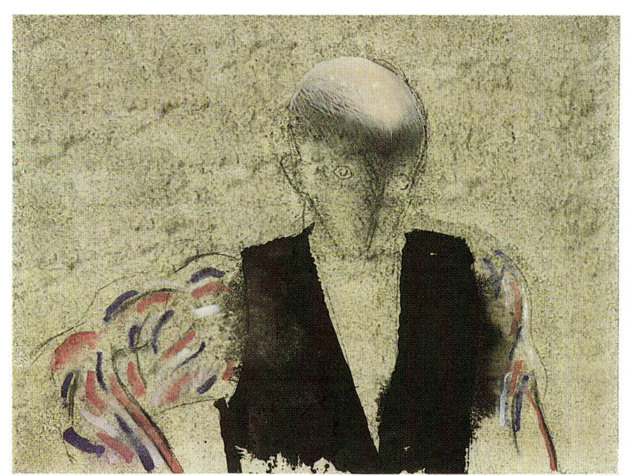

50. *Gang (E)*, 1981
Gouache on paper
21-5/8 × 29-1/2" (55 × 75 cm)
Collection of the artist

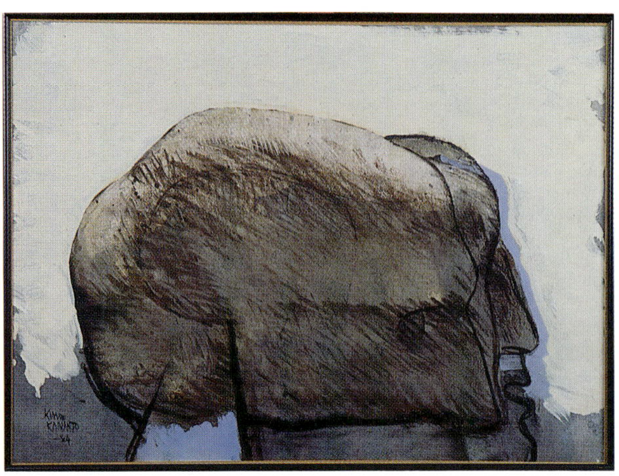

51. *Falang*, 1984
Acrylic and black chalk on paper
19-1/4 × 27-1/8" (49 × 69 cm)
Collection of the artist

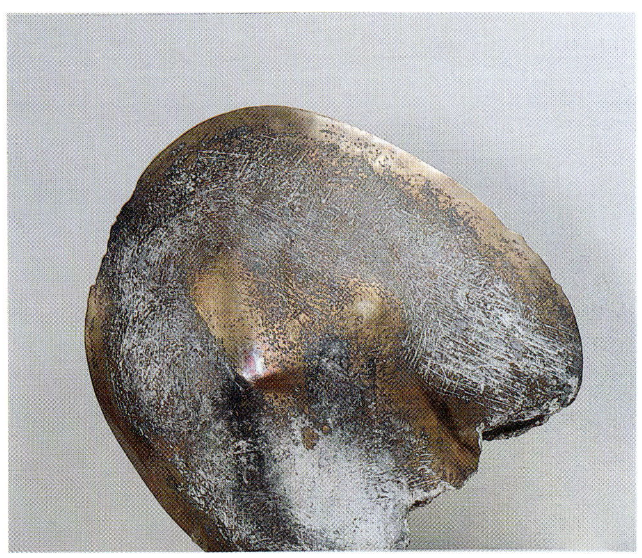

52. *Scallop*, 1985
Bronze
h. 29-1/2" (h. 75 cm)
Collection of the artist

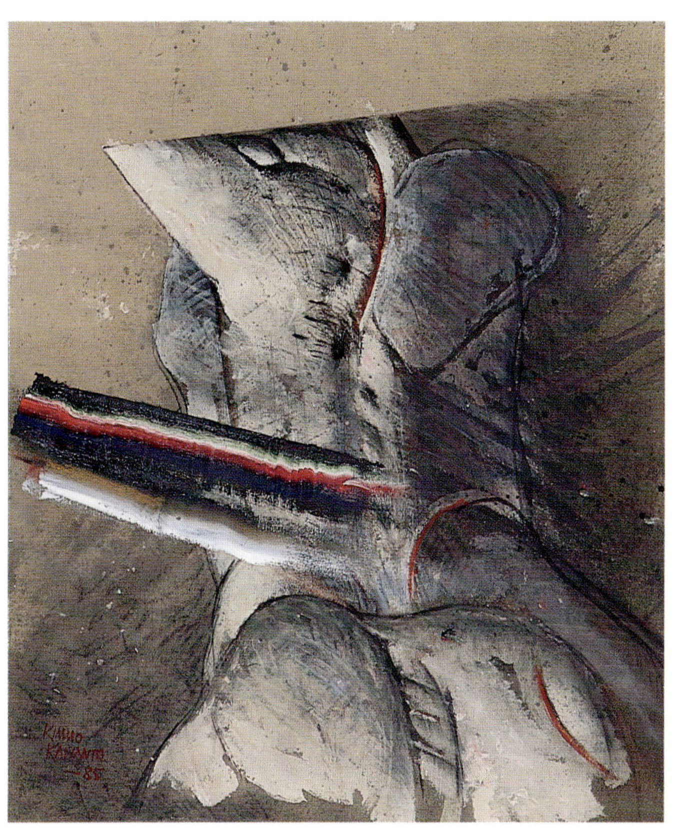

53. *Parade*, 1985
Acrylic on canvas
55-1/8 × 47-1/4" (140 × 120 cm)
Collection of Sara Hilden Art Museum, Tampere;
Collection Sara Hildén

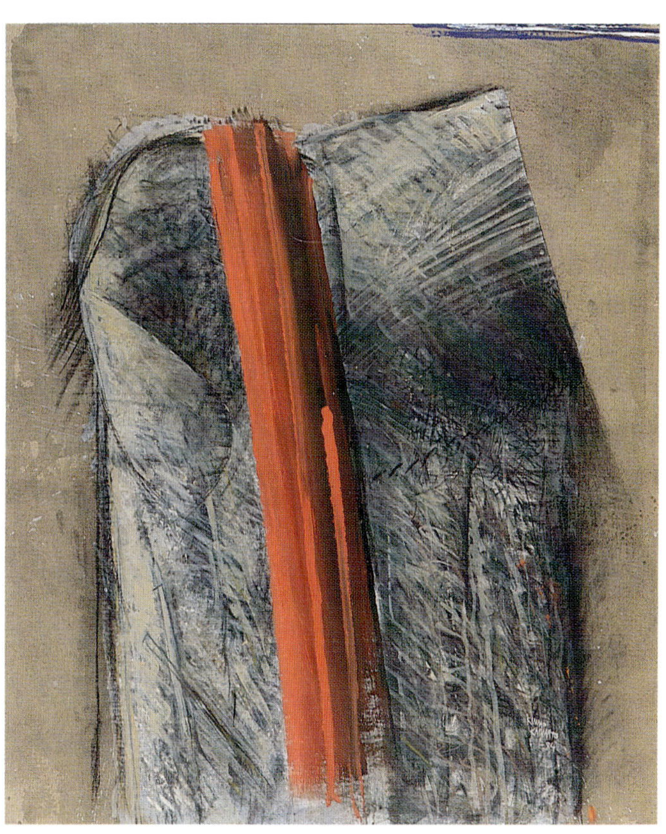

54. *Tacitus*, 1985
Acrylic on canvas
55-1/8 × 47-1/4" (140 × 120 cm)
Collection of Sara Hilden Art Museum, Tampere;
Collection Sara Hildén

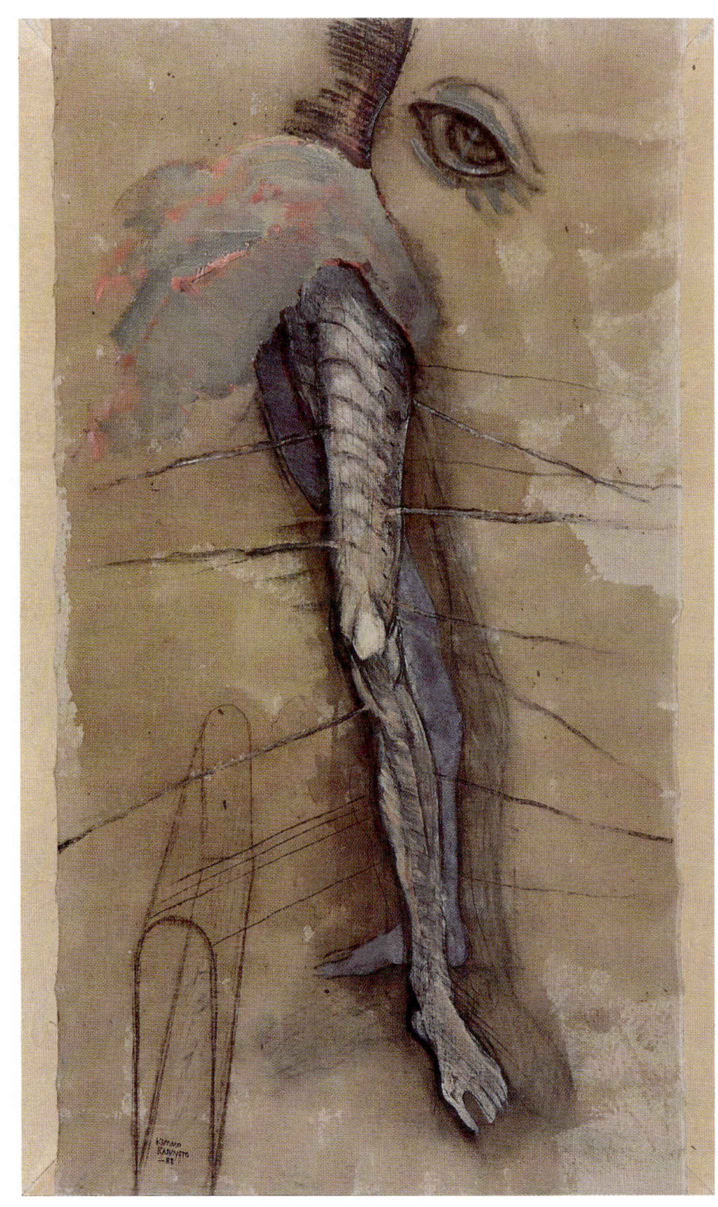

55. *Saint Sebastian II*, 1988
Acrylic on canvas
76-3/8 × 47-1/4" (194 × 120 cm)
Collection of Sara Hilden Art Museum, Tampere;
Collection Sara Hildén

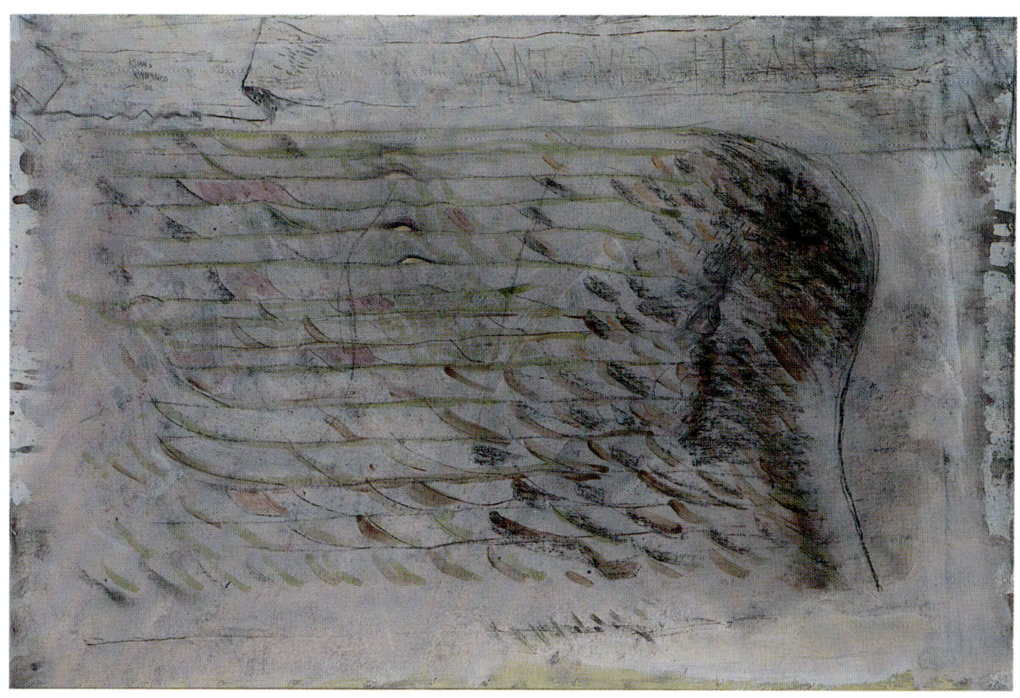

56. *The Annunciation*, 1988
Acrylic on canvas
39-3/8 × 60-1/4" (100 × 153 cm)
Collection of the artist

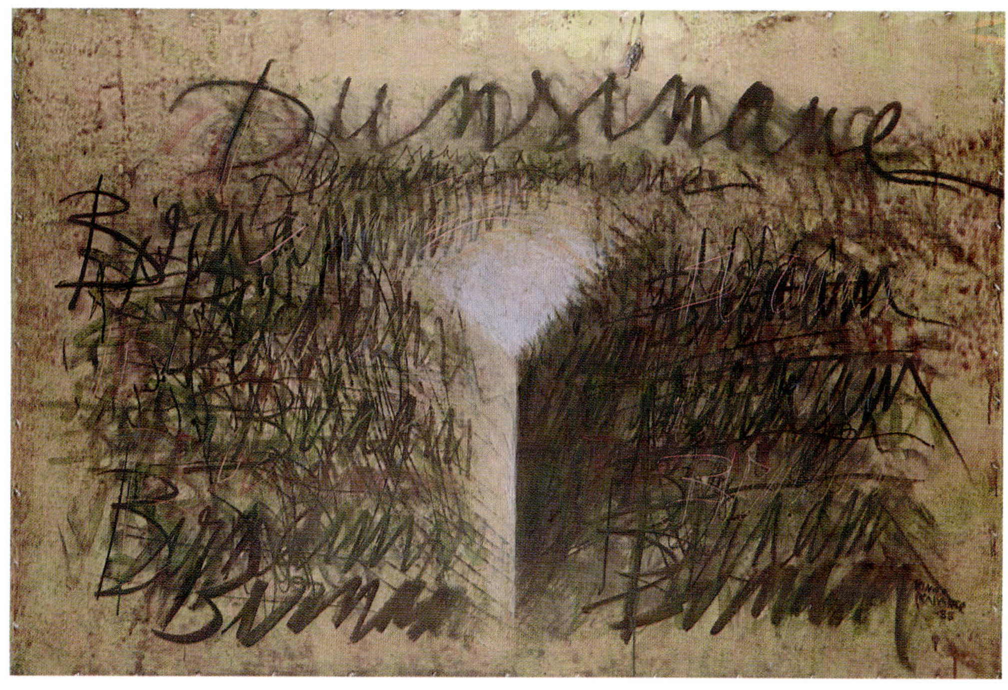

57. *The Great Birnam Wood*, 1988
Acrylic and charcoal on canvas
39-3/8 × 59-7/8" (100 × 152 cm)
Collection of Erkki Reponen

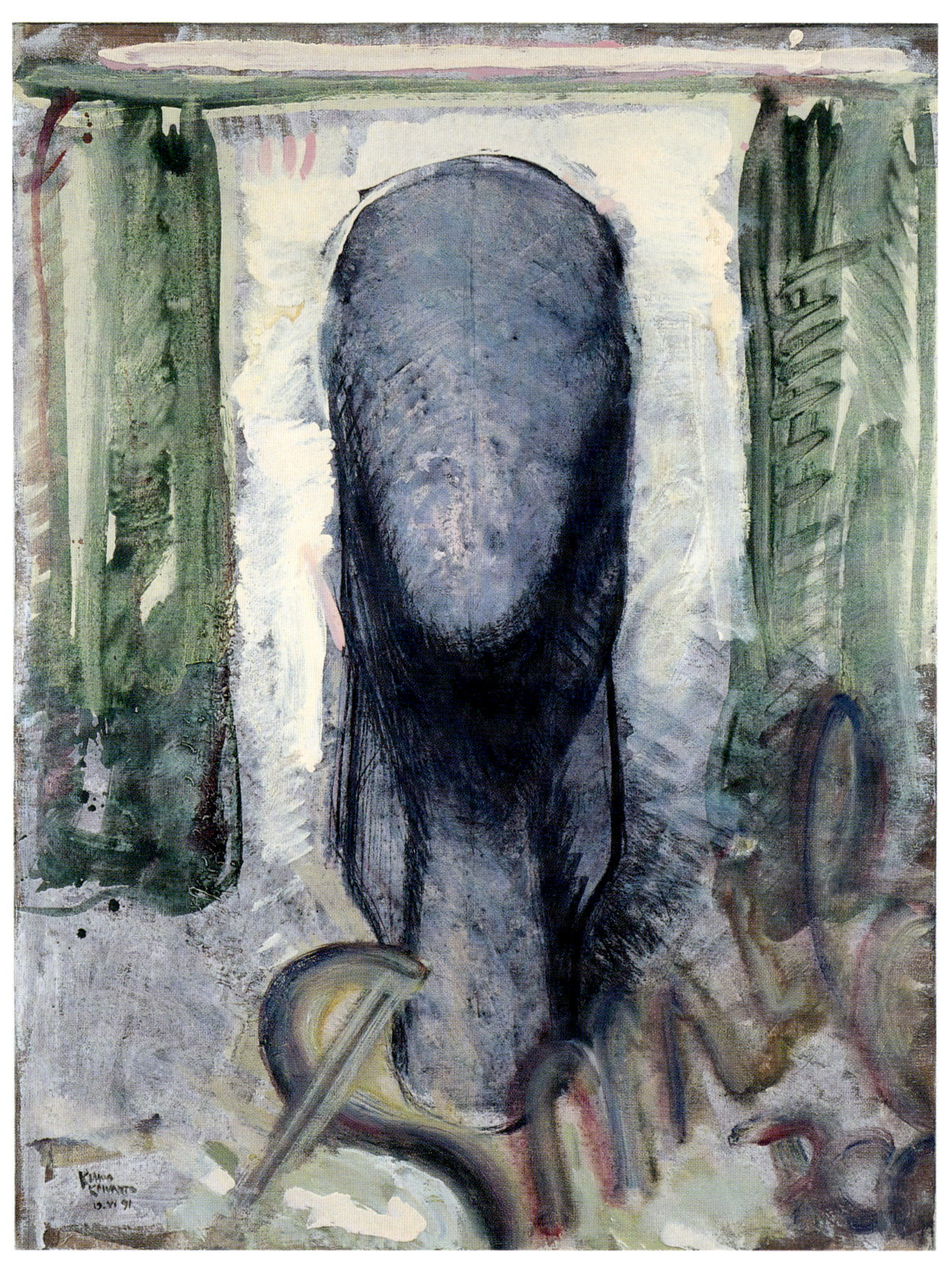

58. *Smile, Poet! (Homage to Pentti Saarikoski)*, 1991
Acrylic on canvas
72 × 56-1/4" (183 × 143 cm)
Collection of the artist

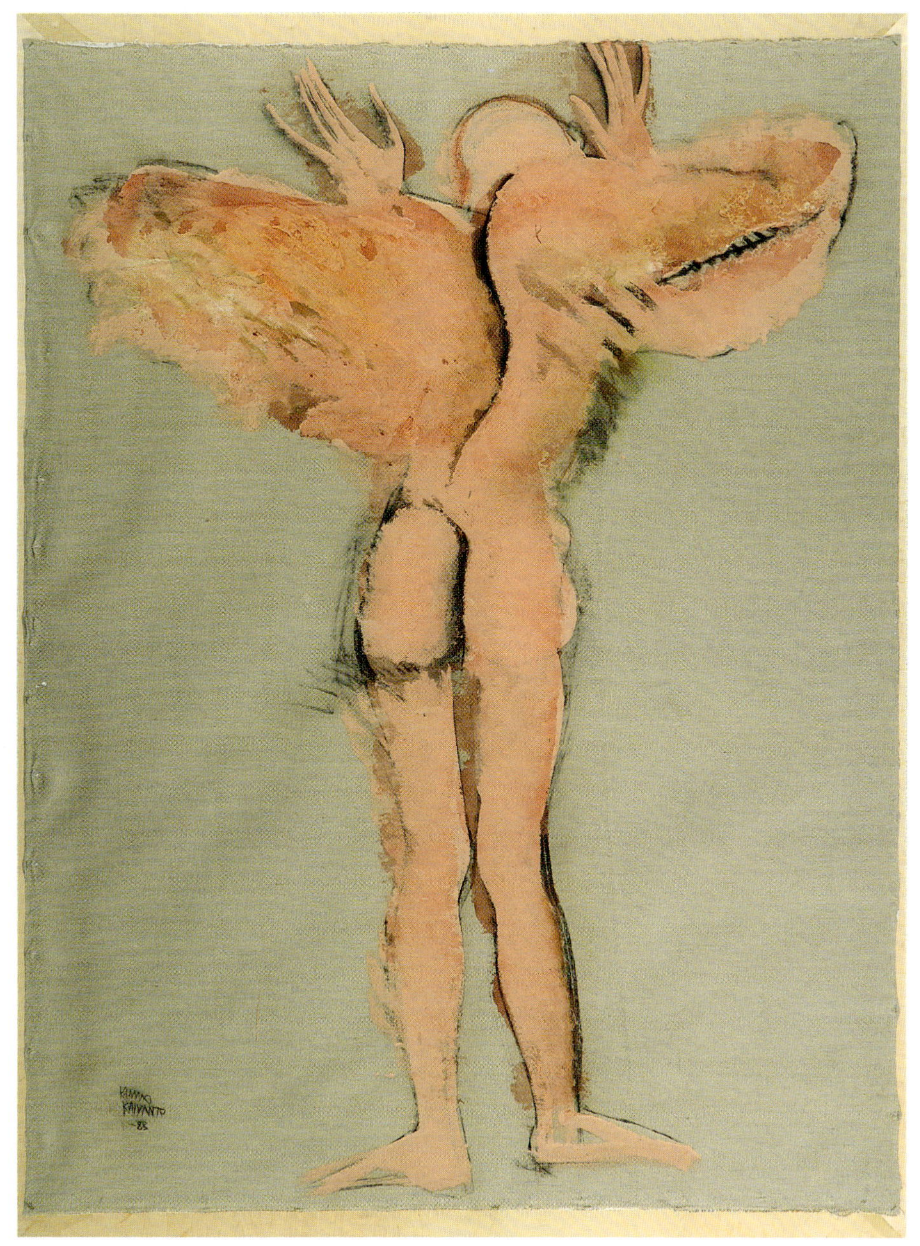

59. *The Caryatid*, 1988
Acrylic on canvas
80-3/4 × 60-1/4" (205 × 153 cm)
Collection of Sara Hilden Art Museum, Tampere;
Collection Sara Hildén

Bibliography

Compiled by
Jari Björklöv
Edited by Reiko Tomii

This bibliography is divided into nine sections:
A. Exhibition Catalogues and Related Material
B. Books on and about the Artist
C. Publications Illustrated by the Artist
D. Articles by the Artist
E. Articles on and about the Artist (Art-related Periodicals)
F. Articles on and about the Artist (General Magazines)
G. Articles on and about the Artist (Newspapers)
H. Oral Documentation
I. Audio-Visual Documentation

Entries within each section are chronologically arranged and sequentially numbered. Multiple citations for any given date, however, are organized alphabetically by author or editor, and where author or editor is unknown, by title of the work. In sections E. through I., a single dagger indicates substantial mention of the artist and a double dagger cursory mention; unmarked entries are entirely devoted to the artist. All items listed here have been verified against primary sources at the Central Art Archives and the Archives of Broadcasting in Helsinki, and/or personal papers and documents in the artist's possession.

A. Exhibition Catalogues and Related Material

1956

A.1 [Leaflet with checklist] *Tampereen Taiteilijaseuran 25. vuosinäyttely* (25th annual exhibition of the Tampere Artists' Association). Tampere: Kirjastotalo, 20-28 Oct. 1956.

1957

A.2 [Leaflet with checklist] *Nuorten 15. Näyttely/De Ungas 15. Utställning* (15th Young Artists' Exhibition). Helsinki: Taidehalli, 14-29 Sept. 1957.

A.3 [Leaflet with checklist] *Suomen Kuvataidejärjestöjen Liiton vuosinäyttely* (Annual exhibition of the Union of Finnish Visual Arts Organizations). Lahti: Taidemuseo, 2-17 Nov. 1957.

A.4 [Leaflet with checklist] *Tampereen Taiteilijaseuran 26. vuosinäyttely* (26th annual exhibition of the Tampere Artists' Association). Tampere: Kirjastotalo, 16 Nov-1 Dec. 1957.

1958

A.5 [Leaflet with checklist] *Suomen Taiteilijain 64. Näyttely/Finska Konstnärernas 64. Utställning* (64th Exhibition of Finnish Artists' [Association]). Helsinki: Taidehalli, 4-23 Feb. 1958.

A.6 [Leaflet with checklist] *Mikkelin Taideyhdistys: XIII vuosinäyttely* (Mikkeli Art Society: 13th annual exhibition). Mikkeli, 23-30 Mar. 1958.

A.7 [Leaflet with checklist] *Taidenäyttely* (Exhibition [of the group "Seven Artists"]). Tampere: Kirjastotalo, 13-21 Sept.

1958.

A.8 [Exhibition catalogue] *Suomen Kuvataidejärjestöjen Liiton 20-vuotisjuhlanäyttely* (20th anniversary exhibition of the Union of Finnish Visual Arts Organizations). Foreword by W.A. Eloniemi. Hämeenlinna: Taidemuseo, 1-16 Nov. 1958.

A.9 [Leaflet with checklist] *Tampereen Taiteilijaseuran 27. vuosinäyttely* (27th annual exhibition of the Tampere Artists' Association). Tampere: Kirjastotalo, 22-30 Nov. 1958.

1959

A.10 [Exhibition catalogue] *Expoziţia de Arta Plastica Contemporana Finlandeza* (Exhibition of Finnish contemporary art). Bucharest: Sala Dalles, May 1959.

A.11 [Invitation] *Kimmo Kaivanto*. Helsinki: Taidesalonki Pinx, 5 Sept. 1959.

A.12 [Leaflet with checklist] *Kimmo Kaivanto*. Helsinki: Taidesalonki Pinx, 5-18 Sept. 1959.

A.13 [Leaflet with checklist] *Tampereen Taiteilijaseuran 28. vuosinäyttely* (28th annual exhibition of the Tampere Artists' Association). Tampere: Kirjastotalo, 1-11 Oct. 1959.

A.14 [Exhibition catalogue] *Kolmivuotisnäyttely/Treårsutställning* (Triennial [of the Fine Arts Academy of Finland]). Helsinki: Ateneum, 16 Oct.-15 Nov. 1959.

A.15 [Leaflet with checklist] *Suomen Kuvataidejärjestöjen Liiton vuosinäyttely* (Annual exhibition of the Union of Finnish Visual Arts Organizations). Kuopio, 7-22 Nov. 1959.

1960

A.16   [Leaflet with checklist] *Modernia taidetta* (Modern art). Lahti: Kariniemi, 6 July-11 Sept. 1960.

A.17   [Leaflet with checklist] *Tampereen Taiteilijaseuran 40-vuotisjuhlanäyttely* (40th anniversary exhibition of the Tampere Artists' Association). Tampere: Taidemuseo, 1-16 Oct. 1960.

A.18   [Leaflet with checklist] *Nuorten 17. Näyttely/De Ungas 17. Utställning* (17th Young Artists' Exhibition). Helsinki: Taidehalli, 19 Nov.-11 Dec. 1960.

A.19   [Leaflet with checklist] *Nykytaiteen näyttely* (Exhibition of contemporary art). Foreword by Tytti af Forselles. Pori: Kauppaoppilaitos, 20-25 Nov. 1960.

1961

A.20   [Leaflet with checklist] *Kimmo Kaivanto: Maalauksia, grafiikkaa* (Paintings, graphics). Tampere: Kirjastotalo, 23 Sept.-1 Oct. 1961.

A.21   [Leaflet with checklist] *Kimmo Kaivanto*. Helsinki: Taidesalonki Pinx, 3-16 Nov. 1961.

A.22   [Leaflet with checklist] *Tampereen Taiteilijaseuran 30. vuosinäyttely* (30th annual exhibition of the Tampere Artists' Association). Tampere: Kirjastotalo, 1961.

1962

A.23   [Exhibition catalogue] *Kolmivuotisnäyttely/Treårsutställning* (Triennial [of the Fine Arts Academy of Finland]). Helsinki: Ateneum, 13 Oct.-11 Nov. 1962.

A.24   [Leaflet with checklist] *Tampereen Taiteilijaseuran 31. vuosinäyttely* (31st annual exhibition of the Tampere Artists' Association). Tampere: Kirjastotalo, 27 Oct.-4 Nov. 1962.

A.25   [Leaflet with checklist] *Tamperelaista taidetta* (Art from Tampere). Turku: Taidemuseo, 11-25 Nov. 1962.

A.26   [Leaflet with checklist] *Wystawa Prac Artystów z Tampere Finlandia* (Exhibition of Artists from Tampere, Finland). Foreword by Olavi Veistäjä. Łódź: Galeria Sztuki, 7-16 Dec. 1962.

A.27   [Leaflet with checklist] *Taiteilijat piirtävät/Konstnärena tecknar* (Artists are drawing). Suomen Taideakatemian kiertonäyttely 14/1962 (Exhibition circulated by the Fine Arts Academy of Finland no. 14, 1962).

1963

A.28   [Leaflet with checklist] *Tampereen nykytaidetta* (Contemporary art of Tampere). Tampere: Kirjastotalo, June-Aug. 1963.

A.29   [Leaflet with checklist] *VII Bienal de São Paulo* (7th São Paulo Biennial). São Paulo, Sept.-Dec. 1963.

A.30   [Leaflet with checklist] *Maalauksia, veistoksia, grafiikkaa* (Paintings, sculpture, graphics). Tampere: Kirjastotalo, 14-22 Sept. 1963.

A.31   [Leaflet with checklist] *Kimmo Kaivanto*. Helsinki: Taidesalonki Pinx, 12-24 Oct. 1963.

A.32   [Leaflet with checklist] *Mikkelin Taideyhdistys: XVIII vuosinäyttely* (Mikkeli Art Society: 18th annual exhibition). Mikkeli, 3-10 Nov. 1963.

A.33   [Exhibition catalogue] *Suomen kuvataidejärjestöjen liiton 25-vuotisjuhlanäyttely* (25th anniversary exhibition of the Union of Finnish Visual Arts Organizations). Tampere: Taidemuseo, 16-27 Nov. 1963.

1964

A.34   [Leaflet with checklist] *Tampereen taidetta* (Art from Tampere). Imatra: Taidemuseo, 21 Feb.-1 Mar. 1964.

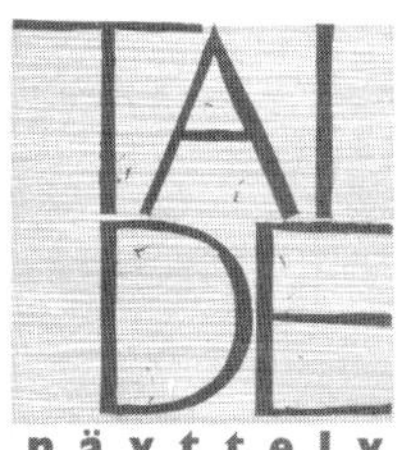

A.7

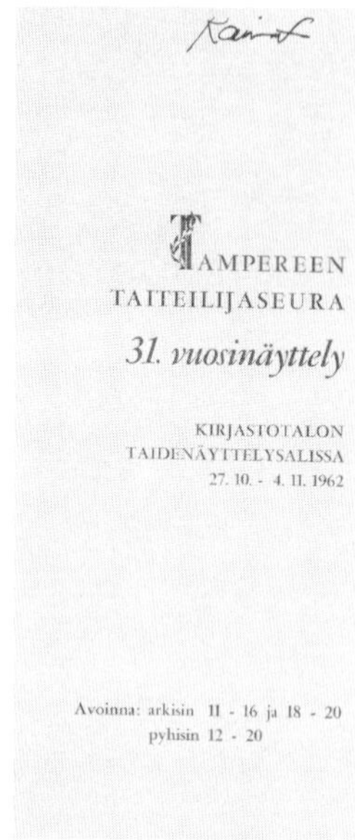

A.24

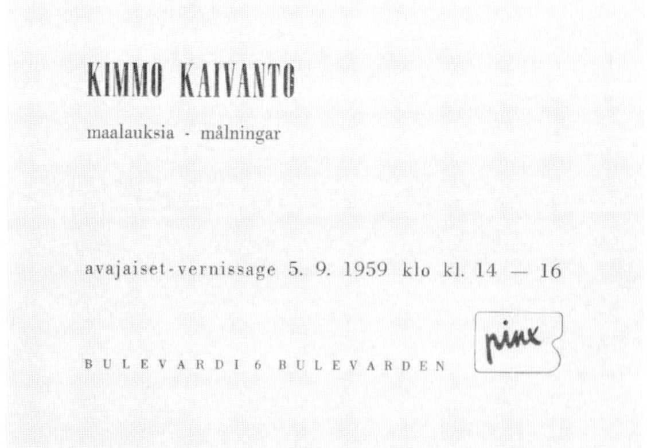

A.11

A.35   [Exhibition catalogue] *Maaliskuulaiset/Martianerna* (March Group). Texts by Pekka Suhonen and Erik Kruskopf. Helsinki: Taidehalli, 11-23 Mar. 1964 and Stockholm: Svea Galleriet 9-31 Jan. 1965.

A.36   [Exhibition catalogue] *Maaliskuulaiset/Martianerna: Ny Finsk Konst* (March Group: New Finnish Art). Texts by Erik Kruskopf and Pekka Suhonen. Helsinki: Taidehalli, 11-23 Mar. 1964; Joensuu: Turtiaisen Taidekokoelmat, 3-10 Aug. 1964; Lohja: Kirjasto 22-29 Nov. 1964; Stockholm: Svea Galleriet 9-31 Jan. 1965; and Turku: Taidemuseo, 12-28 Feb. 1965.

A.37   [Leaflet with checklist]. *Tampereen nykytaidetta* (Contemporary art of Tampere). Tampere: Kirjastotalo, 15 June-31 Aug. 1964.

A.38   [Leaflet with checklist] *Nordisk Konstutställning* (Exhibition of Nordic art). Hässelby: Hässelby Slott, Oct. 1964.

A.39   [Leaflet with checklist] *Kain Tapper/Kimmo Kaivanto*. Tampere: Kirjastotalo, 14-22 Nov 1964.

A.40   [Exhibition catalogue] *Taidemaalari työskentelee/Målaren i arbete* (Painter at work). Helsinki: Taidehalli, 21 Nov.-13 Dec. 1964.

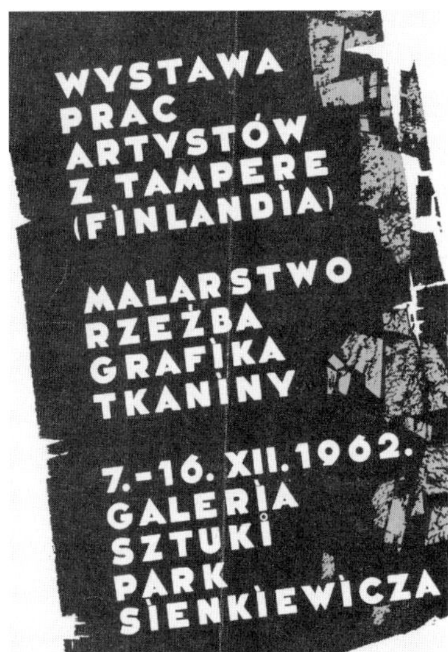

A.26

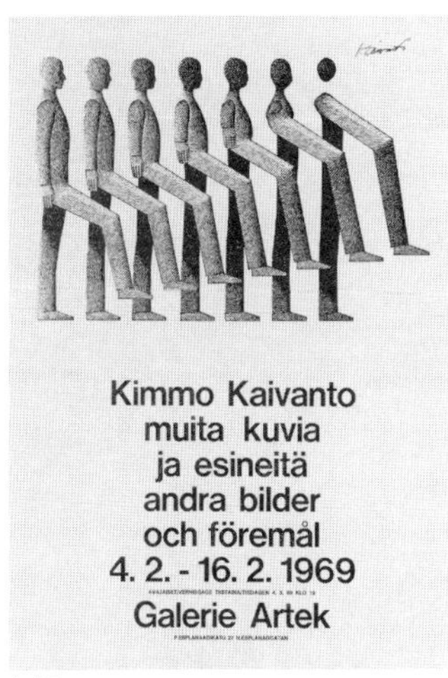

A.70

1965

A.41   [Leaflet with checklist] *Taidepäivien näyttely/Kulturdagarnas utställning* (Art Festival Exhibition). Vaasa, 30 Jan.-7 Feb. 1965.

A.42   [Leaflet with checklist] *Tampereen taidetta* (Art from Tampere). Jyväskylä: Keski-Suomen museo, 2-11 Apr. 1965.

A.43   [Exhibition catalogue] *Moderne Finnische Kunst* (Modern Finnish art). Hamburg: Kunsthaus, 13 Apr.-5 May 1965.

A.44   [Exhibition catalogue] *Finnische Grafik in Hamburg 1965* (Finnish graphic art in Hamburg 1965). Hamburg: BP Clubheim, 11-28 May 1965.

A.45   [Leaflet with checklist] *Tampereen nykytaidetta* (Contemporary art in Tampere). Tampere: Kirjastotalo, 15 June-31 Aug. 1965.

A.46   [Leaflet with checklist] *Kimmo Kaivanto*. Helsinki: Taidesalonki Pinx, 16-27 Oct. 1965.

A.47   [Exhibition catalogue] *Kolmivuotisnäyttely/Treårsutställning* (Triennial [of the Fine Arts Academy of Finland]). Helsinki: Ateneum, 30 Oct.-28 Nov. 1965.

A.48   [Leaflet with checklist] *Tampereen Taiteilijaseuran 34. vuosinäyttely* (34th annual exhibition of the Tampere Artists' Association). Tampere: Kirjastotalo, 27 Nov.-6 Dec. 1965.

1966

A.49   [Leaflet with checklist] *Kolmivuotisnäyttely/Treårsutställning* (Triennial [of the Fine Arts Academy of Finland]). Lahti: Taidemuseo 13-23 Jan. 1966; Turku: Taidemuseo, 28 Jan.-6 Feb. 1966; Hämeenlinna: Taidemuseo, 10-20 Feb. 1966; Tampere: Taidemuseo, 26 Feb.-12 Mar. 1966; Oulu: Taidemuseo, 17-27 Mar. 1966; and Kuopio, 29 Mar.-10 Apr. 1966.

A.50   [Leaflet with checklist] *Lappeenrannan Taiteilijaseuran vuosinäyttely* (Annual exhibition of the Lappeenranta Artists' Association). Lappeenranta, 27 Feb.-13 Mar. 1966.

A.51   [Leaflet with checklist] *Nykytaidetta Ateneumin kokoelmista* (Contemporary art from the collections of the Ateneum [Art Museum]). Joensuu: Turtiaisen taidekokoelmat, 29 July-4 Aug. 1966.

A.52   [Leaflet with checklist] *Tampereen Nykytaiteen Museon kesä 1966* (Summer 1966 at the Tampere Modern Art Museum). Tampere: Nykytaiteen museo, Summer 1966.

A.53   [Leaflet with checklist] *Suomalaista piirustustaidetta/Finländsk teckningskonst* (Finnish drawings). Kuopio: Kaupungintalo, 3-6 Sept. 1966; Varkaus: Taidemuseo, 11-25 Sept. 1966; Rovaniemi: Kirjastotalo, 15-23 Apr. 1967.

A.54   [Leaflet with checklist] *Maaliskuulaiset* (March Group). Foreword by Olli Valkonen. Tampere: Nykytaiteen museo, 23 Sept.-30 Oct. 1966.

A.55   [Exhibition catalogue] *Näyttely 66/Utställning 66* (Exhibition 66). Forewords by Seppo Niinivaara and C-J. af Forselles. Helsinki: Taidehalli, 19 Nov.-4 Dec. 1966.

A.56   [Exhibition catalogue] *Współczesna plastyka finlandii* (Contemporary Finnish art). Foreword by Olli Valkonen. [Poland], 1966.

1967

A.57   [Leaflet with checklist] *Kimmo Kaivanto*. Hämeenlinna: Taidemuseo, 13-23 Jan. 1967.

A.58   [Leaflet with checklist] *Tampereen taide 1917-1967* (Art of Tampere 1917-1967). Tampere: Taidemuseo, 26 Feb.-19 Mar. 1967.

A.59   [Exhibition catalogue] *Sara Hildénin kokoelma Hämeenlinnan taidemuseossa* (The Sara Hildén Collection at the Hämeenlinna Art Museum). Foreword by E.J. Vehmas. Hämeenlinna: Taidemuseo, 5-27 Mar. 1967.

A.60   [Exhibition catalogue] *Nordisk konst 1967* (Nordic Art 1967). Foreword by Tage Hedqvist. Stockholm: Liljevalchs Konsthall, 27 Apr.-28 May 1967.

A.61   [Leaflet with checklist] *Tampereen Nykytaiteen Museon kesä 1967: Seitsämän tamperelaista kuvataiteilijaa* (Summer 1967 at Tampere Modern Art Museum: Seven Tampere artists). Tampere: Taidemuseo, Summer 1967.

A.62   [Leaflet with checklist] *Finländskt 60-tal* (Finnish sixties). Foreword by Erik Bergh. Maarianhamina: Ålands Konstmuseum, 24 Sept.-8 Oct. 1967.

A.63   [Leaflet with checklist] *Turun Taideyhdistyksen vuosinäyttely/Konstföreningens i Åbo årsutställning* (Annual exhibition of the Turku Art Society). Turku: Taidemuseo, 10 Nov.-10 Dec. 1967.

A.64   [Exhibition catalogue] *IIIéme Grand Prix International d'Art Contemporain* (3rd International Grand Prix of Contemporary Art). Monaco: Palais des Congres, 15 Nov.-15 Dec. 1967.

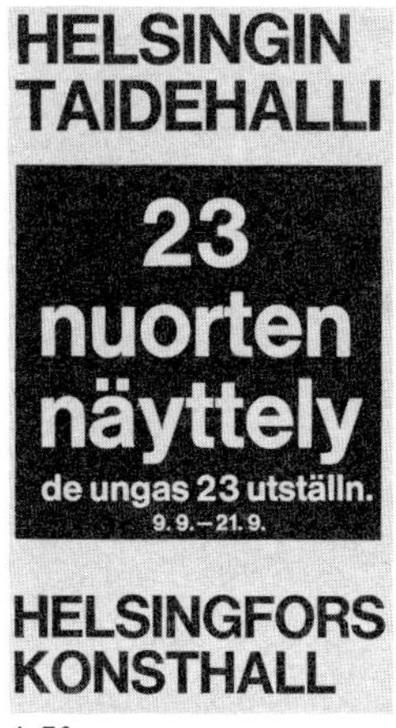

A.73

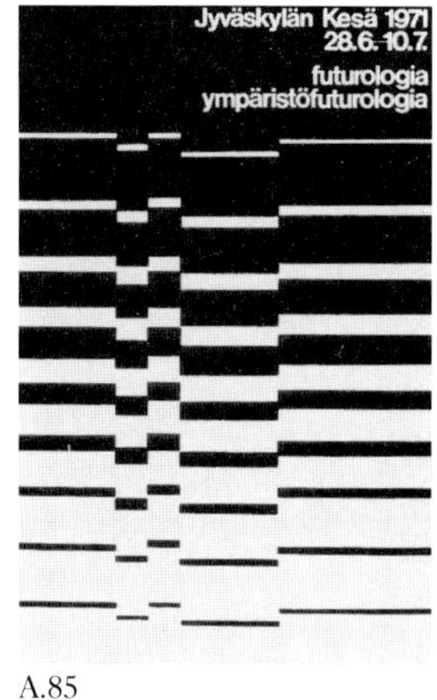

A.85

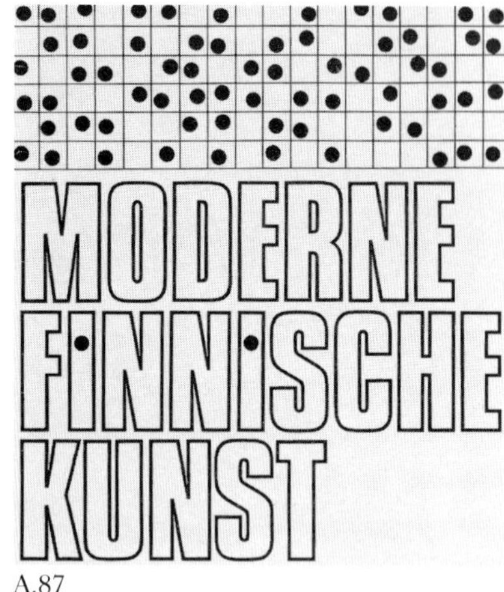

A.87

1968

A.65 [Exhibition catalogue] *Suomen Kuvataidejärjestöjen Liiton 30-vuotisnäyttely* (30th annual exhibition of the Union of Finnish Visual Arts Organizations). Helsinki: Taidehalli, 23 Feb.-10 Mar. 1968.

A.66 [Exhibition catalogue] *Ars Baltica*. Foreword by Torvald Lönnefalk. Visby: Gotlands Fornsal, 16 June-25 Aug. 1968.

A.67 [Exhibition catalogue] *Catalogo della XXXIV Esposizione Biennale Internazionale d'Arte Venezia* (Catalogue of the 35th exhibition of the international Venice Biennale). Venice, 22 June-20 Oct. 1968.

A.68 [Exhibition catalogue] *Biennale XXIV Venezia: Finlandia* (24th Venice Biennale: Finland). Venice, [22 June-25 Aug. 1968].

A.69 [Exhibition catalogue] *Kolmivuotisnäyttely/Treårsutställning* (Triennial [of the Fine Arts Academy of Finland]). Foreword by Olli Valkonen. Helsinki: Ateneum, 1 Nov.-1 Dec. 1968.

1969

A.70 [Leaflet with checklist] *Kimmo Kaivanto: Muita kuvia ja esineitä/Andra bilder och föremål* (Other pictures and objects). Texts by Yrjö Littunen and the artist. Helsinki: Galerie Artek, 4-16 Feb. 1969.

A.71 [Exhibition catalogue] *Moderne Kunst aus Finnland* (Modern art from Finland). Introduction by Leena Savolainen. Kiel: Kunsthalle, 21 June-27 July 1969.

A.72 [Exhibition catalogue] *Purnu 69*. Foreword by Olli Valkonen. Orivesi: Purnu, 28 June-24 Aug. 1969.

A.73 [Leaflet with checklist] *Nuorten 23. Näyttely/De Ungas 23. Utställning* (23rd Young Artists' Exhibition). Helsinki: Taidehalli, 9-21. Sept. 1969.

A.74 [Exhibition catalogue] *Kuvan sanoma* (A picture's message). Suomen Taideakatemian kiertonäyttely 32/1969 (Exhibition circulated by the Fine Arts Academy of Finland, no. 32, 1969). Texts by Soili Sinisalo and others.

1970

A.75 [Exhibition catalogue] *Nordisk kunst* (Nordic art). Copenhagen: Charlottenborg, 19 Apr.-18 May. 1969.

A.76 [Leaflet with checklist] *Helsinki taide 60-70/Helsingfors konst 60-70/Helsinki art 60-70*. Foreword by Kari Jylhä. Helsinki: Taidehalli, 14 May-4 June 1970.

A.77 [Leaflet with checklist] *Tampereen Taiteilijaseuran 50-vuotisjuhlanäyttely* (50th anniversary exhibition of the Tampere Artists' Association). Tampere: Taidemuseo, 19 Sept.-11 Oct. 1970.

A.78 [Exhibition catalogue] *VIII. Internationale Graphikausstellung* (8th International Exhibition of Graphic Art). Foreword by Kristian Sotriffer. Vienna: Europahaus, 1970.

A.79 [Exhibition catalogue] *Kineettisiä kuvia* (Kinetic pictures). Suomen Taideakatemian kiertonäyttely 33/1970 (Exhibition circulated by the Fine Arts Academy of Finland, no. 33, 1970).

A.80 [Leaflet with checklist] *Maisema/Landskap* (Landscape). Suomen Taideakatemian kiertonäyttely 34/1970 (Exhibition circulated by the Fine Arts Academy of Finland, no. 34, 1970).

A.81 [Exhibition catalogue] *Peinture Finlandaise Contemporaine/Hedendaagse Finse Schilderkunst* (Contemporary Finnish Painting). Introduction by Sakari Saarikivi. Brussels and Antwerp, 1970.

1971

A.82 [Invitation] *Kimmo Kaivanto: Sormet pelissä/Fingrarna med i spelet* (Fingers at play). Helsinki: Amos Andersonin Taidemuseo, 4 Feb. 1971.

A.83 [Exhibition catalogue] *Kimmo Kaivanto: Sormet pelissä/Fingrarna med i spelet* (Fingers at play). Texts by the artist and others. Helsinki: Amos Andersonin Taidemuseo, 5 Feb.-7 Mar. 1971 and Tampere: Nykytaiteen museo, 12 Mar.-13 Apr. 1971.

A.84 [Exhibition catalogue] *Purnu 71*. Foreword by Olavi Veistäjä. Orivesi: Purnu, 5 June-22 Aug. 1971.

A.85 [Exhibition catalogue] *Jyväskylän Kesä: Kupla* (Jyväskylä Summer Festival: A Bubble). Jyväskylä: Yliopiston campus, 28 June-10 July 1971.

A.86 [Leaflet with checklist] *5 Künstler aus Finnland* (5 Artists from Finland). Essen: Haus Industrieform, 12-28 Nov. 1971.

A.87 [Exhibition catalogue] *Moderne Finnische Kunst* (Modern Finnish Art). Foreword by Maaretta Jaukkuri. Fulda and Bonn, 1971.

1972

A.88 [Leaflet with checklist] *Tampereen taidetta* (Art from Tampere). Hämeenlinna: Taidemuseo, 5-20 Jan. 1972.

A.89 [Exhibition catalogue] *Heden Daagse Finse Kunst* (Contemporary Finnish Art). Introduction by Maaretta Jaukkuri. The Hague: Pulchri Studio, 8-29 Jan. 1972.

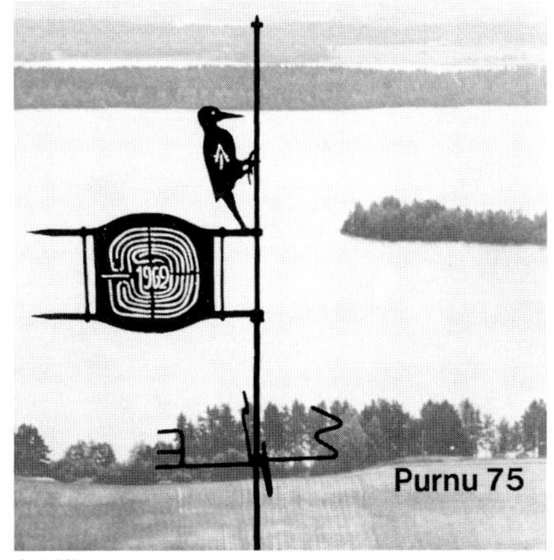

A.107

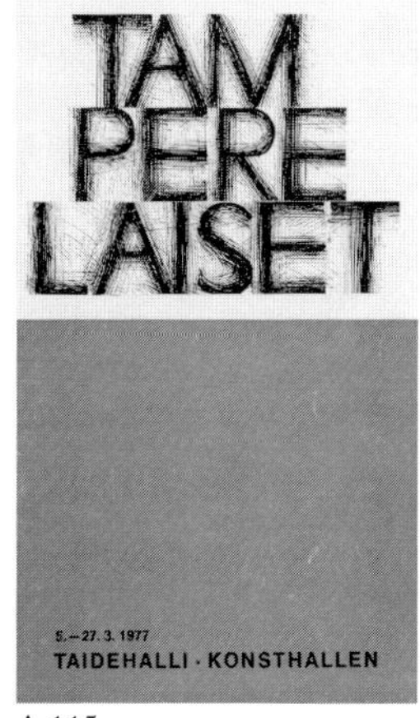

A.115

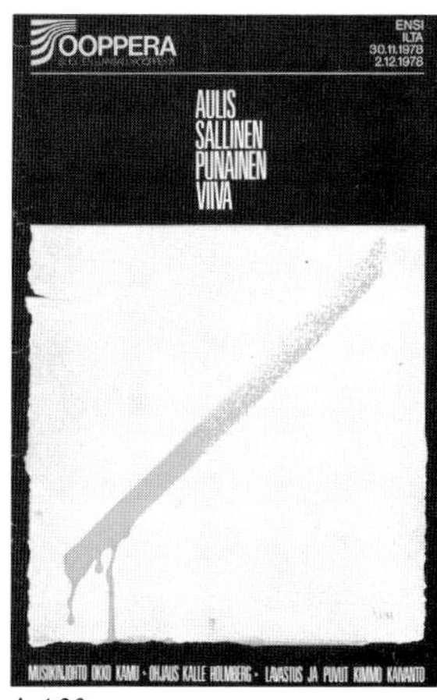

A.123

A.90 [Leaflet with checklist] *Kimmo Kaivanto: Menneen kesän kuvia/Bilder från sommaren som var* (Pictures of the past summer). Helsinki: Galerie Artek, 7-21 Mar. 1972.

A.91 [Exhibition catalogue] *Vedos '72* (Print '72). Helsinki: Taidehalli, 10-26 Mar. 1972.

A.92 [Leaflet with checklist] *Kesänäyttely/Sommarutställning* (Summer exhibition). Noormarkku: Villa Mairea, 1 July-20 Aug. 1972.

1973

A.93 [Leaflet with checklist] *Art from Finland.* New York: Finch College Museum of Art, 10 May-17 June 1973.

A.94 [Exhibition catalogue] *Purnu 73.* Foreword by E.J. Vehmas. Orivesi: Purnu, 8 June-2 Sept. 1973.

A.95 [Exhibition catalogue] *Turun Taidegraafikot ry: 40-vuotisjuhlanäyttely* (Graphic Artists of Turku [registered organization]: 40th anniversary exhibition). Foreword by Erik Bergh. Turku: Taidemuseo, 1-25 Nov. 1973 and Hämeenlinna: Taidemuseo, 29 Nov.-12 Dec. 1973.

A.96 [Exhibition catalogue] *Unga Finska Bilder* (Young Finnish Painting). Riksutställningar, no. 1136 (State exhibiition [of Sweden], no. 1136). Foreword by Bengt von Bonsdorff. 1973.

1974

A.97 [Leaflet] *Elf Finnische Graphiker* (Eleven Finnish Graphic Artists). Bonn: Galerie Pudelko, 6-25 Feb. 1974.

A.98 [Exhibition catalogue] *Ars 74.* Foreword by Salme Sarajas-Korte. Helsinki: Ateneumin taidemuseo, 15 Feb.-31 Mar. 1974.

A.99 [Exhibition catalogue] *Kunstszene Finnland* (Finnish Art Scene). Düsseldorf: Kunstmuseum, 24 Apr.-3 June 1974.

A.100 [Exhibition catalogue] *Pirkanpohjan kesänäyttely: Suomalaista nykytaidetta Ähtärissä* (Summer exhibition at Pirkanpohja: Contemporary Finnish art in Ähtäri). Ähtäri: Pirkanpohja, 26 May-4 Aug. 1974.

A.101 [Leaflet with checklist] *Taidenäyttely* (Art exhibition). Lapinlahti: Halosten Museosäätiö, 14 June-31 July 1974.

A.102 [Exhibition catalogue] *Workaday Finland.* Foreword by Maaretta Jaukkuri. London: Institute of Contemporary Arts, 4 Oct.-3 Nov. 1974.

A.103 [Leaflet with checklist] *Kimmo Kaivanto.* Poems by Juhani Peltonen. Helsinki: Taidehalli, 29 Nov.-15 Dec. 1974.

A.104 [Leaflet with checklist] *Arkipäivän Suomi/Vardagens Finland* (Workaday Finland). Foreword by Maaretta Jaukkuri. Södertälje: Konsthall, 30 Nov. 1974-5 Jan. 1975.

A.105 [Exhibition catalogue] *Finsk i dag* (Finland today). Foreword by Bengt von Bonsdorff. Copenhagen: Galerie Asbæk, 11 Dec. 1974-25 Jan. 1975.

A.106 [Exhibition catalogue] *Kukkasia* (Little flowers). Suomen Taideakatemian kiertonäyttely 52/1974 (Exhibition circulated by the Fine Arts Academy of Finland, no. 52, 1974).

1975

A.107 [Exhibition catalogue] *Purnu 75.* Foreword by Erik Kruskopf. Orivesi: Purnu, 7 June-7 Sept. 1975.

A.108 [Leaflet with checklist] *Kimmo Kaivanto.* Kotka: Teatteritalon näyttelyhalli, 2-16 Nov. 1975.

A.109 [Exhibition catalogue] *Facettes de Finlande: 10 ans d'art finlandais* (Facets of Finland: A decade of Finnish art). Ed. by Salme Sarajas-Korte and Tuula Arkio. Paris: Musée Galliéra, 17 Dec. 1975-18 Jan. 1976.

A.110 [Exhibition catalogue] *Naisia taiteessa* (Women in art). Suomen Taideakatemian kiertonäyttely 54/1975 (Exhibition circulated by the Fine Arts Academy of Finland, no. 54, 1975).

1976

A.111 [Leaflet with checklist] *Kuukauden piirtäjä/Månadens tecknare* (Draftsman of the month). Turku: Taidemuseo, Apr. 1976.

A.112 [Exhibition catalogue] *Facets–Finland: 10 Artists of the Last 10 Years.* Ed. by Salme Sarajas-Korte and Tuula Arkio. Dublin: Hugh Lane Municipal Gallery of Modern Art, 7-29 May. 1976 and Belfast: Gallery of the Arts Council of Northern Ireland, 4 June-3 July 1976.

A.113 [Exhibition catalogue] *La Biennale di Venezia '76: Finlandia, Svezia, Norvegia/The Venice Biennale 1976: Finland, Sweden, Norway.* Venice, June 1976.

A.114 [Leaflet with checklist] *Kimmo Kaivanto.* Jyväskylä: Alvar Aalto-museo, 17 Sept.-3 Oct. 1976.

1977

A.115 [Leaflet with checklist] *Tamperelaiset* (Artists from Tampere). Foreword by Kirsti Melartin. Helsinki: Taidehalli, 5-27 Mar. 1977.

A.116 [Exhibition catalogue] *Pohjolan Taidegraafikot: 40-*

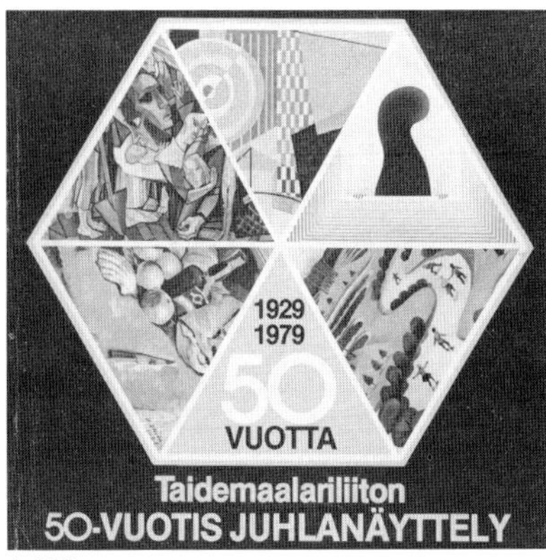

A.133

A.131 [Program] *The Finnish National Opera & Ballet* ["The Last Temptations" by Joonas Kokkonen, "The Red Line" by Aulis Sallinen and "Gayane" by Aram Khachaturian]. London: Saddler's Wells Theatre, 12-16 June 1979.

A.132 [Exhibition catalogue] *Tampere 200v taiteilijain kuvaamana* (200 years of Tampere painted by artists). Ed. by Anneli Ilmonen. Tampere: Taidemuseo, 25 Sept.-21 Nov. 1979.

A.133 [Exhibition catalogue] *Taidemaalariliiton 50-vuotisjuhlanäyttely* (50th anniversary exhibition of the [Finnish] Painters' Union). Helsinki: Taidehalli, 13 Oct.-4 Nov. 1979; Turku: Taidemuseo, 17 Nov. 1979-6 Jan. 1980; Tampere: Taidemuseo, 16 Jan.-10 Feb. 1980; Hämeenlinna: Taidemuseo, 16 Feb.-2 Mar. 1980; Kemi: Taidemuseo, 15 Mar.-7 Apr.1980; Jyväskylä: Alvar Aalto-museo, 18 Apr.-4 May 1980; and Lappeenranta: Etelä-Karjalan museo, 17 May-15 June 1980.

vuotisjuhlanäyttely/Nordisk Grafik Union: 40-årsjubileumutställning (Nordic Graphic Art Union: 40th anniversary exhibition). Helsinki: Taidehalli, 2-24 Apr. 1977.

A.117 [Leaflet with checklist] *Suomalaisia akvarelleja 1900-luvulta/20th Century Finnish Water-Colors.* Jyväskylä: Keski-Suomen Museo, 28 June-17 July 1977.

A.118 [Invitation] *Kimmo Kaivanto: Seinämaalaus, Tori* (The mural "Square"). Tampere: Nykytaiteen museo, 23 Sept. 1977.

A.119 [Leaflet] *Kimmo Kaivanto: Seinämaalaus, Tori* (The mural "Square"). Text by Pekka Paavola. Tampere: Nykytaiteen museo, 24 Sept.-30 Oct. 1977.

A.120 [Exhibition catalogue] *Finsk bild* (Finnish pictures). Introduction by Jaakko Lintinen. Stockholm: Liljevalchs Konsthall, 25 Nov. 1977-8 Jan. 1978.

A.121 [Exhibition catalogue] *Sculptures Miniatures & Feuilles Graphiques de Finlande* (Finnish Miniature Sculpture and Graphics). Circulated by Suomen Taiteilijaseura in France, 1977-78.

1978

A.122 [Leaflet with checklist] *Mitali- ja graafiikkanäyttely* (Medal and graphic art exhibition). 27 Apr.-11 May 1978.

A.123 [Program] *Aulis Sallinen: Punainen viiva* (Aulis Sallinen: The Red Line). Helsinki: Suomen Kansallisooppera, 30 Nov. 1978 and 2 Dec. 1978 [premiere].

A.124 [Exhibition catalogue] *Skopin taidetta/Scabs konstverk* (Art from the SKOP Collection). Foreword by Matti Ranki. Helsinki: Taidehalli, 2-26 Dec. 1978.

A.125 [Exhibition catalogue] *Neljätoista suomalaista runoilijaa ja taiteilijaa* (Fourteen Finnish poets and visual artists). Foreword by Leena Peltola. 1978.

A.126 [Exhibition catalogue] *8. Biennale der Ostseeländer: Suomi-Finland* (8th biennale of the Baltic Countries: Suomi-Finland). 1978.

1979

A.127 [Leaflet with checklist] *Allende-museo Suomi/Allende-museet Finland* (Allende museum Finland). Helsinki: Taidehalli, 6-28 Jan. 1979.

A.128 [Leaflet with checklist] *Tampereen Taidemuseo vierailee* (Tampere Art Museum visits). Hämeenlinna: Taidemuseo, 8-28 Mar. 1979.

A.129 [Exhibition catalogue] *Finsk Bild* (Finnish pictures). Introduction by Maaretta Jaukkuri. Oslo: Kunsternes Hus, 28 Apr.-2 June 1979.

A.130 [Exhibition catalogue] *Purnu 79.* Foreword by Anneli Ilmonen. Orivesi: Purnu, 9 June-19 Aug. 1979.

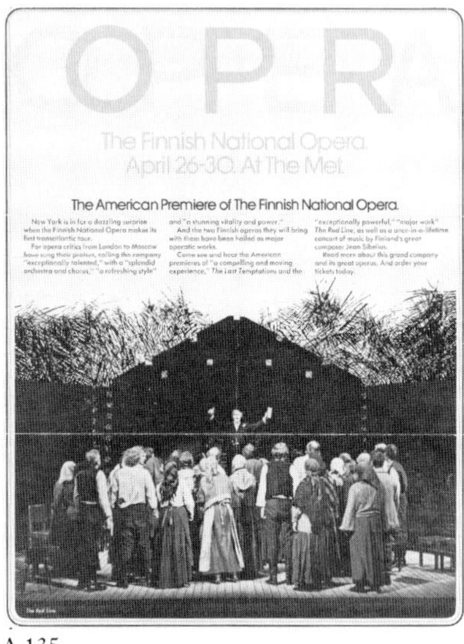

A.135

A.134 [Leaflet with checklist] *Kimmo Kaivanto.* Turku: Galerie Grafiart, 22 Nov.-11 Dec. 1979.

1980

A.135 [Program] *Det röda strecket* (The Red Line). Stockholm: Stora Teatern, 12 Jan. 1980 [premiere].

A.136 [Leaflet with checklist] *Tamperelaiset/12 från Tampere* (Tampere artists/12 from Tampere). Foreword by Pekka Paavola. Vaasa: Pohjanmaan museo, 5-30 Mar. 1980.

A.137 [Exhibition catalogue] *Kokeileva 60-luku/Experimenterande 60-tal* (Experimental sixties). Texts by Salme Sarajas-Korte, Leena Ahtola-Moorhouse and Soili Sinisalo. Helsinki: Ateneumin taidemuseo, 8 May-8 June 1980 and Turku: Taidemuseo, 15 June-21 Sept. 1980.

A.138 [Exhibition catalogue] *Suomalaista kuvataidetta/Modern Finnish Art.* Foreword by Kari Juva. Valkeakoski: Voipaalan Taidekeskus, 17 May-31 Aug. 1980.

A.139 [Exhibition catalogue] *Idyllistä ahdistukseen* (From idyll to oppression). Foreword by Pekka Helin. Tampere: Nykytaiteen museo, 30 May-31 Aug. 1980.

A.140 [Exhibition catalogue] *Kuvan maailma, maailmankuva* (The world of pictures, a picture of the world). Foreword by Jaakko Lintinen. Jyväskylä: Alvar Aalto-museo, 24 June-13 July 1980.

A.141 [Exhibition catalogue] *Porin taidemuseon vihkiäisnäyttely/Björnborgs konstmuseums invigningsutställning/Pori Art Museum Inaugural Exhibition.* Foreword by Salme Sarajas-Korte. Pori: Taidemuseo, 25 Sept.-22 Nov. 1981.

A.142 [Exhibition catalogue] *Ruovesi taiteilijoiden kuvaamana* (Ruovesi painted by artists). Ed. by Anneli Ilmonen, Elli Perkko and Anneli von Pfaler. Ruovesi: Säästöpankki, 23 Oct.-9 Nov. 1980; Virrat: Kaupungintalo, 11-23 Nov. 1980; and Mänttä: Gösta Serlachiuksen taidemuseo, 25 Nov.-9 Dec. 1980.

1981

A.143 [Exhibition catalogue] *Kimmo Kaivanto.* Text by Erik Kruskopf. Södertälje: Konsthall, 24 Jan.-5 Mar. 1981.

A.144 [Exhibition catalogue] *Puupiirros Suomessa/Träsnittet i finsk*

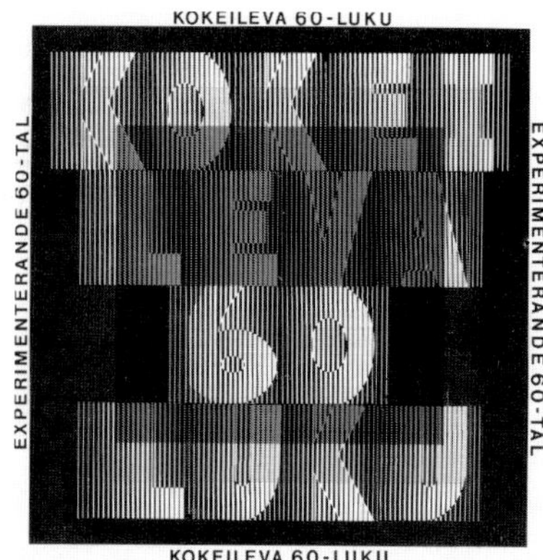

A.137

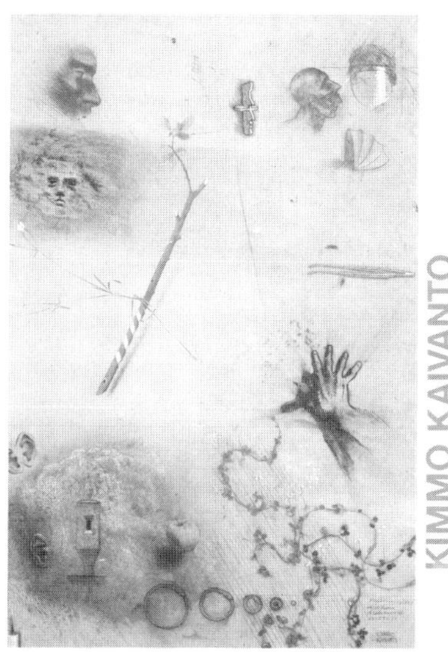

A.143

konst (Woodcut in Finnish art). Introduction by Leena Peltola. Helsinki: Sinebrychoffin taidemuseo, 12 Mar.-3 May 1981.

A.145 [Exhibition catalogue] *Purnu 81.* Foreword by Paavo Suvanto. Orivesi: Purnu, 4 June-23 Aug. 1981.

1982

A.146 [Leaflet with checklist] *Moderne Finnische Graphik* (Finnish contemporary graphic art). Foreword by Bengt von Bonsdorff. Erlangen e. V.: Kunstverein, 6-30 July 1982.

A.147 [Exhibition catalogue] *Kimmo Kaivanto: Vuoden taiteilija/Årets konstnär/Artist of the Year.* Texts by Soili Sinisalo and Jaakko Lintinen. Helsinki: Taidehalli, 19 Aug.-19 Sept. 1982.

A.148 [Exhibition catalogue] *Kimmo Kaivanto.* Text by Timo Vuorikoski. Tampere: Sara Hildénin taidemuseo, 2 Oct.-28 Nov. 1982.

A.149 [Exhibition catalogue] *Rauhan puolesta* (For peace). Tuusula: Tuusulan kunnantalo and Suomen kuntainliiton kunnallisopisto, 16-31 Oct. 1982.

A.150 [Leaflet] *Nytt på papper* (New works on paper). Foreword by Ingrid Mesterton. Göteborg: Konsthallen, 14 Nov.-27 Dec. 1981.

A.151 [Exhibition catalogue] *Sex finska grafiker/Kuusi suomalaista graafikkoa* (Six Finnish print-makers). Foreword by J.O. Mallander. Helsinki: Pohjoismainen Taidekeskus, 1982.

1983

A.152 [Exhibition catalogue] *Pyhäniemi '83.* Foreword by Maija-Riitta Kallio. Hollola: Pyhäniemen kartano, 15 May-11 Sept. 1983.

A.153 [Order form] *Ooppera: The Finnish National Opera.* New York: Metropolitan Opera, 26-30 Apr. [1983].

1984

A.154 [Exhibition catalogue] *Suvremena finska umjetnost/Sodobna finska umetnost* (Contemporary Finnish art). Zagreb: Galerije Grada, 6-30 Sept. 1984; Sarajevo: Umjetnički Paviljon, 2-18 Nov. 1984; and Ljubljana: Cankarjev Dom, 28 Nov.-23 Dec. 1984.

A.155 [Exhibition catalogue] *Löytöretki maisemaan: Suomalaisuus kuvataiteessa 1700-luvulta nykypäivään* (Journey into the landscape: Finnishness in visual arts from the 18th century to our time). Ed. by Anneli Ilmonen. Tampere: Taidemuseo, 17 Sept.-20 Nov. 1984.

1985

A.156 [Leaflet with checklist] *Pyhäniemi '85.* Foreword by Heikki Tuominen. Hollola: Pyhäniemen kartano, 1 June-1 Sept. 1985.

A.157 [Exhibition catalogue] *Purnu 86.* Forewords by Risto Tainio and Hannu Kilpeläinen. Orivesi: Purnu, Summer 1986.

A.158 [Exhibition catalogue] *Forum + Art: Kimmo Kaivanto.* Text by Kaj Kalin and the artist. Helsinki: Amos Andersonin Taidemuseo, 15 Nov. 1985-5 Jan. 1986.

1987

A.159 [Exhibition catalogue] *Kimmo Kaivanto.* Kuopio: Taidemuseo, 3 Apr.-3 May 1987.

1988

A.160 [Exhibition catalogue] *Suomalainen maisema/Det finska landskapet/The Finnish Landscape/Die finnische Landschaft.* Text by Leena Lindqvist. Punkaharju: Retretti, Summer 1988.

A.161 [Exhibition catalogue] *Kimmo Kaivanto: Maalauksia/Recent Paintings.* Text by the artist. Helsinki: Galleria Bronda, 11 Nov.-4 Dec. 1988.

A.162 [Exhibition catalogue] *Maalauksen uusi kieli: Suomalaista modernismia 1956-61/Måleriets nya språk: Finländsk modernism 1956-61* (The new language of painting: Finnish modernism 1956-61). Texts by Aune Jääskinen and Ulla Vihanta. Suomen Taideakatemian kiertonäyttely 85/1988 (Exhibition circulated by the Fine Arts Academy of Finland, no. 85, 1988).

1989

A.163   [Exhibition catalogue] *Maaliskuulaiset ja 60-luku/Martianerna och 60-talet* (The March Group and the 1960s). Text by Leena Peltola. Helsinki: Taidehalli, 11 Mar.-9 Apr. 1989.

1990

A.164   [Exhibition catalogue] *Nordiskt 60-tal: Uppbrott och konfrontation/Pohjolan 60-luku: Murros ja vastus/The Nordic '60s: Upheaval and Confrontation.* Reykjavik: Listasafn Islands, 3 Mar.-1 Apr. 1990; Hoevikodden: Kunstsentret Hoevikodden, 28 Apr.-17 June 1990; Odense: Kunsthallen Brandts klaederfabrik, 29 June-19 Aug. 1990; Stockholm: Kulturhuset, 7 Sept.-4 Nov. 1990; and Helsinki: Taidehalli, 20 Nov.-31 Dec. 1990.

A.165   [Invitation] *Vuosisata kansallistaidetta/Ett sekel: Kansalliskonst/A Century of Finnish Art.* Helsinki: Taidehalli, 7 June 1990.

A.166   [Exhibition catalogue] *Tampereen Taiteilijaseura 1920-1990. Korvesta maailmalle* (The Tampere Artists' Association 1920-1990. From the wilderness to the wide world). Text by Pekka Helin. Tampere: Pyynikinlinna, 6-30 Sept. 1990 and Taidekeskus Mältinranta, 21 Sept.-30 Oct. 1990.

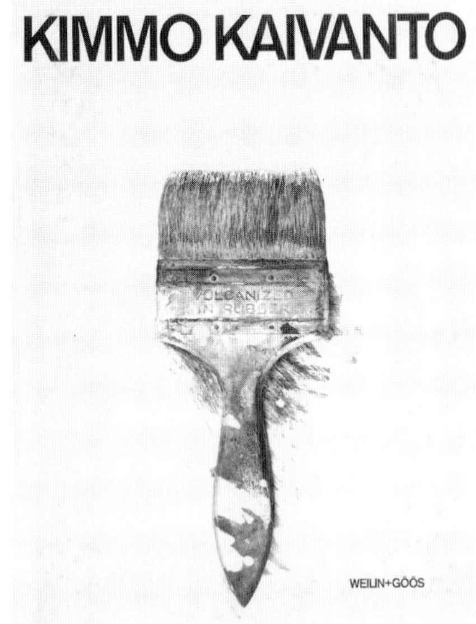

B.50

B. Books on and about the Artist

1958

B.1   Krohn, Alf, ed. *Suomen Taide 1957-1958: Vuosikirja* (Yearbook of Finnish Art 1957-1958). Helsinki: Suomen Taiteilijaseura, 1958: 117.

1959

B.2   Valkonen, Olli, ed. *Suomen Taide 1958-1959: Vuosikirja* (Yearbook of Finnish Art 1958-1959). Helsinki: Suomen Taiteilijaseura, 1959: 80, 103, 168.

1960

B.3   Valkonen, Olli, ed. *Suomen Taide 1960: Vuosikirja* (Yearbook of Finnish Art 1960). Helsinki: Suomen Taiteilijaseura, 1960: 94, 98, 131.

1961

B.4   Koroma, Kaarlo, ed. *Suomen taidetta 1950-luvulla* (Finnish art in the 1950s). Helsinki: Werner Söderström Oy, 1961: 82.

B.5   *Suomen Taide 1961: Vuosikirja* (Yearbook of Finnish Art 1961). Helsinki: Suomen Taiteilijaseura, 1961: 74, 135.

1962

B.6   Koroma, Kaarlo, ed. *Kuvataiteilijat* (Artists' registry). Helsinki: Suomen Taiteilijaseura ry, 1962: 94.

B.7   *Suomen Taide 1962* (Finnish Art 1962). Helsinki: Suomen Taiteilijaseura, 1962: 98, 110, 114, 116, 126, 135.

1963

B.8   Lainio, Eino, ed. *Suomalaista käyttögrafiikkaa/Finnish Graphic Design.* Helsinki: Taidepiirtäjäin liitto Grafia, 1963: 55, 56.

B.9   *Suomen Taide 1963: Vuosikirja* (Yearbook of Finnish Art 1963). Helsinki: Suomen Taiteilijaseura, 1963: 18, 20, 114, 116, 125, 126.

1964

B.10   *Suomen Taide 1964: Vuosikirja* (Yearbook of Finnish Art 1964). Helsinki: Suomen Taiteilijaseura, 1964: 28, 76, 78, 80, 100, 133, 134, 140, 143.

1965

B.11   *Suomen Taide 1965: Vuosikirja* (Yearbook of Finnish Art 1965). Helsinki: Suomen Taiteilijaseura, 1965: 118, 129, 131.

1966

B.12   *Suomen Taide 1966: Vuosikirja* (Yearbook of Finnish Art 1966). Helsinki: Suomen Taiteilijaseura, 1966: 62, 88, 89, 100, 118, 124, 126, 128, 131, 135.

1967

B.13   *Suomen piirustustaide Schaumanista Rantaseen/Finnish Drawings from Schauman to Rantanen.* Foreword by Sakari Saarikivi. Helsinki: Werner Söderström Oy, 1967: 192, 207.

B.14   *Suomen Taide 1967: Vuosikirja* (Yearbook of Finnish Art 1967). Helsinki: Suomen Taiteilijaseura, 1967: 44, 71, 120, 126, 132, 133, 134, 136, 137.

B.15   Tolvanen, Jouko. *Taidesanakirja* (Dictionary of art). Helsinki: Otava, 1967: 406.

1968

B.16   *Ateneumin Taidemuseo/Konstmuseet i Ateneum/The Art Gallery of Ateneum.* Helsinki: Ateneumin Taidemuseo, 1968.

B.17   *Hämeenlinnan Taidemuseo* (Hämeenlinna Art Museum). Hämeenlinna: Taidemuseo, 1968.

B.18   *Suomen Taide 1968: Vuosikirja* (Yearbook of Finnish Art 1968). Helsinki: Suomen Taiteilijaseura, 1968: 21, 51, 53, 54, 119, 128, 129, 132, 134, 135, 138, 145.

1969

B.19   *Suomen Taide 1969: Vuosikirja* (Yearbook of Finnish Art 1969). Helsinki: Suomen Taiteilijaseura, 1969: 45, 81, 115, 127, 129, 139, 144.

1970

B.20   Boulton-Smith, John. *Uutta suomalaista*

maalaustaidetta/Modern Finnish Painting. Helsinki: Tammi, 1970: 44-45, plates 61-62.

B.21 Helin, Martti and Hämeranta, Tauno. *Tampereen Taiteilijaseura 1920-1970* (The Tampere Artists' Association 1920-1970). Tampere: Tampereen Taiteilijaseura, 1970.

B.22 *Kuka kukin on/Who's Who in Finland*. Helsinki: Otava, 1970: 351-52.

B.23 Lindström, Aune, ed. *Fokus taide 1* (Focus art 1). Helsinki: Otava, 1970: 720, 723.

B.24 Lindström, Aune, ed. *Fokus taide 2* (Focus art 2). Helsinki: Otava, 1970: 634.

B.25 Lintinen, Jaakko, ed. *Taide 70: Suomen taiteen vuosikirja* (Yearbook of Finnish Art 70). Helsinki: Suomen Taiteilijaseura, 1970: 20, 40, 52, 87.

1971

B.26 Lintinen, Jaakko, ed. *Taide 71: Suomen taiteen vuosikirja* (Yearbook of Finnish Art 71). Helsinki: Suomen Taiteilijaseura, 1971: 31, 64, 72, 76.

1972

B.27 *Kuvataiteilijat 1972* (Artists' registry 1972). Helsinki: Suomen Taiteilijaseura ry, 1972: 98-99.

B.28 Lintinen, Jaakko, ed. *Taide 72: Suomen taiteen vuosikirja* (Yearbook of Finnish Art 72). Helsinki: Suomen Taiteilijaseura, 1972: 31, 65, 76, 80, 82, 84, 87, 91.

1973

B.29 Lintinen, Jaakko, ed. *Taide 73: Suomen taiteen vuosikirja* (Yearbook of Finnish Art 73). Helsinki: Suomen Taiteilijaseura, 1973: 31, 85, 87, 88, 89, 90.

B.30 Sydhoff, Beate. *Bildkonst i Norden 5* (Nordic Visual Arts 5). Stockholm: Prisma, 1973: 267.

1974

B.31 *Kuka kukin on/Who's Who in Finland*. Helsinki: Otava, 1974: 320-21.

B.32 Lintinen, Jaakko, ed. *Taide 74: Suomen taiteen vuosikirja* (Yearbook of Finnish Art 74). Helsinki: Suomen Taiteilijaseura, 1974: 35, 96, 100, 101.

1975

B.33 Lintinen, Jaakko, ed. *Taide 75: Suomen taiteen vuosikirja* (Yearbook of Finnish Art 75). Helsinki: Suomen Taiteilijaseura, 1975: 112, 114, 124, 125.

1976

B.34 Lintinen, Jaakko, ed. *Taide 76: Suomen taiteen vuosikirja* (Yearbook of Finnish Art 76). Helsinki: Suomen Taiteilijaseura, 1976: 60, 109, 120.

B.35 Lindsten, Leo. *Realismin kasvot* (The face of Realism). Helsinki: Suomen Taiteilijaseura ry and Werner Söderström Oy, 1976: 37, 57.

1977

B.36 Fields, Jack and Moore, David. *Finland Creates*. Helsinki: J.K. Gummerus, 1977: 106-107.

B.37 *Kunst i Norden* (Art in the Nordic countries). Helsinki: Nordiska konstförbundet, 1977: 166, 215.

B.38 Lintinen, Jaakko, ed. *Taide 77: Suomen taiteen vuosikirja* (Yearbook of Finnish Art 77). Helsinki: Suomen Taiteilijaseura, 1977: 116, 137, 147, 148, 149.

B.39 Peltola, Leena and Racz, Istvan. *Suomen taidetta 1940-1975* (Finnish art 1940-1975). Helsinki: Otava, 1977: 21, 22, 25, 26, 35, 317, plates 121, 199, 221, 231.

1978

B.40 Lintinen, Jaakko, ed. *Suomen taiteen vuosikirja 1978: Taiteen kuvat ja kuviot/Yearbook of Finnish Art 1978: Finnish Art, Patterns and Images*. Helsinki: Suomen Taiteilijaseura, 1978: 69, 117, 118, 131, 138.

B.41 Peltola, Leena; Murto, Anneli; and Honkanen, Hilkka, eds. *Skopin taidetta* (Art from the SKOP collection). Helsinki: Säästöpankkien Keskus-Osake-Pankki, 1978: 78-79

B.42 Ringbom, Sixten, ed. *Konsten i Finland* (Art in Finland). Helsinki: Holger Schildts Förlag, 1978: 299, 310, plate 637.

B.43 Seppälä, Raimo. *Kustaa oli kunnon mies* (Gustavus was a good man). Helsinki: Otava, 1978.

B.44 *Taidekokoelma Kuntsi/Konstsamling Kuntsi* (The Kuntsi art collection). Vaasa: Kuntsin taidekokoelma, 1978: 10, 13.

1979

B.45 *Kuvataiteilijat 1979* (Artists' registry 1979). Helsinki: Suomen Taiteilijaseura ry, 1979: 136-37.

1980

B.46 Bråhammar, Gunnar and Garmer, Kristina. *Moderna mästare: 33 konstnärer från 33 länder* (Modern masters: 33 artists from 33 countries). Malmö: Galerie Börjeson, 1980: 196-211.

B.47 Vuolanne, Matti. *Suomalaisen kuvataiteen lähdehakemisto* (Index of Finnish art). Helsinki: Lähetyksen Kirjapalvelu Oy, 1980: 71.

1981

B.48 Mäkinen, Marketta, ed. *Jyväskylän kaupungin taidekokoelmat, Alvar Aalto-museo/Jyväskylä Town Art Collection, Alvar Aalto Museum*. Jyväskylä: [The City] and Alvar Aalto-museo, 1981: 4, 6, 65, 68-69.

1982

B.49 Mikkola, Maija-Riitta, ed. *Suomalaista piirustustaidetta* (Finnish drawings). Lahti: Taidemuseo, 1982: 45.

B.50 Sinisalo, Soili and Lintinen, Jaakko. *Kimmo Kaivanto*. Helsinki: Weilin & Göös, 1982.

1983

B.51 Hautala, Jorma; Hienonen, Erkki; and Lintinen, Jaakko, eds. *Taide ja taiteilijat: Suomen taiteen vuosikirja/Art and Artists: Yearbook of Finnish Art*. Helsinki: Suomen Taiteilijaseura, 1983: 64, 67.

B.52 Honkanen, Helmiriitta. *Placatista julisteeksi* (From placards to posters). Helsinki: Otava, 1983: 109, 132.

B.53 Vuorikoski, Timo. *Sara Hildénin taidemuseo/Sara Hildén Art Museum*. Tampere: Sara Hildénin taidemuseo, 1983: 12-13, 46-47.

1984

B.54 Bergh, Erik and Hovi, Päivi, eds. *Turun Taidemuseo, Turun Taideyhdistyksen kokoelmat/Turku Art Museum, The Collections of Turku Art Society*. Turku: Turun Taideyhdistys ry, 1984: 112.

B.55 Ilmonen, Anneli, ed. *Tampereen taidemuseo 50 vuotta* (50th anniversary of Tampere Art Museum). Tampere: Tampereen Taideyhdistys ry, 1984.

B.56 Rantanen, Leena. *Sateenkaari* (The rainbow). Helsinki: Otava, 1984: 60-61.

1985

B.57 Junttila, Marja and Westerlund, Jorma, eds. *Oulun taidemuseo/Oulu City Art Gallery*. Oulu: Taidemuseo, 1985: 73.

B.58   *Taide pohjoismaissa 1945-1980/Konst i Norden 1945-1980/Art in the Nordic Countries 1945-1980.* Helsinki: Pohjoismainen taidekeskus, 1985: 94, 106.

B.59   *Taidepörssi 1985: Suomalaisen maalaustaiteen rekisteri* (1985 "art exchange": Registry of Finnish painting). Helsinki: Oy Infodec Ab, 1985: 60.

1986

B.60   *Aineen Kuvataidesäätiö* (Aine Foundation for Visual Arts). Oulu: Aineen taidemuseo, 1986: 26.

B.61   *Kuka kukin on/Who's Who in Finland.* Helsinki: Otava, 1986: 312.

B.62   *Northern Poles: Breakaways and Breakthroughs in Nordic Painting and Sculpture of the 1970's and 1980's.* Ed. by Torsten Bloendal. Copenhagen: Bloendal, 1986: 176-182, 208, 234.

B.63   Paavola, Irmeli, ed. *Tampereen Nykytaiteen Museo 20 vuotta* (Tampere Modern Art Museum 20 years old). Tampere: Nykytaiteen Museo, 1986: 23, 33.

B.64   Räsänen, Désirée, ed. *Rovaniemen taidemuseo/Rovaniemi Art Museum.* Rovaniemi: Taidemuseo, 1986: 45.

B.65   *Taidepörssi 1986: Suomalaisen maalaustaiteen rekisteri* (1986 "art exchange": Registry of Finnish painting). Helsinki: Oy Infodec Ab, 1986: 53.

B.66   Valkonen, Markku and Valkonen, Olli, eds. *Suomen taide 6* (Finnish art 6). Helsinki: Werner Söderström Oy, 1986: 18, 19, 114-17.

1987

B.67   *Kuvataiteilijat 1986* (Artists' registry 1986). Helsinki: Suomen Taiteilijaseura ry, 1987: 156-57.

B.68   Martin, Timo and Nukari, Matti. *From Idealism to Real Time.* Helsinki: Suomen Yhdyspankki Oy, 1987: 223.

B.69   Repo, Eino S.; Suurpää, Matti; and Valkonen, Markku, eds. *Taiteet Suomea takomassa* (Arts forge Finland). Helsinki: Tammi, 1987: 152, 176.

B.70   *Tampereen Taiteilijaseura 1986* (The Tampere Artists' Association 1986). Tampere: Tampereen Taiteilijaseura ry, 1987: 44, 45.

1988

B.71   Rönkkö, Pekka, ed. *Lapsuuden kuvat* (Pictures of childhood). Helsinki: Mannerheimin Lastensuojeluliitto, 1988: 182-83.

B.72   *Taidepörssi 1988: Suomalaisen maalaustaiteen rekisteri* (1988 "art exchange": Registry of Finnish painting). Helsinki: Oy Infodec Ab, 1988: 70.

1989

B.73   Ilvas, Juha. *Kansallistaidetta: Suomalaista taidetta Kansallis-Osake-Pankin kokoelmissa* (Kansallis-art: The Kansallis Centenary Collection of Finnish art). Helsinki: Kansallis-Osake-Pankki, 1989: 202-203, 355.

B.74   Ilvas, Juha. *The Kansallis Centenary Collection of Finnish Art.* Helsinki: Kansallis-Osake-Pankki, 1989: 202, 355.

B.75   Jauhiainen, Pirkko, ed. *Taidetta* (Art). Helsinki: Raha-automaattiyhdistys, 1989: 28, 43.

B.76   Louna, Lahti and Louna, Matti. *Suomalaisen taideopas* (A Finn's art guide). Helsinki: Tammi, 1989: 43, 139,156.

B.77   *Taidepörssi 1989: Suomalaisen maalaustaiteen rekisteri* (1989 "art exchange": Registry of Finnish painting). Helsinki: Oy Infodec Ab, 1989: 65.

1990

B.78   Ahtola-Moorhouse, Leena; Peltola, Leena; and Sinisalo, Soili. *Taiteen vuoksi* (Because of art). Kerava: Keravan Taide ja Kulttuuriyhdistys ry, 1990: 82-83.

B.79   Ilvas, Juha. *Kansallistaidetta: Suomalaista taidetta Kansallis-Osake-Pankin kokoelmissa, Dokumentaatio-osa, Lähteet ja kirjallisuus* (Kansallis-art: The Kansallis Centenary Collection of Finnish art, Documentation, sources and literature). Helsinki: Kansallis-Osake-Pankki: 1990: 22-23.

B.80   *Kuka kukin on/Who's Who in Finland.* Helsinki: Otava, 1990: 360.

B.81   *Maire Gullichsenin taidesäätiön kokoelma, Porin taidemuseo/The Collection of Maire Gullichsen's Art Foundation, Pori Art Museum.* Foreword by Göran Schildt. Pori: Taidemuseo, 1990: 77, 78.

B.82   Sarajas-Korte, Salme, ed. *Ars Suomen taide 6* (Finnish art 6). Helsinki: Otava, 1990: 143-44, 185-86, 192, 194, 209-210, 214, 220.

B.83   *Taidepörssi 1990: Suomalaisen maalaustaiteen rekisteri* (1990 "art exchange": Registry of Finnish painting). Helsinki: Oy Infodec Ab, 1990: 86.

1991

B.84   *Kuvataiteilijat 1991* (Artists' registry 1991). Helsinki: Kustannusosakeyhtiö Taide, 1991: 160-61.

B.85   Lepistö, Vappu. *Kuvataiteilijat taidemaailmassa* (Artists in the art world). Helsinki: Tutkijaliitto, 1991.

B.86   *Taidepörssi 1991: Suomalaisen maalaustaiteen rekisteri* (1991 "art exchange." Registry of Finnish painting). Helsinki: Oy Infodec Ab, 1991: 95.

B.87   *Taiteen pikkujättiläinen* (Little encyclopedia of art). Helsinki: Werner Söderström Oy, 1991: 389, 704, 705, 854.

C. Publications Illustrated by the Artist

1960

C.1   Kuusi, Matti, ed. *Suomen kansan vertauksia* (Finnish folk allegories). Helsinki: Suomalaisen Kirjallisuuden Seura, 1960.

1970

C.2   [Cover commissioned for] A.80.

C.3   Peltonen, Juhani. "Norjasta ostettu posliinitonttu" (A porcelain elf bought from Norway). *Eeva*, no. 8 (1970): 38-39.

1971

C.4   *Iiris*, no. 1 (1971): unpaged.

C.5   *Paletten*, no. 4 (1971): cover.

C.6   *The Times Literary Supplement: Scandinavian Writing Today*, 10 Sept. 1971: cover.

1972

C.7   *Kouluohjelmat*, no. 3 (1972): back cover.

C.8   *Nutida Musik*, no. 2 (1972-73): cover.

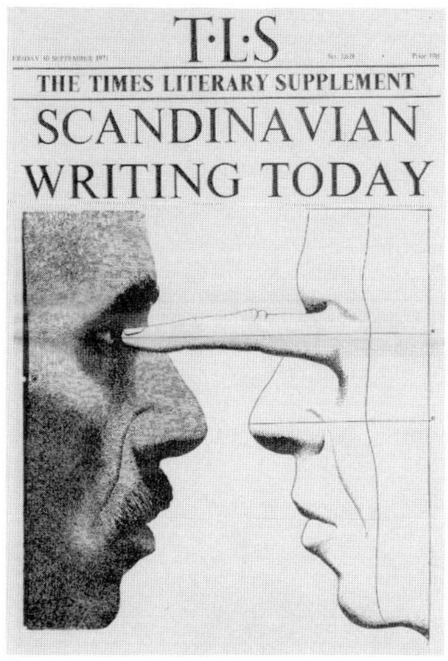

C.6

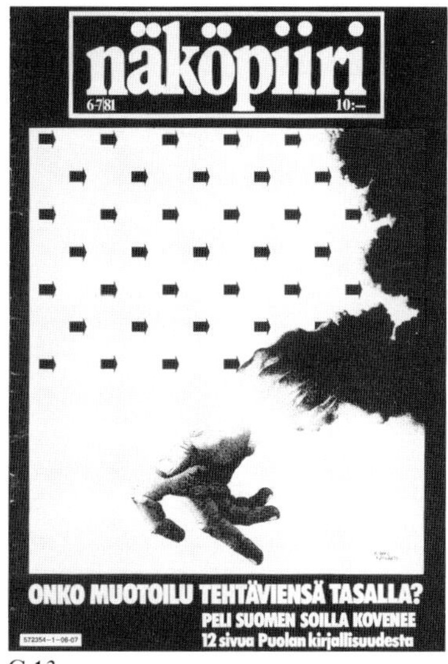

C.13

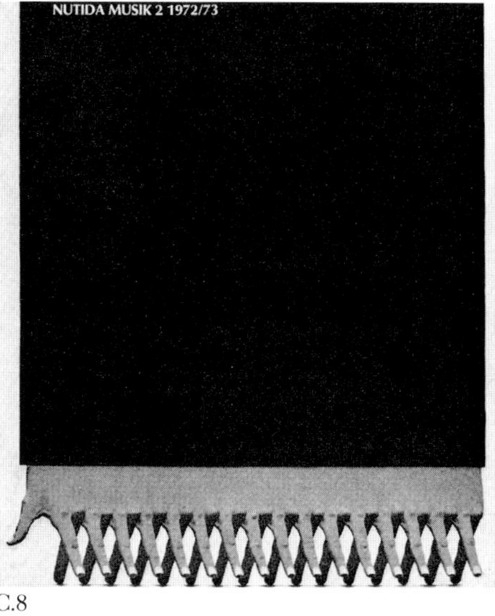

C.8

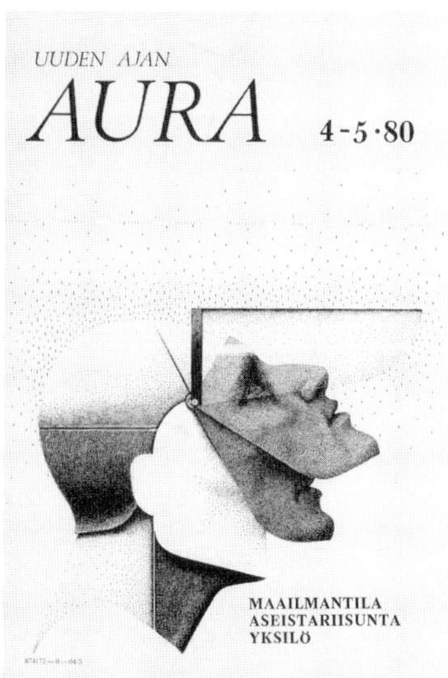

C.12

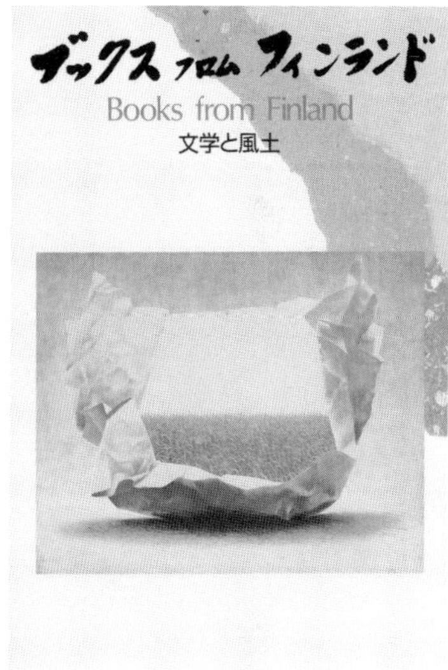

C.17

1973

C.9 *Nya Argus*, no. 3 (Mar. 1973): cover.

1977

C.10 *Kurikka*, no. 5 (1977): cover.

1978

C.11 [Cover for] A.123.

1980

C.12 *Uuden Ajan Aura*, nos. 4-5 (1980): unpaged, cover.

1981

C.13 *Näköpiiri*, nos. 6-7 (1981): cover.

1982

C.14 Kytöhonka, Arto. *Toinen teos* (Another work). Hausjärvi: Äitini Talo, 1982.

C.15 *Taide*, no. 3 (1982): cover.

1983

C.16 *Tehy*, no. 3 (1983): cover.

1984

C.17 *Books from Finland* [special issue in Japanese], (1984): cover.

1985

C.18 *Images from Finland: Poetry and Graphics* [special issue of books from Finland], (1985): cover.

C.19 [Brochure] *Festa*. Tampere: Mannerheimin Lastensuojeluliitto, 1985: cover.

1987

C.20 *Lentosuunta*, no. 3 (1987): cover.

1988

C.21 *Elias*, no. 1 (1988): cover.

C.22 Manner, Eeva-Liisa. *Hevonen, minun ystäväni* (My friend, the horse). Helsinki: Tammi, 1988.

C.23 *Yliopisto*, no. 9 (18 Mar. 1988): cover.

D. Articles by the Artist

1966

D.1 "Mielipiteitä valtion taidekomitean mietinnöstä" (Opinions on the State Art Committee report). *Taide* 7, no. 1 (1966): 38.

1967

D.2 "Taiteilijan Tampere" (An artist's Tampere). *Taide* 8, no. 3 (1967): 144-45.

1968

D.3 "10-vuotiaan sotakuvat" (Ten-year-old boy's pictures of war). *Iiris*, no. 3 (1968): 5.

1969

D.4 "Muita kuvia ja esineitä/Andra bilder och föremål" (Other pictures and objects). In A.70.

D.5 "Havahdummeko..." (Shall we awake...). In A.74.

1971

D.6 "4.2.1969...." In A.83.

D.7 "Sormet sanoo soo, soo, soo" (Fingers say: no, no, no). *Taide* 12, no. 2 (1971): 3-4.

1973

D.8 "Suomalaisia nykyrealisteja" (Finnish contemporary Realists). *Taide* 14, no. 3 (1973): 36-38.

1975

D.9 "Idea meren kuolemaan" (An idea for "When the Sea Dies"). *Taide* 16, no. 1 (1975): 5-8.

1976

D.10 "A questo punto.../At this stage...." In A.113.

1980

D.11 *Pippuripaletti* (A pepper-palette). Tampere: Taidemuseon Ystävät, 1980: 36-37.

1982

D.12 "Ainakin tämä mielessäni" (At least this is on my mind). *Vartija*, nos. 5-6 (1982): 294.

D.13 "Merkintöjä päiväkirjastani/Anteckningar våren 1980/Notes spring 1980." In B.50.

1983

D.14 "Taiteilijan ammattikuva" (The image of the artist's profession). *Taide* 24, no. 3 (1983): 22.

1984

D.15 "Mielikuvia Zefyroksen vaiheista" (Mental images of the phases of the Zefyros). *Sokeri Pohjalla*, no. 1 (1984): 19.

D.16 "Minä ja valokuva" (The photograph and I). *Valokuvauksen vuosikirja 1984* (Photography yearbook 1984). Helsinki: Suomen valokuvataiteen museon säätiö, 1984: 97.

D.17 "Onnen saaristo" (The archipelago of happiness). *Helsingin Sanomat*, 19 July 1984.

1988

D.18 "Tyypilliset kysymykset/The Typical Questions." In A.161.

E. Articles on and about the Artist (Art-related Periodicals)

1961

E.1 "Näyttelyt" (Exhibitions). *Taide* 2, no. 4 (1961): 165, 166.†

1963

E.2 "Näyttelyitä" (Exhibitions). *Taide* 4, no. 3 (1963): 134.‡

1965

E.3 Valkonen, Olli. "Näyttelykatsaus" (Exhibition survey). *Taide* 6, no. 1 (1965): 41.‡

E.4 "Näyttelykuvia" (Pictures from exhibitions). *Taide* 6, no. 3 (1965): 135.‡

E.5 Alitalo, Heikki. "Näyttelykatsaus" (Exhibition survey). *Taide* 6, no. 4 (1965): 183, 185.†

E.6 "Pariisin kansainvälinen nuorten biennale" (International young artists' biennial in Paris). *Taide* 6, no. 4 (1965): 180-81.‡

E.7 Orley, Georges. "The 4th Biennale of Paris." *Studio International* 170, no. 871 (Nov. 1965): 202-203.‡

1966

E.8 Alitalo, Heikki. "Näyttelykatsaus" (Exhibition survey). *Taide* 7, no. 1 (1966): 42.‡

E.9 "Valtion taidekilpailu 1965" (State Art Competition 1965). *Taide* 7, no. 1 (1966): 24-27.‡

E.10 Kruskopf, Erik. "Taiteilijoita/Artistes Finlandais" (Finnish artists). *Taide* 7, no. 2 (1966): 66-76.†

E.11 Valkonen, Olli. "Kimmo Kaivanto." *Taide* 7, no. 3 (1966): 111-16.

1967

E.12 Helin, Martti. "Näyttelykatsaus: Tampere" (Exhibition survey: Tampere). *Taide* 8, no. 1 (1967): 46.†

E.13 "Valtion taidekilpailu 1966" (State Art Competition 1966). *Taide* 8, no. 1 (1967): 28-31.‡

E.14 Helin, Martti. "Näyttelykatsaus: Tampere" (Exhibition survey: Tampere). *Taide* 8, no. 2 (1967): 108.‡

E.15 Niinivaara, Seppo. "Näyttelykatsaus" (Exhibition survey). *Taide* 8, no. 2 (1967): 98.‡

E.16 Helin, Martti. "Näyttelykatsaus: Tampere" (Exhibition survey: Tampere). *Taide* 8, no. 3 (1967): 161.†

E.17 Valkonen, Olli. "Näyttelykatsaus" (Exhibition survey). *Taide* 8, no. 3 (1967): 155.‡

E.18 Helin, Martti. "Näyttelykatsaus: Tampere" (Exhibition survey: Tampere). *Taide* 8, no. 4 (1967): 223.‡

1968

E.19 "Tapahtumia" (Events). *Taide* 9, no. 1 (1968): 49.†

E.20 "Valtion taidekilpailu 1967" (State Art Competition 1967). *Taide* 9, no. 1 (1968): 20-21.‡

E.21 "Suomen taide ulkomailla" (Finnish art abroad). *Taide* 9, no. 2 (1968): 96-97.†

E.22 "Suomi Venetsian 34. Biennaalissa 1968" (Finland at the 34th Venice Biennale of 1968). *Taide* 9, no. 2 (1968): 64-67.†

E.23 Valkonen, Olli. "Venetsian 34. Biennaali" (34th Venice Biennale). *Taide* 9, no. 2 (1968): 124-25.‡

1969

E.24 "Kimmo Kaivanto." *Taide* 10, no. 2 (1969): 52.

E.25 "Finland på Lousiana" (Finland at Lousiana). *Louisiana Revy*, no. 2 (1969): 39-40.‡

E.26 Valkonen, Markku. "Taide-yhteiskunta" (Art society). *Taide* 10, no. 3 (1969): 142-43.†

E.27 "Kulttuurimme kuva Tanskassa" (Our cultural image in Denmark). *Taide* 10, no. 4 (1969): 198-200.‡

1970

E.28 "Tapahtumia" (Events). *Taide* 11, no. 1 (1970): 42, 47.‡

E.29 Näsänen, Perttu. "Kuva on väline" (An image is an instrument). *Taide* 11, no. 2 (1970): 20-22.‡

E.30 Siegel, Jeanne. "The Fine Arts of Finland." *Arts Magazine* 44, no. 4 (Feb. 1970): 48-50.†

1971

E.31 "Ajankohtainen kuvakatsaus" (Current picture survey). *Taide* 12, no. 1 (1971): 15.‡

E.32 Kruskopf, Erik. "Missä olemme, mihin menemme?" (Where are we, where are we going?). *Taide* 12, no. 1 (1971): 34-41.†

E.33 Hamberg, Lars. "Kimmo Kaivanto–Artist." *Kunst og Kultur* 54, no. 2 (1971): 121-31.

E.34 Näsänen, Perttu. "Sormet pelissä, mutta kenen sormet ja missä pelissä?" (Fingers at play, but whose fingers and at what play?). *Taide* 12, no. 2 (1971): 2-3.

E.35 Näsänen, Perttu. "Keskustelua" (Conversation). *Taide* 12, no. 3 (1971): 52.

E.36 "Realismi: Mitä se on?" (Realism: What is it?). *Taide* 12, no. 4 (1971): 21-25.†

E.37 Mallander, Jan-Olof. "Ett hål i isen" (A hole in the ice). *Paletten*, no. 4 (1971): 32-34.

1972

E.38 "Helsingin kaupungintalon julkisia teoksia/The new acquisitions of art in the City Hall of Helsinki." *Taide* 13, no. 1 (1972): 42.†

E.39 "Tapahtumia" (Events). *Taide* 13, no. 4 (1972): 41, 44.†

1973

E.40 "Tapahtumia" (Events). *Taide* 14, no. 1 (1973): 7.‡

E.41 "Tämän päivän maisemamaalaus" (Landscape painting today). *Taide* 14, no. 1 (1973): 48.‡

1974

E.42 "Ars 74." *Taide* 15, no. 1 (1974): 10.‡

E.43 Mallander, J.O. "Ars 74." *Taide* 15, no. 2 (1974): 55-56.‡

E.44 Peltonen, Juhani. "Kokoelmien kohtaaminen" (The meeting of collections), *Taidehalli 74* (1974).

1975

E.45 Kruskopf, Erik. "Tätä näyttelyä ette nähneet" (You didn't see this exhibition). *Taide* 16, no. 1 (1975): 4-12.

E.46 "Naista ympäröivät myytit" (Myths surrounding women). *Taide* 16, no. 5 (1975): 30.‡

E.47 Suhonen, Pekka. "Kuvia ja myyttejä" (Images and myths). *Taide* 16, no. 5 (1975): 21.‡

1976

E.48 Broner, Kaisa. "Ajatuksia ympäristöstä, taiteesta ja Venetsian biennaalista" (Thoughts about environment, art and the Venice Biennale). *Taide* 17, no. 4 (1976): 16-23.‡

1977

E.49 "Julkisia teoksia" (Public art). *Taide* 18, no. 1 (1977): 11-13.†

E.50 Valkonen, Markku. "Aavistamattomiin tähtisumuihin ja takaisin" (To the unknown nebulas and back), *Taide* 18, no. 6 (1977): 25-31.‡

1978

E.51 Salonen, Marja. "Kuvia ruudussa" (Pictures on TV). *Taide* 19, no. 2 (1978): 51-53.‡

E.52 Hamberg, Lars. "Tammerfors–Tampere." *F 15 Kontakt*, nos. 4-5 (1978).†

1979

E.53 Lintinen, Jaakko. "Näillä näkymillä menee hyvin" (So far, so good). *Taide* 20, no. 1 (1979): 6-14.†

E.54 "Taiteen puolesta" (For art). *Valokuva*, no. 6 (1979): 34.‡

1980

E.55 Kivirinta, Marja-Terttu. "Punaisen viivan supergrafiikkaa" (Super graphics of the Red Line). *Taide* 21, no. 3 (1980): 34-35.

1982

E.56 Pallasmaa, Ullamaria. "Kuljen virrassa, suunnan tiedän..." (I follow the tide, I know the course...). *Taide* 23, no. 3 (1982): 18-23.

E.57 "Mix Books." *Form–Function–Finland*, no. 4 (1982): 42.†

1984

E.58 Sarje, Kimmo. "Kirjoja" (Books). *Taide* 25, no.1 (1984): 54-55.

1988

E.59 Drougge, Per. "Invandrarna och konsten" (Immigrants and art). *Om Konst och Annat i Stockholms Län* 5, nos. 1-2 (1988): 5-10.†

E.60 "Kuvakatsaus" (Survey of pictures). *Taide* 29, no. 5 (1988): 49.

1991

E.61 Lintinen, Jaakko. "70-luvun realismeja etsimässä" (Looking for Realism of the 1970s). *Taide* 31, no. 3 (1991): 49-53.†

F. Articles on and about the Artist (General Magazines)

1958

F.1 Kosonen, Pekka. "Tampereen taiteen seitsemän veljestä" (The seven brothers of Tampere art). *Viikko Sanomat*, no. 44 (31 Oct. 1958): 28-29.†

1961

F.2 S-nen. "Koti ja ateljee" (Home and studio). *Kaunis Koti*, no. 1 (1961): 44-47.

F.3 Tanttu, Juha. "Melkein tuntemattomia" (Almost unknown). *Suomen Kuvalehti*, no. 47 (25 Nov. 1961): 1-4.†

1962

F.4   Tarkka, Antti. "Tutustumme Tampereen Taiteilijaseuraan" (Getting acquainted with the Tampere Artists' Association). *Yhdyslanka*, no. 1 (1962).†

1963

F.5   Sauri, Eero. "Kymmenen taiteilijan talo" (The house of ten artists). *Kuvaposti*, no. 9 (1963): 23-26.†

F.6   Tapper, Kain. "Vieraalla maalla" (Traveling abroad). *Viikkolehti*, no. 13 (31 Mar. 1963): 8.‡

1966

F.7   Tikkanen, Birgitta. "Mikä on tärkeää?" (What is important?). *Me Naiset*, no. 11 (1966).†

1967

F.8   Elimäki, Karin. "Kimmo Kaivanto." *Kauppa ja Koti*, no. 3 (1967).

1968

F.9   Luukela, Arja. "Ensi kesänä Biennaalissa" (At the Biennial this summer), *Avotakka*, no. 4 (Apr. 1968): 60-62, 65.†

1969

F.10   Elfving, Ebba. "Ett levande museum" (A living museum). *Astra*, no. 3 (1969).‡

F.11   Mattsson, Maija-Liisa. "Kimmo Kaivanto ajattelee kuvia" (Kimmo Kaivanto thinks in pictures). *Anna*, no. 10 (11 Mar. 1969): 36-39.

F.12   "Kimmo Kaivanto, 37." *Suomen Kuvalehti*, no. 31 (1 Aug. 1969): 28.

F.13   Kirjavainen, Tuula. "Soipa teräs" (Sounding steel). *Suomalainen*, no. 4 (Nov. 1969): 26.

1970

F.14   Lindegren, Riitta. "Sara Hildén, suuri mesenaatti" (Sara Hildén, a great patron). *Anna*, no. 44 (3 Nov. 1970): 18-21.‡

1971

F.15   Lehtola, Erkki. "Kimmo Kaivanto." *Radar*, no. 1 (1971): 20-23.

F.16   Riitta. "Kimmon sormet pelissä" (Kimmo's fingers at play). *Anna*, no. 7 (1971).

F.17   Lintinen, Jaakko. "Images of violence." *Look at Finland*, no. 2 (1971).

F.18   Suhonen, Pekka. "Toiveet ja politiikka" (Hope and politics). *Aika*, no. 2 (1971).‡

F.19   Kinnunen, Raila. "Pirtti" (A living room). *Hopeapeili*, no. 10 (11 Nov. 1971): 12-15.

F.20   Saure, Salme. "Lainassa" (On loan). *Hopeapeili*, no. 13 (1971).†

1972

F.21   Niiniluoto, Maarit. "Sormet sormien lomaan" (Linked fingers). *Suomen Kuvalehti*, no. 2 (14 Jan. 1972): 22-23.

F.22   "Kuvantekijät" (Picture makers). *Seura*, no. 5 (1972).‡

F.23   Poukkula, Aila. "Antisankari ajassamme" (Today's anti-hero). *Uusi Nainen*, no. 8 (1972): 18-19.†

F.24   Kinnunen, Raila. "Kimmo Kaivanto." *Eeva*, no. 10 (Oct. 1972): 86-91.

1973

F.25   "Apuraha ei saa olla lohdutuspalkinto syrjitylle" (A grant should not be a consolation prize for the less-favored). *Katso*,

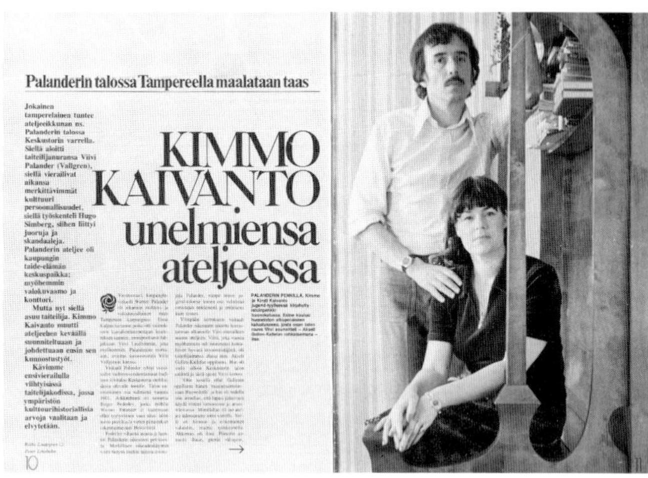

F.30

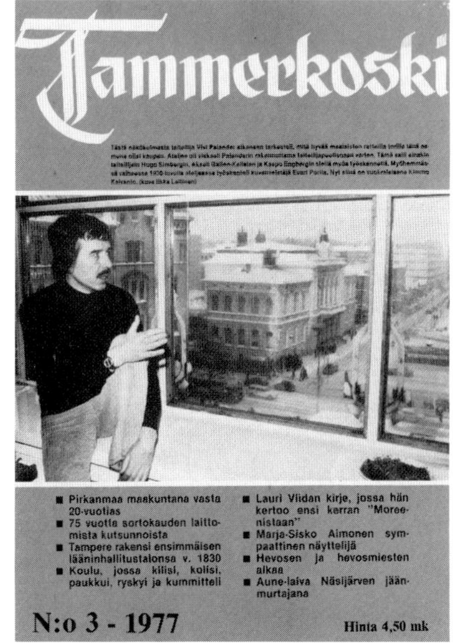

F.36

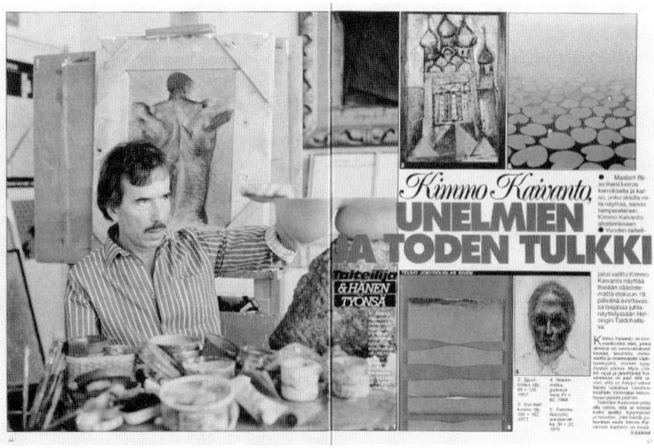

F.55

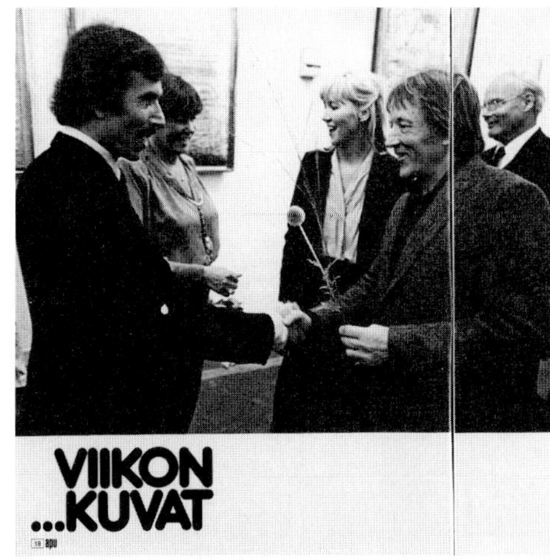

F.61

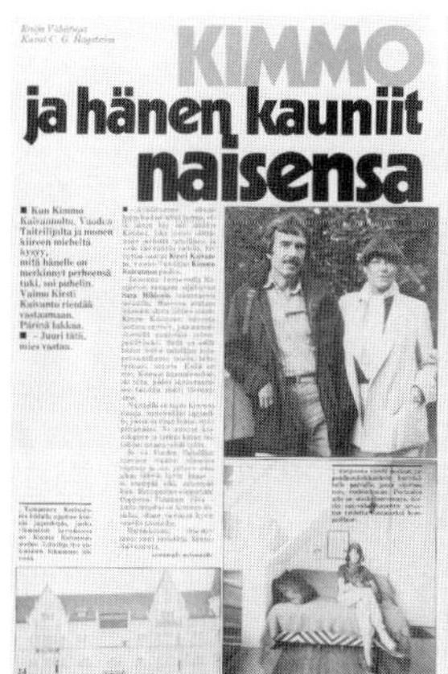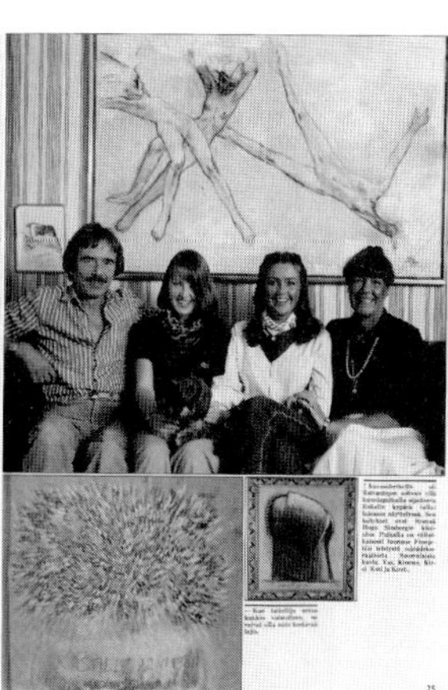

F.62

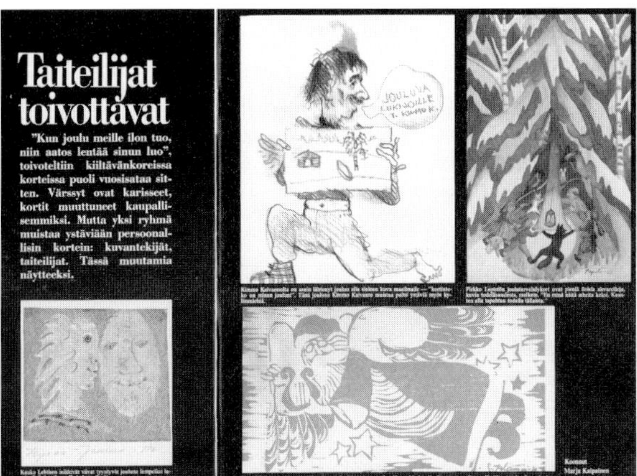

F.72

no. 1 (1-7 Jan. 1973): 8-9.

F.26 Vehviläinen, Matti. "Taiteilijan vuodet" (Artist's years). *VIP*, no. 10 (Oct. 1973): 32-34.

1974

F.27 Mattila, Arja. "Muna" (An egg). *Jaana*, nos. 15-16 (1974).†

F.28 "Viiden kuvantekijän terveiset" (Greetings from five artists). *Oma Markka*, no. 10 (1974).†

F.29 "Viikon henkilö: Kimmo Kaivanto" (Person of the week: Kimmo Kaivanto). *Me Naiset*, no. 49 (5 Dec. 1974): 19.

1975

F.30 Lindegren, Riitta. "Kimmo Kaivanto unelmiensa ateljeessa" (Kimmo Kaivanto at the studio of his dreams). *Jaana*, no. 23 (3 June 1975), 10-15.

F.31 Poijärvi, Eevamaija. "Nöyryys" (Humility). *Kaks' plus*, no.10 (Oct. 1975): 30-34.†

F.32 Vähätupa, Raija. "Vastakohdat terävöityneet" (The opposites sharpened). *Katso*, no. 18 (1975).

1976

F.33 Nevalainen, Eila. "Kaivannon kuvissa on ihmisten Tampere" (People's Tampere in Kaivanto's pictures). *Me*, no. 15 (11 Aug. 1976): 12-15.

F.34 Honkanen, Helmiriitta. "Julisteen kehitys" (The development of the poster). *Markkinointi*, no. 5 (1976).

F.35 "Tampereen menneisyyden taiteellinen läpileikkaus" (An artistic cross-section of Tampere's past). *Tampereen Vilkku*, no. 5 (Dec. 1976): 4-6, cover.

1977

F.36 Jokinen, Helvi. "Kimmo Kaivannon uskalias kulttuuriteko" (Kimmo Kaivanto's bold cultural act). *Tammerkoski*, no. 3 (1977): 8-9, cover.

F.37 Jokela, Eila. "Koski ja tori" (The rapids and the square). *Kotiliesi*, no. 8 (Apr. 1977): 24-28, 129.

F.38 Jyväkorpi, Pirkko. "Taiteilija kasvaa monen monta kertaa" (An artist grows many times). *Työväen Joululehti* (Dec. 1977): 32-37.

F.39 Parkkinen, Pekka. "Kimmo Kaivannon pariisilainen tukikohta" (Kimmo Kaivanto's Parisian base). *Suomen Kuvalehti*, nos. 51-52 (23 Dec. 1977): 76-78.

1978

F.40 "Tamperelaistui taas" (In Tampere again). *Hymy*, no. 3 (1978).

F.41 Harju, Rauno. "Punaisen Viivan All Stars-joukkue" (All-star cast of "The Red Line"). *Jaana*, no. 48 (30 Nov. 1978): 8-10.†

F.42 Rajala, Panu. "Punainen viiva" (The Red Line). *Teatteri*, nos. 11-12 (12 Dec. 1978): 4-7.†

1979

F.43 "Vasarapyörä on 200-vuotiaan Tampereen juhlavuoden tunnus" (Water wheel is the symbol of Tampere's bicentennial anniversary). *Mainosuutiset*, no. 1 (1979).

F.44 Karlsson, Hasse. "Viiva hitaasti" (A line slowly). *Status* 1, no. 3 (1979): 58-61.

F.45 "Ihmisten Tampere 200 vuotta" (People's Tampere: 200 years old). *Jaana*, no. 40 (4 Oct. 1979): 6.†

F.46 Jäämeri, Hannele. "Erään kaupungin piirteet" (The features of a town). *Suomen Kuvalehti*, no. 45 (9 Nov. 1979): 12-17.‡

1980

F.47   Jyväkorpi, Pirkko. "Kaikilla on tarve luoda" (Everyone has the need to create). *Sosialistinen Aikakausilehti*, no. 4 (1980): 14-16.

1981

F.48   "Taidenäyttely merellä" (A [floating] art exhibition on the sea). *Finnjet-kokousuutiset*, no. 3 (1981).

F.49   Korhonen, Linda. "Ystävyyttä" (Friendship). *Me Naiset*, nos. 51-52 (17 Dec. 1981): 62-65.

1982

F.50   Larres, Matti. "Take me to the Woods." *Finnish Business Report*, (Sept. 1982): 30.

F.51   Kirstilä, Pentti. "Vuoden taiteilija Kimmo Kaivanto" (Kimmo Kaivanto, Artist of the Year). *YV*, no. 3 (Mar. 1982): 44-47.

F.52   Hellevaara, Kerttu. "Kimmo Kaivanto on vuoden taiteilija" (Kimmo Kaivanto is "Artist of the Year"). *Hokki*, no. 4 (May 1982): 16-17.

F.53   "Kimmo Kaivanto, Artist of the Year 1982." *Suomi-Finland USA*, nos. 5-6 (1982): 2-4, 6.

F.54   "Rauhanpäivän juliste" (The "Peace Day" poster). *Sanomalehtimies/Journalisten*, no. 20 (18 Oct. 1982): 1.†

F.55   Joki, Teuvo. "Kimmo Kaivanto." *Anna*, no. 29 (20 July 1982): 66-69.

F.56   Coogan, Hertta. "The Private Eye in Public." *Blue Wings*, nos. 7-9 (July-Sept. 1982): 20-23.

F.57   Virtanen, Heini. "Kimmo Kaivanto: Vuoden taiteilija" (Kimmo Kaivanto: Artist of the Year). *Näköpiiri*, no. 8 (1982).

F.58   Syréen, Pekka. "Vuoden taiteilija purjehtija ja luonnonystävä" ("Artist of the Year" is a sailor and a friend of nature). *Ännä*, no. 2 (1982): 6-8.

F.59   Saarikoski, Tuula. "Kimmo Kaivanto." *Jaana*, no. 34 (19 Aug. 1982): 22-23.

F.60   Pyysalo, Riitta. "Olen taivaanrannan maalari" (I am the painter of the horizon). *Suomen Kuvalehti*, no. 34 (20 Aug. 1982): 8-12.

F.61   "Viikon...kuvat: Vuoden kukkapuska" (Pictures of the week: Bouquet of the year). *Apu*, no. 35 (27 Aug. 1982): 18-19.

F.62   Vähätupa, Raija. "Kimmo ja hänen kauniit naisensa" (Kimmo and his beautiful women). *Eeva*, no. 10 (Oct. 1982): 24-29.

F.63   "Piirtoja vuoden taiteilijasta Kimmo Kaivannosta" (Notes on Kimmo Kaivanto, Artist of the Year). *Tammerkoski*, no. 10 (1982).

F.64   Lapintie, Kimmo. "Kosketuksen päässä ihminen" (A man you can reach out and touch). *Aviisi*, no. 14 (1982).

F.65   "Kimmo Kaivanto omissa maisemissaan" (Kimmo Kaivanto in his own landscapes). *Veikkaus–Lotto*, no. 47 (1982).

F.66   Winther, Annika. "Master of Metamorphoses/Le Maitre des métamorphoses/Meister der Metamorphose." *Welcome to Finland*, 1982.

1983

F.67   Renvall, Mika. "Kimmo Kaivanto." *Orja*, no. 1 (1983): 12-13.

F.68   Salminen, Hannu. "Kimmo Kaivanto haluaa risteillä vapaasti kuvallisessa maailmassa" (Kimmo Kaivanto wants to sail freely in the pictorial world). *Suomen Sanomat/Finlandsnytt*, no. 1 (1983).

F.69   Boulton-Smith, John. "Kimmo Kaivanto: Metamorphoses." *Books from Finland*, no. 4 (1983).

F.70   Pallasmaa, Ullamari. "Inside and outside a landscape." *Look at Finland*, no. 4 (1983).

F.71   Laaksonen, Riitta. "ARS:ssa tavanomainenkin on epätavallista" (Even the usual is unusual at the Ars [exhibition]). *Kymppi*, no. 5 (1983): 53-54.†

F.72   Kaipainen, Marja. "Taiteilijat toivottavat" (Artists' holiday wish). *Helsingin Sanomat–Kuukausiliite*, no. 12 (Dec, 1983): 66-67.†

1984

F.73   Mustonen, Irmeli. "Katso, näe, koe" (Look, see, experience). *Sokeri Pohjalla*, no. 1 (1984): 16-19.

F.74   "Ajantieto" (Chronicles). *Helsingin Sanomat–Kuukausiliite*, no. 11 (Nov. 1984): 9-17.†

1985

F.75   "Kirja, ystävämme" (Book, a friend of ours). *Kinski*, no. 1 (1985): 30-31.†

F.76   Katavisto, Anja. "Kimmo Kaivanto." *Öljyposti*, no. 4 (1985): 28-31.

1986

F.77   Huovinen, Maarit. "Kimmo Kaivanto." *Lääkäri ja Vapaa-aika*, no. 1 (1986): 14-18.

F.78   "Taiteilija Kimmo Kaivanto" (Kimmo Kaivanto, the artist). *Mestari-Tappara*, no. 9 (Sept. 1986): 20-21.

1987

F.79   Huovinen, Maarit. "Kimmo Kaivanto selkäleikkauksen jälkeen" (Kimmo Kaivanto after his back surgery). *Kotiliesi*, no. 7 (3 Apr. 1987): 38-40.

F.80   Rosenholm, Heljä. "Hänen katseensa on kirkas ja valoisa" (His gaze is clear and light). *Seura*, 8 July 1987.†

F.81   Härkönen, Terttu. "Joskus kaikki särkyy" (Sometimes everything is shattered). *Askel*, no. 10 (2 Oct. 1987): 16-19, 23.

1988

F.82   Karttila, Hertta. "Kimmo Kaivanto." *Yhteishyvä*, no. 1 (13 Jan. 1988): 6-7, 10.

F.83   "Biogenesis: Elämän alku" (Biogenesis: The beginning of life). *Sokeri Pohjalla*, no. 5 (1988).

F.84   Pyysalo, Riitta. "Fantasioita naisesta" (Fantasies about a woman). *Suomen Kuvalehti*, no. 48 (2 Dec. 1988): 34-35.

1989

F.85   Penttilä, Riitta. "Maaliskuun maisema" (The landscape of the March Group). *Me*, no. 3 (1 Mar. 1989): 6-9.‡

F.86   Kaipiainen, Irene. "Viivan merkitys on horisontti" (The meaning of the line is the horizon). *Yliopisto Uutiset*, no. 22 (1989).

1990

F.87   Tirkkonen, Marja-Liisa. "Yksityistä ylistystä" (Private praise). *Me Naiset*, no. 15 (6 Apr. 1990): 16-18.

1991

F.88   Hartiala, Pirkko. "Kuuluisat siniset" (The famous blues). *Gloria*, no. 5 (May 1991): 74-78.†

G. Articles on and about the Artist (Newspapers)

1956

G.1   V[eistä]jä, O[lavi]. "Tampereen taiteilijaseuran 25. vuosinäyttely" (25th annual exhibition of the Tampere Artists' Association). *Aamulehti*, 25 Oct. 1956.‡

1957

G.2   Saarikivi, Sakari. "Nuorten 15. näyttely" (15th Young Artists' exhibition). *Helsingin Sanomat*, 22 Sept. 1957.‡

G.3   V[ehmas], E[inari] J. "Nuorten näyttely" (Young Artists' exhibition). *Uusi Suomi*, 26 Sept. 1957.‡

G.4   Laine, Osmo. "Kuvataidejärjestöjen liiton näyttely Lahdessa" (Exhibition of the Union of [Finnish] Visual Arts Organizations in Lahti). *Turun Sanomat*, 8 Nov. 1957.‡

G.5   "Suomen Kuvataidejärjestöjen liiton yhdeksäs vuosinäyttely" (9th annual exhibition of the Union of Finnish Visual Arts Organizations). *Etelä-Suomen Sanomat*, 10 Nov. 1957.‡

G.6   Tolvanen, Jouko. "Maakuntien taiteen katselmus" (A provincial art survey). *Lahti*, 10 Nov. 1957.‡

G.7   V[eistä]jä, O[lavi]. "Tamperelaista kuvataidetta" (Visual art in Tampere). *Aamulehti*, 27 Nov. 1957.‡

G.8   H[alme], V[ilh]o. "Taiteilijaseuran vuosinäyttely" (Annual exhibition of the [Tampere] Artists' Association). *Kansan Lehti*, 28 Nov. 1957.‡

1958

G.9   P[ajastie], E[ila]. "Grå konst i grå miljö" (Dull art in dull surroundings). *Nya Pressen*, 15 Feb. 1958.‡

G.10   Valkonen, Olli. "Vuosinäyttely" (Annual exhibition [of the Artists' Association of Finland]). *Suomen Sosialidemokraatti*, 15 Feb. 1958.‡

G.11   V[ehmas], E[inari] J. "Suomen Taiteilijain 64. näyttely" (64th annual exhibition of the Artists' [Association of Finland]). *Uusi Suomi*, 16 Feb. 1958.‡

G.12   Saarikivi, Sakari. "Suomen taiteilijain 64. näyttely" (64th exhibition of the Finnish Artists' [Association]). *Helsingin Sanomat*, 19 Feb. 1958.‡

G.13   Uexküll, Petra. "Yhden värin maalareita" (One-color painters). *Ilta-Sanomat*, 19 Feb. 1958.‡

G.14   K[ruskopf], E[rik]. "Plus och minus på årsexpo" (Plus and minus in the annual exhibition [of the Artists' Association of Finland]). *Hufvudstadsbladet*, 21 Feb. 1958.‡

G.15   Favén, Mauri. "Suomen taiteilijain 64. näyttely" (64th annual exhibition of Finnish Artists' [Association]). *Kansan Uutiset*, 23 Feb. 1958.‡

G.16   Häkli, Tauno. "Mikkelin Taideyhdistyksen XIII vuosinäyttely rikas ja antoisa" (Rich and rewarding 13th annual exhibition of the Mikkeli Art Society). *Länsi-Savo*, 25 Mar. 1958.‡

G.17   L., U. "Nouseva maalari" (An emerging painter). *Tamperelainen*, 14 Aug. 1958.

G.18   "Nuorekasta rohkeutta ja voimaa" (Youthful courage and strength). *Suomen Sosialidemokraatti*, 13 Sept. 1958.‡

G.19   Teikari. "Seitsämän tamperelaista taiteilijaa yllättää" ("Seven Artists" of Tampere surprise). *Aamulehti*, 13 Sept. 1958.‡

G.20   "Seitsemän tamperelaisen taiteilijan yhteisnäyttely" (Exhibition of "Seven Artists" group of Tampere). *Aamulehti*, 14 Sept. 1958.‡

G.21   "Syyskuun taideavaus Tampereella" (Opening the September exhibition season in Tampere). *Uusi Suomi*, 14 Sept. 1958.‡

G.22   V[eistä]jä, O[lavi]. "Voimalla seitsemän miehen" (By the strength of seven men). *Aamulehti*, 18 Sept. 1958.†

G.23   Uexküll, Petra. "Voimakasta, mutta viljeltymätöntä on nykypäivän maalaus Tampereella" (Contemporary painting in Tampere is strong but uncultivated). *Ilta-Sanomat*, 18 Sept. 1958.†

G.24   R., S. "Merkitävä näyttely Tampereella" (A notable exhibition in Tampere). *Keskisuomalainen*, 19 Sept. 1958.‡

G.25   "Seitsemän taiteilijan näyttely" (Exhibition of "Seven Artists"). *Aamulehti*, 20 Sept. 1958.‡

G.26   H[alme], V[ilh]o. "Seitsemän taiteilijaa kirjastotalossa" ("Seven Artists" at the Library). *Kansan Lehti*, 21 Sept. 1958.†

G.27   DHI. "Jubileumsexpo i Tavastehus" (Jubilee exhibition in Hämeenlinna). *Hufvudstadsbladet*, 3 Nov. 1958.‡

G.28   Koivuniemi, Henni. "Suomen Kuvataidejärjestöjen Liiton 20-vuotisnäyttely Hämenlinnassa" (20th annual exhibition of the Union of Finnish Visual Arts Organizations in Hämeenlinna). *Satakunnan Kansa*, 5 Nov. 1958.‡

G.29   V-nen., E. "Kuvataidejärjestöjen Liiton 20-vuotisjuhlanäyttely" (20th anniversary exhibition of the Union of [Finnish] Visual Arts Organizations). *Hämeen Kansa*, 8 Nov. 1958.‡

G.30   V[ehmas], E[inari] J. "Kuvataidejärjestöjen liiton juhlanäyttely Hämeenlinnassa" (Jubilee exhibition of the Union of [Finnish] Visual Arts Organizations in Hämeenlinna). *Uusi Suomi*, 9 Nov. 1958.‡

G.31   K[ovane]n, T[apio] E. "Husan taidenäyttely Jämsässä" (Husa's exhibition at Jämsä). *Koillis-Häme*, 11 Nov. 1958.‡

G.32   Heinänen, Urho. "Kuvataidejärjestöjen juhlanäyttely" (Jubilee exhibition of the Union of [Finnish] Visual Arts Organizations). *Hämeen Sanomat*, 13 Nov. 1958.†

G.33   V[eistä]jä, O[lavi]. "Tamperelaista nykytaidetta: Taiteilijaseuran 27:s vuosinäyttely" (Contemporary art in Tampere: 27th annual exhibition of the [Tampere] Artists' Association). *Aamulehti*, 27 Nov. 1958‡

G.34   R., S. "Tampereen taiteilijaseuran vuosinäyttely" (Annual exhibition of the Tampere Artists' Association). *Keskisuomalainen*, 28 Nov. 1958.‡

G.35   H[alme], V[ilh]o. "Taiteilijaseuran 27. näyttely" (27th exhibition of the [Tampere] Artists' Association). *Kansan Lehti*, 30 Nov. 1958.‡

1959

G.36   S-a., E. "Tamperelaistaidetta Valkeakoskella" (Art from Tampere shown at Valkeakoski). *Hämeen Kansa*, 22 Feb. 1959.‡

G.37   "Kimmo Kaivannon työ orpokoti Kalliolaan" (A work by Kimmo Kaivanto to the Kalliola Orphanage). *Aamulehti*, 6 June 1959.

G.38   "Kolmisenkymmentä värikylläistä maalausta ja piirrosta vuosilta 1957-59..." (About thirty colorful paintings and drawings from the years 1957-59...). *Helsingin Sanomat*, 7 Sept. 1959.

G.39   P[ajastie], E[ila]. "En kolorist stämmer upp" (A colorist makes an impression). *Nya Pressen*, 9 Sept. 1959.

G.40   Uexküll, Petra. "Punainen sipulikirkko" (A red onion-domed church). *Ilta-Sanomat*, 11 Sept. 1959.

G.41   Saarikivi, S[akari]. "Viikon taidenäyttelyjä: Kimmo

Kaivanto" (This week's exhibitions: Kimmo Kaivanto). *Helsingin Sanomat*, 12 Sept. 1959.

G.42 F., M. "Näyttelykauden alku: Kimmo Kaivanto" (The beginning of the exhibition season: Kimmo Kaivanto). *Kansan Uutiset*, 13 Sept. 1959.

G.43 Gulin, Åke. "Konstkrönika" (Art chronicles). *Hufvudstadsbladet*, 13 Sept. 1959.

G.44 V[ehmas], E[inari] J. "Viikon taidenäyttelyjä: Kimmo Kaivanto" (This week's exhibitions: Kimmo Kaivanto). *Uusi Suomi*, 13 Sept. 1959.

G.45 "Kimmo Kaivannolla antoisa näyttely" (A rewarding exhibition by Kimmo Kaivanto). *Kansan Lehti*, 15 Sept. 1959.

G.46 "Kimmo Kaivannolla näyttely Helsingissä." (Kimmo Kaivanto's exhibition in Helsinki). *Aamulehti*, 17 Sept. 1959.

G.47 B[lomstedt], J[uhana]. "Kimmo Kaivanto." *Suomen Sosialidemokraatti*, 20 Sept. 1959.

G.48 R., S. "Taidetta" (Art). *Keskisuomalainen*, 6 Oct. 1959.†

G.49 K[ruskopf], E[rik]. "Ungt och medelmåttigt från tre magra konstår" (Young and mediocre from three poor years of art). *Hufvudstadsbladet*, 17 Oct. 1959.‡

G.50 V[eistä]jä, O[lavi]. "Tamperelaista nykytaidetta" (Contemporary art in Tampere). *Aamulehti*, 7 Oct. 1959.‡

G.51 H[alme], V[ilh]o. "Taiteilijaseuran 28:s näyttely" (28th exhibition of the [Tampere] Artists' Association). *Kansan Lehti*, 11 Oct. 1959.†

G.52 Niinivaara, Seppo. "Tampereen Taiteilijaseuran vuosinäyttely" (Annual exhibition of the Tampere Artists' Association). *Tamperelainen*, 22 Oct. 1959.†

G.53 K[ruskopf], E[rik]. "Konstmönstring i Kuopio" (Art survey in Kuopio). *Hufvudstadsbladet*, 13 Nov. 1959.‡

G.54 Puustinen, Irma. "Paljon katsottavaa, runsaasti katsojia Kuvataidejärjestöjen liiton näyttelyssä" (Much to see, plenty of spectators at the exhibition of the Union of [Finnish] Visual Arts Organizations). *Savon Sanomat*, 14 Nov. 1959.

G.55 O-. "Pomintoja Kuopion taidenäyttelystä" (Extracts of the exhibition in Kuopio). *Päivän Sanomat*, 26 Nov. 1959.†

G.56 "Kimmo Kaivanto voitti Saukonpuiston koulun seinäkoristelukilpailun" (Kimmo Kaivanto won the Saukonpuisto School mural competition). *Aamulehti*, 18 Dec. 1959.

1960

G.57 H-mi., E. "Taiteemme kolmivuotiskatselmus" (The Triennial of our art). *Aamulehti*, 20 Feb. 1960.‡

G.58 "Modernismia Kariniemessä" (Modern art at Kariniemi). *Lahti*, 10 July 1960.‡

G.59 "Saukonpuiston koulun koristelu suoritettiin kolmessa eri vaiheessa" (The Saukonpuisto School mural was painted in three different phases). *Aamulehti*, 21 Sept. 1960.

G.60 Halme, Vilho. "40 vuotta tamperelaistaidetta" (40 years of Tampere art). *Kansan Lehti*, 16 Oct. 1960.†

G.61 V[eistä]jä, O[lavi]. "Tampereen kuvataiteen katselmus" (A survey of visual arts in Tampere). *Aamulehti*, 16 Oct. 1960.‡

G.62 Peltonen, J. "Tamperelaisten juhlanäyttely" (Jubilee exhibition of the Tampere Artists' [Association]). *Uusi Suomi*, 23 Oct. 1960.‡

G.63 Kruskopf, Erik. "Ung konst med färg" (Young art with color). *Hufvudstadsbladet*, 20 Nov. 1960.‡

G.64 Uexküll, Petra. "Nuorten näyttely" (Young Artists' exhibition). *Ilta-Sanomat*, 26 Nov. 1960.‡

G.65 Vehmas, Einari. "Viikon taidenäyttelyistä" (About this week's exhibitions). *Helsingin Sanomat*, 27 Nov. 1960.‡

G.66 Niinivaara, Seppo. "Nuorten näyttely" (Young Artists' exhibition). *Suomen Sosialidemokraatti*, 28 Nov. 1960.‡

G.67 Pajastie, Eila. "Färg utan föremål triumferar i Konsthall" (Color without goal triumphs at the [Helsinki] Art Hall). *Nya Pressen*, 28 Nov. 1960.‡

G.68 Saarikivi, Sakari. "Nuorten näyttely" (Young Artists' exhibition). *Uusi Suomi*, 28 Nov. 1960.‡

G.69 S., I. "Nuorten kuvataidetta Helsingissä" (Young Artists' exhibition in Helsinki). *Aamulehti*, 13 Dec. 1960.‡

1961

G.70 "Nykytaide tarvitsee tilaa Tampereella" (Contemporary art needs a place of its own in Tampere). *Tamperelainen*, 21 Apr. 1961.

G.71 "1,25 miljoonaa apurahoiksi" (1.25 million for grants). *Suomen Sosialidemokraatti*, 26 May 1961.‡

G.72 "Nykytaiteen näyttely avoinna Taidehallissa koko kesän" (Contemporary art exhibition is open at the [Helsinki] Art Hall all summer). *Helsingin Sanomat*, 23 June 1961.‡

G.73 J-u. "Kimmo Kaivanto Kirjastotalolla" (Kimmo Kaivanto's exhibition at the Library). *Kansan Lehti*, 23 sept. 1961.

G.74 T-ri. "Tamperelainen ja oululainen" (An artist from Tampere and another from Oulu). *Aamulehti*, 23 Sept. 1961.

G.75 V[eistä]jä, O[lavi]. "Värisävyjen maalari" (Painter of many shades). *Aamulehti*, 24 Sept. 1961.

G.76 "Kaksi taidenäyttelyä Tampereella ja kolmas avataan huomenna" (Two exhibitions in Tampere and the third one to open tomorrow). *Aamulehti*, 29 Sept. 1961.†

G.77 H[alme], V[ilh]o. "Kimmo Kaivannon näyttely" (Kimmo Kaivanto's exhibition). *Kansan Lehti*, 29 Sept. 1961.

G.78 R., S. "Tamperelaisia taidenäyttelyitä" (Exhibition of Tampere artists). *Keskisuomalainen*, 30 Sept. 1961.

G.79 "Tampereen taidenäyttelyt" (Art exhibitions in Tampere). *Aamulehti*, 1 Oct. 1961.†

G.80 "Korkeapainetta Tampereen taidemuseossa" (Fine weather at the Tampere Art Museum). *Aamulehti*, 17 Oct. 1961.‡

G.81 "Suurikokoinen seinämaalaus Koukkuniemen vanhainkotiin" (A large-sized mural for the Koukkuniemi Home for the Aged). *Aamulehti*, 2 Nov. 1961.†

G.82 "Taidenäyttelyt" (Art exhibitions). *Helsingin Sanomat*, 3 Nov. 1961.‡

G.83 "Eilen avattiin Pinxissä maalaustaiteemme nuorta koulua edustavan Kimmo Kaivannon näyttelyä" (Yesterday an exhibition by Kimmo Kaivanto representing our new school of painting opened at the Pinx). *Uusi Suomi*, 6 Nov. 1961.

G.84 Uexküll, Petra. "Kimmo Kaivanto." *Ilta-Sanomat*, 9 Nov. 1961.

G.85 Vehmas, Einari. "Viikon taidenäyttelyitä: Kimmo Kaivanto" (This week's exhibitions: Kimmo Kaivanto). *Uusi Suomi*, 9 Nov. 1961.

G.86 A-o., H. "Kimmo Kaivanto." *Kansan Uutiset*, 10 Nov. 1961.

G.87 Valkonen, Olli. "Taidenäyttelyt: Kimmo Kaivanto" (Art exhibitions: Kimmo Kaivanto). *Helsingin Sanomat*, 10 Nov. 1961.

G.88 Mykiö [Nummi, Lassi]. "Sattui silmiin" (It caught the eye). *Kauppalehti*, 11 Nov. 1961.†

G.89 P[ajastie], E[ila]. "Personliga uttryckets närvaro och avsaknad" (Presence and absence of personal expression). *Nya Pressen*, 13 Nov. 1961.

G.90 Gulin, Åke. "Konstkrönika" (Art chronicles).

Hufvudstadsbladet, 14 Nov. 1961.

G.91 Parko, Severi. "Kimmo Kaivanto." *Suomen Sosialidemokraatti*, 15 Nov. 1961.

G.92 Parkola, Severi. "Siveltimen kertomaa" (Told by a brush). *Päivän Sanomat*, 15 Nov. 1961.

G.93 Ripsaluoma, Sirkka. "Tamperelaisten vuosinäyttely" (Annual exhibition of the Tampere Artists' [Association]). *Keskisuomalainen*, 29 Nov. 1961‡

G.94 V[eistä]jä, O[lavi]. "Tampereen Taiteilijaseuran vuosinäyttely" (Annual exhibition of the Tampere Artists' Association). *Aamulehti*, 1 Dec. 1961.‡

G.95 H[alme], V[ilh]o. "Taiteilijaseuran 30. katselmus" (30th annual exhibition of the [Tampere] Artists' exhibition). *Kansan Lehti*, 3 Dec. 1961.‡

G.96 Valkonen, Olli. "Tasainen taidekilpailu" (An even [State] Art Competition). *Helsingin Sanomat*, 30 Dec. 1961.‡

1962

G.97 "Suomen taidetta näytteillä USA:ssa" (Finnish art shown in the U.S.A.). *Turun Sanomat*, 28 Jan. 1962.‡

G.98 "Tamperelaisten Kiovan-näyttely" (The Kiova exhibition of the Tampere artists). *Keskisuomalainen*, 17 Feb.1962.‡

G.99 Ripsaluoma, Sirkka. "Kymmenen taiteilijan talo" (A house of ten artists). *Keskisuomalainen*, 18 Feb. 1962.†

G.100 Kujanen, T.E. "9 maalarin ja graafikon taidenäyttely Jämsässä" (An exhibition of nine painters and printmakers at Jämsä). *Keskisuomalainen*, 30 Feb. 1962.‡

G.101 L., T. "Taiteilijaseuran vuosinäyttely" (Annual exhibition of the [Lahti] Artists' Association). *Lahti*, 7 Mar. 1962.‡

G.102 Kujanen, T.E. "9 maalarin ja graafikon näyttely Jämsässä" (Exhibition of nine painters and printmakers in Jämsä). *Keskisuomalainen*, 30 Mar. 1962.‡

G.103 "Koukkuniemen seinämaalaus on valmistunut" (The Koukkuniemi mural is completed). *Aamulehti*, 18 May 1962.

G.104 "Koukkuniemen uusin monumentaalitaideteos paljastettiin eilen" (Newest monumental art work unveiled at Koukkuniemi yesterday). *Kansan Lehti*, 1 Oct. 1962.

G.105 "Tampereen uusin seinämaalaus" (The newest mural in Tampere). *Aamulehti*, 1 Oct. 1962.

G.106 Kruskopf, Erik. "Treårsexpon" (The Triennial). *Hufvudstadsbladet*, 14 Oct. 1962.‡

G.107 Vehmas, Einari. "Kolmivuotisnäyttely Ateneumissa" (Triennial at the Ateneum). *Uusi Suomi*, 14 Oct. 1962.‡

G.108 Valkonen, Olli. "Suomen kuvataiteen Triennale" (Triennial of Finnish visual arts). *Helsingin Sanomat*, 24 Oct. 1962.‡

G.109 "Tampereen näyttelyssä 16 taiteilijan teoksia" (Works by 16 different artists on exhibit in Tampere). *Helsingin Sanomat*, 28 Oct. 1962.‡

G.110 K[ruskopf], E[rik]. "Konsttävlingkaos" (A chaotic art competition). *Hufvudstadsbladet*, 31 Oct. 1962.‡

G.111 "Niukka sato" (A scanty crop). *Kansan Lehti*, 2 Nov. 1962.‡

G.112 Nummi, Lassi. "Isoiset informalistit ja konkreetikkojen kriisi: I kierros Ateneumin kolmivuotisnäyttelyssä" (Informalists are big, Concretists in crisis: The first round in Ateneum's triennial). *Kauppalehti*, 2 Nov. 1962.‡

G.113 T-a., A. "Kirkonkylätaidetta" (Village art). *Tamperelainen*, 2 Nov. 1962.‡

G.114 V[eistä]jä, O[lavi]. "Tamperelaista nykytaidetta" (Contemporary art in Tampere). *Aamulehti*, 2 Nov. 1962.‡

G.115 P[ajastie], E[ila]. "Informalismens genombrott ett faktum på treårsexpon" (Informalism's breakthrough is a reality at the triennial). *Nya Pressen*, 5 Nov. 1962.‡

G.116 Villehartti, Veli. "Värikästä ja elävää tamperelaista taidetta turkulaisia virkistämään" (Colorful and lively art from Tampere to cheer up the people of Turku). *Turun Sanomat*, 11 Nov. 1962.†

G.117 "Konserttisali vai kiviseita" (Concert hall or stone Seita [goddess]). *Yykoo*, 13 Nov. 1962.†

G.118 Laine, Osmo. "Tampereen taidetta II" (Art from Tampere II). *Turun Sanomat*, 18 Nov. 1962.‡

G.119 P., S. "Tampereen Taiteilijaseuran näyttely" (Exhibition of the Tampere Artists' Association). *Turun Päivälehti*, 18 Nov. 1962.†

G.120 R[autiainen], K[alle]. "Tampereen Taiteilijaseuran näyttely" (Exhibition of the Tampere Artists' Association). *Uusi Aura*, 18 Nov. 1962.†

1963

G.121 "158 teosta esillä Suomen Taiteilijain näyttelyssä" (158 different works shown at the exhibition of the Finnish Artists' [Association]). *Uusi Suomi*, 26 Jan. 1963.‡

G.122 Kautto, Jussi. "Tilaa huipulla" (Room at the top). *Etelä-Suomen Sanomat*, 19 Feb. 1963.‡

G.123 "Seitsemän taiteilijan ryhmä virkoaa jälleen" (The "Seven Artists" group gets together again). *Aamulehti*, 20 Apr. 1963.‡

G.124 Wutzel, Otto. "Botschaft aus dem Lande der 60.000 Seen" (A legation from the land of 60,000 lakes). *Linzer Volksblatt*, 4 May 1963.‡

G.125 "Nykytaidetta Taidehallissa" (Contemporary art at the [Helsinki] Art Hall). *Uusi Suomi*, 8 July 1963.‡

G.126 Teikari. "Taas voimalla seitsemän miehen" (By the strength of seven men again). *Aamulehti*, 14 Sept. 1963.†

G.127 P., V. "Seitsemän taiteilijaa" (The "Seven Artists" group). *Kansan Lehti*, 19 Sept. 1963.†

G.128 Ala-Outinen, P. "Seitsemän modernistia" (Seven modernists). *Keskisuomalainen*, 20 Sept. 1963.†

G.129 V[eistä]jä, O[lavi]. "Seitsemän taiteilijan näyttely Tampereella" (Exhibition of the "Seven Artists" group of Tampere). *Aamulehti*, 24 Sept. 1963.†

G.130 "Taidenäyttelyt" (Art exhibitions). *Helsingin Sanomat*, 11 Oct. 1963.‡

G.131 "Viikon näyttelyitä" (This week's exhibitions). *Suomen Sosialidemokraatti*, 13 Oct. 1963.‡

G.132 v[on] H[aartman], L[ars]. "Konstkrönika" (Art chronicles). *Hufvudstadsbladet*, 13 Oct. 1963.

G.133 P[ajastie], E[ila]. "Kalligrafiskt och mellanspel" (Calligraphy and interlude). *Nya Pressen*, 16 Oct. 1963.

G.134 K[ova]nen, T[apio]. "Pinxin näyttelyt" (Exhibitions at the Pinx). *Suomen Sosialidemokraatti*, 16 Oct. 1963.

G.135 Valkonen, Olli. "Näyttelykatsaus: Kimmo Kaivanto" (Exhibition survey: Kimmo Kaivanto). *Helsingin Sanomat*, 17 Oct. 1963.

G.136 A-o., H. "Kimmo Kaivanto." *Kansan Uutiset*, 18 Oct. 1963.

G.137 Vehmas, Einari. "Viikon taidenäyttelyistä: Kimmo Kaivanto" (About this week's exhibitions: Kimmo Kaivanto). *Uusi Suomi*, 20 Oct. 1963.

G.138 Nummi, Lassi. "Seikkailuja muotojen ja valon maailmassa" (Adventures in the world of form and light). *Kauppalehti*, 21 Oct. 1963.

G.139 Karreinen, T. "Valkeakoski-viikon taidenäyttelyt" (Exhibitions at the Valkeakoski Festival). *Valkeakosken Sanomat*, 23 Oct. 1963.†

G.140 Kärkkäinen, Seppo. "Taidenäyttelyitä" (Art exhibitions). *Päivän Sanomat*, 25 Oct. 1963.

G.141 V[eistä]jä, O[lavi]. "Abstraktin maalauksen läpimurto" (Abstract painting's breakthrough). *Aamulehti*, 22 Nov. 1963.†

G.142 Laine, Osmo. "Suomen Kuvataidejärjestöjen Liiton näyttely Tampereella" (Exhibition of the Union of Finnish Visual Arts Organizations in Tampere). *Turun Sanomat*, 24 Nov. 1963.‡

G.143 P., V. "Kuvataidejärjestöjen Liiton näyttely I" (Exhibition of the Union of [Finnish] Visual Arts Organizations). *Kansan Lehti*, 24 Nov. 1963.†

G.144 Vehmas, Einari. "Kuvataidejärjestöjen liiton juhlanäyttely Tampereella" (Jubilee exhibition of the Union of [Finnish] Visual Arts Organizations in Tampere). *Uusi Suomi*, 25 Nov. 1963.‡

G.145 "Ateljeetalon yhteisnäyttely" (Group exhibition at the Studio House). *Aamulehti*, 14 Dec. 1963.†

G.146 "Suomen Taiteilijaseuran hallitus jakoi apurahoja" (The Finnish Artists' Association board awards grants). *Uusi Suomi*, 17 Dec. 1963.‡

1964

G.147 -a-a. "Tamperelaista taidetta Imatran Taidemuseossa" (Art from Tampere at the Imatra Art Museum). *Ylä-Vuoksi*, 21 Feb. 1964.‡

G.148 Pajastie, Eila. "13 Martianer" (13 members of the March Group). *Nya Pressen*, 11 Mar. 1964.‡

G.149 v[on] H[aartman], L[ars]. "Informalistisk mönstring" (Informalist survey). *Hufvudstadsbladet*, 13 Mar. 1964.†

G.150 Reijonen, Tuuli. "Näyttelykierros" (Exhibition circuit). *Helsingin Sanomat*, 16 Mar. 1964.‡

G.151 Roitto, Aatos. "'Maaliskuulaiset' Helsingin Taidehallissa" ("The March Group" at the Helsinki Art Hall). *Maaseudun Tulevaisuus*, 17 Mar. 1964.‡

G.152 Kovanen, Tapani. "Maaliskuulaiset" (The March Group). *Suomen Sosialidemokraatti*, 20 Mar. 1964.‡

G.153 Routio, A.I. "Näyttelykatsaus" (Exhibition survey). *Kauppalehti*, 21 Mar. 1964.‡

G.154 Vehmas, Einari. "Maaliskuulaiset: Uusi ryhmä" (Artists of March: A new group). *Uusi Suomi*, 22 Mar. 1964.‡

G.155 W[ichma]n, E[va]. "Maaliskuulaiset" (The March Group). *Kansan Uutiset*, 22 Mar. 1964.‡

G.156 "Suomesta taidetta Hässelbyn linnaan" (Finnish Art at Hässelby castle). *Uusi Suomi*, 8 June 1964.‡

G.157 "Apurahoja kuvataiteilijoille" (Grants for artists). *Aamulehti*, 19 June 1964.‡

G.158 H[elin], M[artti]. "Tampereen nykytaidetta" (Contemporary art in Tampere). *Aamulehti*, 4 July 1964.‡

G.159 "Modernin taiteen vahvoja nimiä" (The big names of modern art). *Karjalainen*, 4 Aug. 1964.‡

G.160 Vuorinen, Aimo. "Taidenäyttely" (Art exhibition). *Etelä-Saimaa*, 23 Sept. 1964.†

G.161 K., J. "Arvokkaalla näyttelyllä avattiin kuvataiteen syyssesonki Lappeenrannassa" (Autumn art season opened with a valuable exhibition in Lappeenranta). *Karjala*, 1 Oct. 1964.‡

G.162 Teikari. "Veistäjä ja maalari" (Sculptor and painter). *Aamulehti*, 14 Nov. 1964.†

G.163 "Nordisk konst på expo i Mölndal" (Exhibition of Nordic art to Mölndal). *Hufvudstadsbladet*, 15 Nov. 1964.‡

G.164 "Viisi taidenäyttelyä avoinna Tampereella" (Five exhibitions open in Tampere). *Aamulehti*, 15 Nov. 1964.‡

G.165 "Taidenäyttelyjä Tampereella" (Art exhibitions in Tampere). *Uusi Suomi*, 16 Nov. 1964.‡

G.166 "'Maaliskuulaisten' näyttely Lohjan taideviikon aikana" (Exhibition of the "March Group" at the Lohja Art Festival). *Länsi-Uusimaa*, 17 Nov. 1964.‡

G.167 V[eistä]jä, O[lavi]. "Nykytaidetta: Kain Tapperin ja Kimmo Kaivannon näyttely" (Contemporary art: Exhibition of Kain Tapper and Kimmo Kaivanto). *Aamulehti*, 18 Nov. 1964.†

G.168 P., V. "Kuvataiteviikko Tampereella" (Visual arts in Tampere this week). *Kansan Lehti*, 22 Nov. 1964.†

G.169 "Tampere 23.11.-64." *Ilkka*, 23 Nov. 1964.†

G.170 Reijonen, Tuuli. "Kypsää ja kirjavaa" (Mature and varied). *Helsingin Sanomat*, 25 Nov. 1964.‡

G.171 "Kolmas tamperelaisen kuvataiteen katselmus tänä vuonna" (Third survey this year of visual arts in Tampere). *Aamulehti*, 27 Nov. 1964.‡

G.172 O., K. "Tapper ja Kaivanto" (Tapper and Kaivanto). *Yykoo*, 4 Dec. 1964.†

1965

G.173 "Suomalainen taidenäyttely Tukholmassa" (Exhibition of Finnish art in Stockholm). *Helsingin Sanomat*, 10 Jan. 1965.‡

G.174 "Vaasan Taiteilijaseuran taidepäivien näyttely" (Exhibition of the Vaasa Artists' Association at the Art Festival). *Vaasa*, 15 Jan. 1965.‡

G.175 "Informalism på Vasautställningen" (Informalism at Vaasa exhibition). *Vasabladet*, 3 Feb. 1965.‡

G.176 Laine, Osmo. "Vaasan kuvataidetta" (Art in Vaasa). *Turun Sanomat*, 3 Feb. 1965.‡

G.177 Hanka, Kalervo. "Vaasan kulttuuripäivien taidenäyttely" (Exhibition at the Vaasa Summer Festival). *Kansan Ääni*, 4 Feb. 1965.†

G.178 U., R. "Taidepäivien näyttely" (The exhibition at the [Vaasa] Art Festival). *Ilkka*, 4 Feb. 1965.‡

G.179 G., S.H. "Näyttelyjä maakunnissa" (Exhibitions in the provinces). *Helsingin Sanomat*, 8 Feb. 1965.‡

G.180 Laine, Osmo. "Uusi luonto" (New nature). *Turun Sanomat*, 25 Feb. 1965.†

G.181 V-ri., E.J. "Maaliskuulaiset" (The March Group). *Suomen Sosialidemokraatti*, 25 Feb. 1965.‡

G.182 "Taidemaalariliiton vuosikokous" (The annual meeting of the Painters' Union). *Suomen Sosialidemokraatti*, 3 Apr. 1965.‡

G.183 "Tamperelaisen taiteen laatua" (The quality of art in Tampere). *Kansan Lehti*, 10 Apr. 1965.‡

G.184 "Kolme maalausta Pellervon kouluun" (Three paintings to the Pellervo School). *Aamulehti*, 1 June 1965.‡

G.185 "Tampereen nykytaiteen näyttely" (Exhibition of contemporary art in Tampere). *Uusi Suomi*, 15 June 1965.‡

G.186 "Suomalaista taidetta Jugoslaviassa" (Finnish art in Yugoslavia). *Helsingin Sanomat*, 17 June 1965.‡

G.187 "Taidettamme Hampurissa" (Our art in Hamburg). *Helsingin Sanomat*, 24 June 1965.‡

G.188 H[elin], M[artti]. "Tamperelaista nykytaidetta" (Contemporary art in Tampere). *Aamulehti*, 20 July 1965.‡

G.189 "Taidenäyttelykausi alkaa ensi viikolla Helsingissä" (Exhibition season begins in Helsinki next week). *Aamulehti*, 19 Aug. 1965.‡

G.190 Mäki, Hilkka. "Pariisin IV biennaalin taidepalkinnot jaettu" (Fourth Paris Biennial art prize awarded). *Helsingin Sanomat*, 9 Oct. 1965.‡

G.191 A-o., H. "Taidekierros" (Art circuit). *Kansan Uutiset*, 21 Oct.

1965.

G.192 Kovanen, Tapani. "Kimmo Kaivanto." *Suomen Sosialidemokraatti*, 23 Oct. 1965.

G.193 Reijonen, Tuuli. "Viikon taidetta" (Art this week). *Helsingin Sanomat*, 23 Oct. 1965.†

G.194 Routio, A.I. "Nuori ruotsalainen linja" (The new Swedish look). *Kauppalehti*, 23 Oct. 1965.

G.195 Niinivara, Seppo. "Viikon näyttelykatsaus: Kimmo Kaivanto" (This week's exhibition survey: Kimmo Kaivanto). *Uusi Suomi*, 24 Oct. 1965.

G.196 v[on] H[aartman], L[ars]. "Konstkrönika" (Art chronicles). *Hufvudstadsbladet*, 24 Oct. 1965.

G.197 P[ajastie], E[ila]. "Fint i Smått" (Quite fine). *Nya Pressen*, 25 Oct. 1965.

G.198 Sinisalo, Soili. "Lyyrisiä impressioita" (Lyrical impressions). *Ylioppilaslehti*, 25 Oct. 1965.

G.199 Sinisalo, Soili. "Kimmo Kaivannon maalauksia" (Kimmo Kaivanto's paintings). *Aamulehti*, 26 Oct. 1965.

G.200 Söderblom, Arja. "Kuvataidekierros: Kimmo Kaivanto" (Exhibition circuit: Kimmo Kaivanto). *Päivän Sanomat*, 26 Oct. 1965.

G.201 Saarikivi, Sakari. "Taideakatemian kolmivuotisnäytely II" (The Triennial of the Fine Arts Academy II). *Helsingin Sanomat*, 10 Nov. 1965.‡

G.202 Vehmas, Einari. "Kolmivuotisnäyttely ja 'reputetut'" (The Triennial and the "rejected"). *Uusi Suomi*, 14 Nov. 1965.‡

G.203 Kaitala, V.M. "Helsingin kuudes triennaale" (6th Triennial of Helsinki). *Kansan Lehti*, 21 Nov. 1965.‡

G.204 Sinisalo, Soili. "Kolmivuotiskatselmus" (The Triennial). *Aamulehti*, 24 Nov. 1965.‡

G.205 V[eistä]jä, O[lavi]. "Tamperelaista kuvataidetta" (Visual arts in Tampere). *Aamulehti*, 2 Dec. 1965.‡

G.206 Kivilahti-Parland, Camilla. "Konst: Kimmo Kaivanto" (Art: Kimmo Kaivanto). *Folktidningen Ny Tid*, 3 Dec. 1965.

G.207 Heinänen, Urho. "Tampereen Taiteilijaseuran vuosinäyttely" (Annual exhibition of the Tampere Artists' Association). *Hämeen Sanomat*, 6 Dec. 1965.‡

G.208 Niinivaara, Seppo. "Valtion taidekilpailun teokset Taidehallissa" (The entries for State Art Competition shown at the [Helsinki] Art Hall). *Uusi Suomi*, 19 Dec. 1965.‡

G.209 Kaitala, V.M. "Valtion taidekilpailu" (State Art Competition). *Kansan Lehti*, 23 Dec. 1965.‡

1966

G.210 Reijonen, Tuuli. "Sara Hildén-Enrothin taidekokoelma" (Sara Hildén-Enroth art collection). *Helsingin Sanomat*, 4 Feb. 1966.‡

G.211 Suvioja, Mika. "Oivallinen läpileikkaus" (An excellent cross-section). *Etelä-Suomen Sanomat*, 6 Feb. 1966.‡

G.212 Niinivaara, Seppo. "Sara Hildénin kotimaiset teokset" (Finnish art at the Sara Hildén Collection). *Uusi Suomi*, 13 Feb. 1966.‡

G.213 "Taiteilija Kimmo Kaivannon näyttely" (Kimmo Kaivanto's exhibition). *Valkeakosken Sanomat*, 16 Feb. 1966.

G.214 "Taidemaalariliiton vuosikokous" (The annual meeting of the Painters' Union). *Suomen Sosialidemokraatti*, 17 Feb. 1966.‡

G.215 "Taidenäyttelyjä" (Art exhibitions). *Aamulehti*, 17 Feb. 1966.‡

G.216 "Kimmo Kaivannon taiteen lähtökohta on luonnonelämys" (Nature's atmosphere is the basis for Kimmo Kaivanto's art).

Valkeakosken Sanomat, 19 Feb. 1966.

G.217 "'Aikamme näköaloja': Näyttely Valkeakoskella" ("Today's viewpoints": Exhibition at Valkeakoski). *Kansan Uutiset*, 22 Feb. 1966.†

G.218 Karreinen, T. "Kimmo Kaivannon näyttely" (Kimmo Kaivanto's exhibition). *Valkeakosken Sanomat*, 25 Feb. 1966.

G.219 Heinänen, Urho. "Nykytaiteen museo Tampereella" (Contemporary art museum in Tampere). *Hämeen Sanomat*, 27 Feb. 1966.‡

G.220 Vuorinen, Aimo. "Kolme kutsuttua taiteilijaa" (Three invited artists). *Etelä-Saimaa*, 5 Mar. 1966.†

G.221 W., A. "Tamperelaisten taiteilijain näyttely avattiin Kokkolassa" (Exhibition of Tampere artists opened in Kokkola). *Keskipohjanmaa*, 6 Mar. 1966.‡

G.222 Säde, Raija. "Sara Hildén-Enrothin Säätiön kokoelmat Turun Taidemuseossa" (Sara Hildén-Enroth Collection at the Turku Art Museum). *Päivän Sanomat*, 8 Mar. 1966.‡

G.223 K., J. "Paikallinen juhlanäyttely Lappeenrannassa" (Local jubilee exhibition in Lappeenranta). *Karjala*, 10 Mar. 1966.‡

G.224 "Kuvataide: Robottien yhteiskunnan vastavoima" (Visual arts: Counterforce of the robot society). *Aamulehti*, 4 Apr. 1966.‡

G.225 v[on] H[aartman], L[ars]. "Konstkrönika" (Art chronicles). *Hufvudstadsbladet*, 17 Apr. 1966.‡

G.226 Reijonen, Tuuli. "Taiteilija ateljeessaan" (Artist in his studio). *Helsingin Sanomat*, 29 May 1966.

G.227 "Sata vuotta suomalaista taidetta" (100 years of Finnish art). *Vaasa*, 29 Mar. 1966.‡

G.228 "Näyttelyt jatkuvat" (Exhibitions continue). *Helsingin Sanomat*, 22 June 1966.‡

G.229 A., E. "Nykytaiteen museossa suuri kesänäyttely" (A large summer exhibition at the [Tampere] Modern Art Museum). *Hämeen Sanomat*, 1 July 1966.‡

G.230 Paavola, Irmeli. "Tamperelaista uussatoa" (New crop of Tampere). *Vaasa*, 6 July 1966.†

G.231 Lang, Rudolf. "Skandinavische Maler und Bildhauer stellen im Kunstverein Hannover aus" (Scandinavian painting and sculpture exhibited at the Hannover Art Society). *Hannoversche Allgemeine Zeitung*, 8 July 1966.‡

G.232 Hämäläinen, Timo. "Tamperelaista nykytaidetta" (Contemporary art in Tampere). *Aamulehti*, 27 July 1966.‡

G.233 T., L. "Nykytaidetta Joensuussa" (Contemporary art in Joensuu). *Uusi Suomi*, 31 July 1966.‡

G.234 Paavola, Irmeli. "Kymmenen taiteilijan talo" (The house of ten artists). *Vaasa*, 10 Sept. 1966.†

G.235 "Maaliskuulaisia ja 'Sokea elefantti'" (Members of the March Group and "Blind Elephant"). *Aamulehti*, 23 Sept. 1966.†

G.236 Paavola, Pekka. "Maaliskuulaiset Tampereen syksyssä" (The March Group in the autumn of Tampere). *Satakunnan Kansa*, 29 Sept. 1966.†

G.237 Kaitala, V.M. "Maaliskuuta syksyllä" (March in autumn). *Kansan Lehti*, 2 Oct. 1966.‡

G.238 Paavola, Irmeli. "Maaliskuulaiset" (The March Group). *Vaasa*, 2 Oct. 1966.†

G.239 Mäki-Opas, Irmeli. "Maaliskuulaiset" (The March Group), *Turun Sanomat*, 7 Oct. 1966.†

G.240 Hursti, Seppo. "Tyylikästä näyttelytaidetta" (Stylish exhibition art). *Hämeen Yhteistyö*, 8 Oct. 1966.†

G.241 "Taidetapahtumia" (Art events). *Helsingin Sanomat*, 9 Oct. 1966.‡

G.242 Vihne, Pekka. "Nykytaiteemme kärkiryhmä" (The top

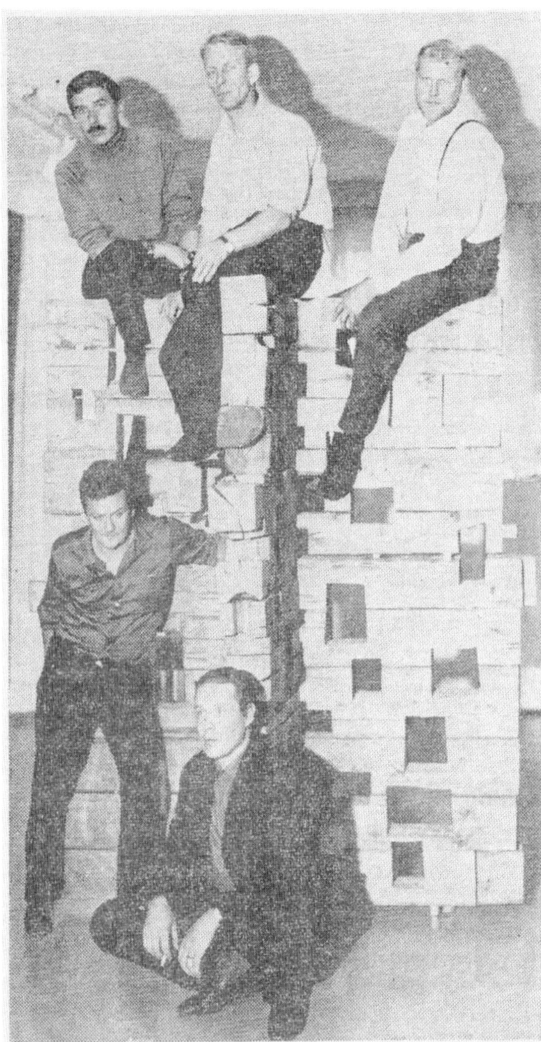

Maaliskuulaisia ja 'Sokea elefantti'

Joukko taiteilijaryhmä 'Maaliskuulaisten' jäseniä ryhtyi tiistaina pystyttämään Tampereen Nykytaiteen Museossa perjantaina avattavaa näyttelyään. Osa heitä ryhmittyi Mauno Hartmanin puuveistoksen 'Sokean elefantin' vaiheille. Veistoksen päällä vas. taidemaalarit Kimmo Kaivanto ja Mauri Favén sekä kuvanveistäjä Mauno Hartman, alhaalla vas. taidemaalarit Jaakko Sievänen ja Kauko Lehtinen. Päivän mittaan saapuivat paikalle vielä taiteilijat Ulla Rantanen, Esko Tirronen, Erkki Heikkilä ja Antti Vuori. Ryhmään kuuluvat lisäksi taidemaalari Reino Hietanen sekä kuvanveistäjät Heikki Häiväoja, Harry Kivijärvi ja Laila Pullinen. Näyttelyyn kertyy 50—60 teosta ja käytössä ovat kaikki museon näyttelytilat.

G.235

group of our contemporary art). *Aamulehti*, 9 Oct. 1966.†

G.243 "Suomalaiset maalaukset yhä teillä tietymättömillä" (Finnish paintings are still missing). *Aamulehti*, 17 Oct. 1966.

G.244 "Skandaali, vai mainostemppu" (A scandal, or a publicity stunt). *Satakunnan Kansa*, 24 Oct. 1966.

G.245 Reijonen, Tuuli. "Maaliskuulaiset" (The March Group). *Helsingin Sanomat*, 25 Oct. 1966.†

G.246 "Taidetapahtumia" (Art events). *Helsingin Sanomat*, 27 Oct. 1966.‡

G.247 P., R. "Maaliskuulaisia Hildén-Enrothin kokoelmassa" (The March Group at the Hildén-Enroth Collection). *Savo*, 28 Oct. 1966.‡

G.248 "Kajaanin taidepäivien monipuolinen näyttely" (A many-sided exhibition at the Kajaani Art Festival). *Kainuun Sanomat*, 29 Oct. 1966.‡

G.249 Karhu, Eeva. "Repinistä Turun taidetapahtumaan" (From Repin to the art event of Turku). *Kymen Sanomat*, 3 Nov. 1966.‡

G.250 "60 vuotta Taidetta kouluihin" (Sixty years of the "Art to Schools" [Society]). *Kansan Uutiset*, 12 Nov. 1966.‡

G.251 "Konstnärerna sin egen jury i gruppexpo" (Artists as their own jury at the group show). *Hufvudstadsbladet*, 18 Nov. 1966.‡

G.252 Kruskopf, Erik. "16 fasetter av vår konst" (16 facets of our art). *Hufvudstadsbladet*, 19 Nov. 1966.‡

G.253 Reijonen, Tuuli. "Yhteisnäyttelyn ongelmat" (The problems of a group exhibition). *Helsingin Sanomat*, 20 Nov. 1966.‡

G.254 Susiluoto, Ahti. "Yksityisnäyttelyt ryhmässä" (One-person exhibitions at the group exhibition). *Kansan Uutiset*, 23 Nov. 1966.†

G.255 Söderblom, Arja. "Juryttömät" (Without the jury). *Päivän Sanomat*, 26 Nov. 1966.†

G.256 Jylhä, Kari. "Näyttely 66 Helsingissä" (Exhibition 66 in Helsinki). *Keskisuomalainen*, 27 Nov. 1966.†

G.257 Valkonen, Olli. "Kypsän tason näyttely" (An exhibition of a high standard). *Uusi Suomi*, 27 Nov. 1966.‡

G.258 Sinisalo, Soili. "Näyttely '66 Helsingissä" (Exhibition '66 in Helsinki). *Aamulehti*, 29 Nov. 1966.‡

G.259 "Valtion taidekilpailun 66 voittaja Pentti Lumikangas" (Pentti Lumikangas, the winner of the 1966 State Art Competition). *Helsingin Sanomat*, 29 Nov. 1966.‡

G.260 W., B. "16 i Konsthallen" (16 [artists] at the [Helsinki] Art Hall). *Västra Nyland*, 30 Nov. 1966.†

G.261 Vuorikoski, Timo. "Tarpeellinen kokeilu" (A necessary experiment). *Ylioppilaslehti*, 2 Dec. 1966.†

G.262 Karjalainen, Eini. "Kemissä odotettu taidetapahtuma" (An anticipated art event in Kemi). *Kansan Tahto*, 4 Dec. 1966.‡

G.263 Paavola Irmeli. "Tamperelaisten vuosinäyttely" (Annual exhibition of the Tampere Artists' Association). *Vaasa*, 8 Dec. 1966.‡

G.264 Vihne, Pekka. "Pettymysten saatto" (A procession of disappointments). *Aamulehti*, 9 Dec. 1966.‡

G.265 Mäki-Opas, Irmeli. "Uudenlainen vuosinäyttely" (A new kind of annual exhibition [by the Tampere Artists' Association]). *Turun Sanomat*, 11 Dec. 1966.‡

1967

G.266 "Tänään on Taiteen päivä" (Today is "Art Day"). *Kansan Lehti*, 4 Jan. 1967.‡

G.267 Högström, Hilkka. "Sara Hildénin kokoelma" (The Sara Hildén Collection). *Vaasa*, 8 Jan. 1967.‡

G.268 "Kimmo Kaivannon töitä esillä Hämeenlinnassa" (Kimmo Kaivanto's works shown in Hämeenlinna). *Hämeen Kansa*, 13 Jan. 1967.

G.269 "Taidemuseossa tapahtui" (It happened at the Art Museum). *Hämeen Sanomat*, 14 Jan. 1967.

G.270 "Taidenäyttely Hämenlinnassa" (Art exhibition in Hämeenlinna). *Suomenmaa*, 14 Jan. 1967.

G.271 "Taidetapahtumia" (Art events). *Helsingin Sanomat*, 14 Jan. 1967.‡

G.272 Heinänen, Urho. "Kimmo Kaivannon taidenäyttely"

(Kimmo Kaivanto's exhibition). *Hämeen Sanomat*, 22 Jan. 1967.

G.273 Sunila, Sakari. "Kymmenen vuotta Kimmo Kaivantoa" (Ten years of Kimmo Kaivanto). *Uusi Suomi*, 22 Jan. 1967.

G.274 K-n., T. "Sara Hildénin suomalainen kokoelma Imatran Taidemuseossa" (Sara Hildén's Finnish collection at the Imatra Art Museum). *Ylä-Vuoksi*, 9 Feb. 1967.‡

G.275 "Tamperelaista kuvataidetta viiden vuosikymmen ajalta" (Five decades of visual arts in Tampere). *Aamulehti*, 25 Feb. 1967.‡

G.276 "Taidemaalarit kokoontuivat" (The painters held their meeting). *Helsingin Sanomat*, 3 Mar. 1967.‡

G.277 "Tampereen taidetta esillä näyttelyssä" (Art from Tampere shown at the exhibition). *Aamulehti*, 3 Mar. 1967.‡

G.278 S., G. "Kansainvälistä kuvataidetta esillä nyt Hämeenlinnassa" (International visual arts on view in Hämeenlinna now). *Turun Sanomat*, 5 Mar. 1967.‡

G.279 Reijonen, Tuuli. "Maaliskuulaiset" (The March Group). *Helsingin Sanomat*, 31 Mar. 1967.†

G.280 Heino, Raimo. "Sara Hildénin kokoelma" (The Sara Hildén Collection). *Hämeen Sanomat*, 2 Apr. 1967.‡

G.281 Vehmas, Einari. "Viikon taidenäyttelyitä" (This week's exhibitions). *Helsingin Sanomat*, 2 Apr. 1967.‡

G.282 Kruskopf, Erik. "Längtan till naturen" (Longing for nature). *Hufvudstadsbladet*, 7 Apr. 1967.‡

G.283 Reinikainen, Raimo. "Maaliskuulaiset" (The March Group). *Kansan Uutiset*, 8 Apr. 1967.†

G.284 Sinisalo, Soili. "'Maaliskuulaiset' Helsingissä" ("The March Group" in Helsinki). *Aamulehti*, 8 Apr. 1967.†

G.285 Kovanen, Tapani. "Maaliskuulaiset Taidehallissa" (The March Group at the [Helsinki] Art Hall). *Suomen Sosialidemokraatti*, 9 Apr. 1967.†

G.286 A-o., H. "Hämäläistaidetta" (Art from Häme). *Kansan Uutiset*, 12 Apr. 1967.‡

G.287 "Taidetapahtumia" (Art events). *Helsingin Sanomat*, 13 Apr. 1967.‡

G.288 Routio, A.I. "Pop levittäytyy esiin" (Pop spreads out). *Kauppalehti*, 14 Apr. 1967.‡

G.289 Sunila, Sakari. "Pienet taidenäyttelyt" (Little exhibitions). *Uusi Suomi*, 14 Apr. 1967.‡

G.290 Åström, Lars Erik. "Konst i Norden" (Art in the North). *Svenska Dagbladet*, 29 Apr. 1967.†

G.291 "Hietalan, Laitalan ja Kaivannon tuotteita Tesomajärven kouluun" (Works by Hietala, Laitala and Kaivanto to the Tesomajärvi school). *Hämeen Yhteistyö*, 30 Apr. 1967.†

G.292 "Kaksi maalausta ja veistos: Taideteoksia Tesomajärven kouluun Tampereella" (Two sculptures and a painting: Works of art to the Tesomajärvi School in Tampere). *Aamulehti*, 30 Apr. 1967.†

G.293 Kaitala, V.M. "Kesän-67 kuvat" (Pictures of summer 67). *Kansan Lehti*, 18 June 1967.†

G.294 Vihne, Pekka. "Seitsemän tamperelaista" ("Seven Artists" of Tampere). *Aamulehti*, 18 June 1967.†

G.295 Paavola, P. "Tamperelaista kesätaidetta" (Summer art of Tampere). *Satakunnan Kansa*, 23 June 1967.‡

G.296 "Taiteilija Kimmo Kaivannon kesää" (Kimmo Kaivanto's summer). *Suomen Sosialidemokraatti*, 30 June 1967.

G.297 Heinänen, Urho. "Tamperelaista nykytaidetta" (Contemporary art in Tampere). *Hämeen Sanomat*, 12 July 1967.†

G.298 "Taidetta" (Art). *Savo*, 13 July 1967.‡

G.299 Sunila, Sakari. "Viettymystä rajoihin" (A fascination with boundaries). *Uusi Suomi*, 19 July 1967.‡

G.300 Paavola, Irmeli. "Seitsemän valittua" (Seven elected persons). *Vaasa*, 6 Aug. 1967.‡

G.301 T., Tuomas "Tamperelaista kermaa" (The cream of Tampere art). *Ilkka*, 13 Aug. 1967.‡

G.302 "'Maanalainen kaupunki' Tampereen Yliopistolle" (The "Underground Town" to Tampere University). *Aamulehti*, 12 Sept. 1967.

G.303 "Tampereen Yliopistolle lahjoitettiin veistos" (Sculptures donated to the Tampere University). *Hämeen Yhteistyö*, 12 Sept. 1967.

G.304 "Maakunnan taidetta esillä Hämeenlinnan taidemuseossa" (Art from the provinces shown at the Hämeenlinna Art Museum). *Hämeen Sanomat*, 20 Sept. 1967.‡

G.305 "Finländsk 60-talskonst i Mariehamn" (Finnish art from the 60s in Maarianhamina). *Åland*, 21 Sept. 1967.‡

G.306 "Maamme ensimmäinen ja ainoa taidenäytelyauto Forssasta" (The first and only exhibition bus in our country is coming from Forssa). *Forssan Lehti*, 30 Sept. 1967.‡

G.307 "Taidetapahtumia" (Art events). *Helsingin Sanomat*, 27 Sept. 1967.‡

G.308 "Kaksi seinämaalausta paljastettiin" (Two murals unveiled). *Aamulehti*, 1 Oct. 1967.†

G.309 Vihne, Pekka. "Näyttely Tampereella" (An exhibition in Tampere). *Aamulehti*, 18 Oct. 1967.‡

G.310 "Hämeen Maakuntanäyttely Forssassa" (Provincial exhibition of Häme in Forssa). *Forssan Lehti*, 22 Oct. 1967.‡

G.311 "Nykytaiteen Museossa keskusteltiin" (Discussion at the [Tampere] Modern Art Museum). *Aamulehti*, 23 Oct. 1967.‡

G.312 Laine, Osmo. "Taideyhdistyksen 75-vuotisnäyttely" (75th annual exhibition of the [Turku] Artists' Association). *Turun Sanomat*, 12 Nov. 1967.†

G.313 Wargh, Carl. "Konstkrönika" (Art chronicles). *Hufvudstadsbladet*, 16 Nov. 1967.‡

G.314 Lindberg, Bo. "Målad geometri, lyrik och religion" (Painted geometry, lyricism and religion). *Åbo Underrättelser*, 19 Nov. 1967.†

G.315 Siukola, Kalle. "Keskinkertainen kokonaisuus" (A mediocre entity). *Aamulehti*, 22 Nov. 1967.†

G.316 Rusko, Jussi. "Näyttelyt Tampereella" (Exhibitions in Tampere). *Hämeen Yhteistyö*, 25 Nov. 1967.‡

G.317 "Apurahoja kuvataiteilijoille" (Grants for artists). *Aamulehti*, 29 Nov. 1967.‡

G.318 Reijonen, Tuuli. "Valtion palkitsemat" (State [Art Competition] prizes). *Helsingin Sanomat*, 16 Dec. 1967.†

G.319 Wargh, Carl. "Konstkrönika" (Art chronicles). *Hufvudstadsbladet*, 22 Dec. 1967.†

1968

G.320 Jylhä, Kari. "Suomen syksy, taiteemme kevät" (Autumn in Finland, spring in our art). *Päivän Sanomat*, 6 Jan. 1968.‡

G.321 Wargh, Carl. "Konstkrönika" (Art chronicles). *Hufvudstadsbladet*, 26 Feb. 1968.‡

G.322 Reijonen, Tuuli. "Kuvataidejärjestöjen Liiton juhlanäyttely" (Jubilee exhibition of the Union of [Finnish] Visual Arts Organizations). *Helsingin Sanomat*, 2 Mar. 1968.‡

G.323 Aurell, Heikki. "30 vuotta kuvataiteiden hyväksi" (30 years for visual arts). *Vaasa*, 3 Mar. 1968.†

G.324 Sinisalo, Soili. "Näyttelyt" (Exhibitions). *Uusi Suomi*, 5 Mar. 1968.‡

G.325 "Taidemaalariliitto" (The Painters' Union [of Finland]). *Aamulehti*, 7 Mar. 1968.‡

G.326 Vainio, Pekka. "Museoiden erikoisuuksia" (Museums' special features). *Tamperelainen*, 14 Mar. 1968.‡

G.327 "Kaivannon teoksia Venetsiaan" (Kaivanto's works to Venice). *Aamulehti*, 16 Mar. 1968.

G.328 "Modernia taidetta kuopiolaiskodeista" (Modern art from the homes of Kuopio). *Savon Sanomat*, 17 Mar. 1968.‡

G.329 "Maaliskuun näyttelyjä" (Exhibitions of March). *Aamulehti*, 24 Mar. 1968.‡

G.330 Sinisalo, Soili. "Näyttelyt" (Exhibitions). *Uusi Suomi*, 4 Apr. 1968.†

G.331 Reijonen, Tuuli. "Näyttelykatsaus" (Exhibition survey). *Helsingin Sanomat*, 6 Apr. 1968.‡

G.332 Lindström, Aune. "Kansanperinne ja kuvataide" (Folklore and visual arts). *Vaasa*, 15 June 1968.‡

G.333 Mahringer, Wolfgang. "Venetsian biennaali hälinän jälkeen" (The Venice Biennale after the clamor). *Helsingin Sanomat*, 13 July 1968.‡

G.334 "Nykytaiteen museon kesä 1968 päättynyt" (The 1968 summer exhibitions close at the [Tampere] Modern Art Museum). *Kansan Lehti*, 30 Aug. 1968.‡

G.335 "Neljä taideteosta paljastettiin" (Four works of art unveiled). *Aamulehti*, 2 Oct. 1968.‡

G.336 "Taidemuseon näyttelyt" (Exhibitions at the [Turku] Art Museum). *Turun Päivälehti*, 7 Nov. 1968.‡

G.337 Vuorikoski, Timo. "Totisesti–kumma näyttely" (Truly an odd exhibition). *Helsingin Sanomat*, 10 Nov. 1968.‡

G.338 Mallander, Jan-Olof. "Symptomatisk treårsutställning" (A symptomatic Triennial). *Hufvudstadsbladet*, 16 Nov. 1968.‡

G.339 Vuorela, Erkki. "Suomen Taideakatemian kolmivuotisnäyttely Ateneumissa" (Triennial of the Fine Arts Academy of Finland). *Veikkaaja*, 25 Nov. 1968.‡

G.340 Siukola, Kalle. "Suomalaisen kuvataiteen kenttä" (The field of Finnish visual arts). *Aamulehti*, 29 Nov. 1968.‡

G.341 Mikkola, Kaisu. "Etelä- ja Keski-Suomen taide 68" (Art in Southern and Central Finland in 1968). *Kaleva*, 31 Dec. 1968.‡

1969

G.342 "Näyttelyt" (Exhibitions). *Helsingin Sanomat*, 2 Feb. 1969.‡

G.343 Bonsdorff, Olavi. "Kaivanto ja kvasitaide" (Kaivanto and quasi-art). *Keskisuomalainen*, 9 Feb. 1969.

G.344 Mallander, Jan-Olof. "En annan Kaivanto" (Another Kaivanto). *Hufvudstadsbladet*, 11 Feb. 1969.

G.345 "Näyttelyjä: Kimmo Kaivanto" (Exhibitions: Kimmo Kaivanto). *Suomen Sosialidemokraatti*, 11 Feb. 1969.

G.346 Reinikainen, Raimo. "Tärkeistä asioista" (On important matters). *Kansan Uutiset*, 11 Feb. 1969.

G.347 Wegelius, Marjaleena. "Tärkeät ja tarpeelliset kuvat" (The important and necessary pictures). *Helsingin Sanomat*, 13 Feb. 1969.

G.348 Routio, A.I. "Vanhaa ja uutta kuvassa" (New and old in the picture). *Kauppalehti*, 14 Feb. 1969.

G.349 Laine, Osmo. "Kimmo Kaivannon esineitä" (Kimmo Kaivanto's objects). *Turun Sanomat*, 16 Feb. 1969.

G.350 Vuorikoski, Timo. "Epäkritiikkiä" (Un-criticism). *Helsingin Sanomat*, 16 Feb. 1969.‡

G.351 "Viisi taiteilijaa, kaksi näyttelyä" (Five artists, two exhibitions). *Aamulehti*, 20 Feb. 1969.

G.352 "Kolme näyttelyä" (Three exhibitions). *Aamulehti*, 22 Feb. 1969.

G.353 Junkola, Miku. "Maapallon tuskaiset muodot" (Anguished forms of the globe). *Satakunnan Kansa*, 23 Feb. 1969.

G.354 Kruskopf, Erik. "Engagerad vilande" (Devoted repose). *Hufvudstadsbladet*, 23 Feb. 1969.

G.355 P., -I. "Muita kuvia ja esineitä" (Other pictures and objects). *Vaasa*, 23 Feb. 1969.

G.356 "Taidemalariliiton vuosikokous" (The annual meeting of the Painters' Union [of Finland]). *Helsingin Sanomat*, 28 Feb. 1969.‡

G.357 Viitala, Raimo. "Kuvataidekatsaus: Tampere" (Art survey: Tampere). *Tyrvään Sanomat*, 1 Mar. 1969.†

G.358 Paavola, Pekka. "Taiteilijan vuorosana" (The artist's chance to speak). *Aamulehti*, 2 Mar. 1969.

G.359 Ala-Outinen, Pertti. "Särkyneet kuviot" (Broken images). *Uusi Aika*, 4 Mar. 1969.

G.360 "Kolme näyttelyä Tampereen Nykytaiteen Museossa" (Three exhibitions at the Tampere Modern Art Museum). *Aamulehti*, 4 Mar. 1969.‡

G.361 "Taidenäyttelyt" (Art exhibitions). *Aviisi*, 7 Mar. 1969.

G.362 "Kaksi näyttelyä avataan" (Two exhibitions will be open). *Aamulehti*, 8 Mar. 1969.‡

G.363 "Kuvataidetta näytteillä" (Visual arts shown). *Aamulehti*, 9 Mar. 1969.†

G.364 Rusko, Jukka. "Tärkeitä kuvia ja esineitä" (Important pictures and objects). *Hämeen Yhteistyö*, 11 Mar. 1969.

G.365 Raitala, Veli-Matti. "Näyttelykuviä" (Pictures at the exhibition). *Kansan Lehti*, 13 Mar. 1969.

G.366 "Kimmo Kaivannon näyttely enää kaksi päivää" (Kimmo Kaivanto's exhibition only two more days). *Aamulehti*, 15 Mar. 1969.

G.367 "Muita kuvia ja esineitä" (Other pictures and objects). *Etelä-Suomen Sanomat*, 15 Mar. 1969.

G.368 Susiluoto, Ahti. "Kuva, tiedonta, protesti: Kimmo Kaivanto" (Picture, information, protest: Kimmo Kaivanto). *Kaleva*, 4 Apr. 1969.

G.369 "Omien kokoelmien näyttely" (Exhibition of [the Tampere Art Museum] Collection). *Aamulehti*, 18 May 1969.‡

G.370 "Museotaidetta" (Museum art). *Turun Ylioppilaslehti*, 2 June 1969.‡

G.371 "Tampereen Nykytaiteen Museo mukana Tampereen messuilla" (The Tampere Modern Art Museum at the Tampere Fair). *Aamulehti*, 5 June 1969.‡

G.372 Paavola, Irmeli. "Purnu luo kesäistä perinnettä" (Purnu creates a summer tradition). *Vaasa*, 6 July 1969.†

G.373 Siukola, Kalle. "Purnun uudet ympyrät" (The new circles of Purnu). *Uusi Suomi*, 10 July 1969.‡

G.374 "Koskien puolesta" (For rapids). *Kainuun Sanomat*, 19 July 1969.‡

G.375 "Purnu 69." *Satakunnan Kansa*, 31 July 1969.†

G.376 "Bildkonst, design, arkitektur samsas på Louisianaexpo" (An Exhibition of visual arts, design and architecture to Louisiana). *Hufvudstadsbladet*, 7 Aug. 1969.‡

G.377 Prepula, Heikki. "Purnu on painava sana" (Purnu is a heavy word). *Kansan Lehti*, 9 Aug. 1969.†

G.378 Veistäjä, Olavi. "Purnu 69." *Aamulehti*, 9 Aug. 1969.‡

G.379 "Ateneumin taidemuseo" (The Ateneum Art Museum). *Helsingin Sanomat*, 10 Sept. 1969.‡

G.380 Kruskopf, Erik. "Bortgallrat engagemang" (Cancelled contract). *Hufvudstadsbladet*, 14 Sept. 1969.‡

G.381 Wegelius, Marjaleena. "Nuorten näyttely vastatuulessa" (The Young Artists' Exhibition got bad reviews). *Helsingin Sanomat*, 14 Sept. 1969.‡

G.382 Kovanen, Tapani. "Nuorten näyttely" (Young Artists' exhibition). *Suomen Sosialidemokraatti*, 18 Sept. 1969.‡

G.383 Paavola, Pekka. "23. Nuorten näyttely Helsingissä" (23rd Young Artists' exhibition). *Aamulehti*, 20 Sept. 1969.‡

G.384 Sinisalo, Soili. "Tapahtui nuorten näyttelyssä" (It happened at the Young Artists' Exhibition). *Uusi Suomi*, 21 Sept. 1969.†

G.385 "Suomalaisen taiteen kuva" (The image of Finnish art). *Aamulehti*, 27 Sept. 1969.‡

G.386 Viitala, Raimo. "30-luvulta meidän päiviimme" (From the thirties to our times). *Tyrvään Sanomat*, 8 Oct. 1969.‡

G.387 "Hämeen läänin taidepalkinto Kimmo Kaivannolle" (Häme Province art prize to Kimmo Kaivanto). *Hämeen Sanomat*, 15 Oct. 1969.†

G.388 Seppälä, Raimo. "Toinen silmä näkee ruman, toinen kauniin" (One eye sees the ugly, the other sees the beautiful). *Aamulehti*, 19 Oct. 1969.

G.389 Wunsch, Kari. "Kuvan sanoma suomalaisessa yhteiskunnassa tässä ja nyt" (The message of a picture in Finnish society here and now). *Liitto*, 25 Oct. 1969.‡

G.390 Laine, Osmo. "Kaivantokatselmus" (Kaivanto survey). *Turun Sanomat*, 26 Oct. 1969.

G.391 "Taidetapahtumia" (Art events). *Helsingin Sanomat*, 31 Oct. 1969.‡

G.392 Heininen, Greta. "Kuvataidepäivien näyttelyt Kankaanpäässä" (Exhibitions at the Kankaanpää Art Festival). *Satakunnan Kansa*, 18 Nov. 1969.‡

G.393 Paavola, Pekka. "Pariisin koulua ja uutta kotimaista" (Paris school and new Finnish art). *Aamulehti*, 19 Nov. 1969.‡

G.394 "Taveldonationer till 37 skolor" (Paintings donated to 37 schools). *Hufvudstadsbladet*, 27 Nov. 1969.‡

G.395 Ylönen, Heikki. "Kimmo Kaivanto." *Itä-Savo*, 28 Nov. 1969.

G.396 "Moniarvoinen ja -ilmeinen kuvataide" (Pluralistic and multi-faceted visual arts). *Satakunnan Kansa*, 6 Dec. 1969.‡

G.397 "Kimmo Kaivanto." *Karjalainen*, 9 Dec. 1969.

G.398 Paavola, Pekka. "Osallistuminen kuvien aiheena" (Participation as a pictorial motif). *Aamulehti*, 11 Dec. 1969.‡

G.399 "Konkretismista uusrealismiin" (From Concretism to new Realism). *Aamulehti*, 13 Dec. 1969.‡

G.400 "Valtion taidepalkinnot 69" (The 1969 State Art [Competition] prizes). *Päivän Sanomat*, 20 Dec. 1969.‡

1970

G.401 "Mielikuvitus, taitavuus, sanottava" (Imagination, skill, message). *Aamulehti*, 6 Jan. 1970.

G.402 Paavola, Pekka. "Tampereen taidekilpailun vaikutelmia" (Impressions of the Tampere Art Competition). *Aamulehti*, 10 Jan. 1970.†

G.403 Kruskopf, Erik. "Konstinköpen 1969" (1969 Art acquisitions). *Hufvudstadsbladet*, 14 Jan. 1970.‡

G.404 "Lyhytelokuvia 21 maasta" (Short films from 21 countries). *Keskisuomalainen*, 25 Jan. 1970.‡

G.405 "Taidenäyttelyjä, oopperaa Tervakoskella" (Art exhibitions, opera at Tervakoski). *Aamulehti*, 29 Jan. 1970.‡

G.406 "Elokuvamiehet osaavat maalata ja rakentaakin" (Filmmakers are able to paint and build). *Hämeen Kansa*, 12 Feb. 1970.‡

G.407 Alhainen, A. "Mesenaatit ovat menneet" (Patrons have gone). *Uusi Suomi*, 17 Feb. 1970.‡

G.408 Heinänen, Urho. "Tervakosken karttuva taidekokoelma" (Growing art collection of the town of Tervakoski). *Hämeen Sanomat*, 22 Feb. 1970.‡

G.409 Rauhala, Lasse. "Suomenselän viikon kolme taidenäyttelyä" (Three exhibitions at the Suomenselkä Festival). *Ilkka*, 26 Feb. 1970.‡

G.410 "Taidemaalariliiton vuosikokouksessa" (At the annual meeting of the Painters' Union). *Helsingin Sanomat*, 27 Feb. 1970.‡

G.411 Isola-Airisto, Irma. "Kirje Riihimäeltä" (A letter from Riihimäki). *Hämeen Sanomat*, 12 Mar. 1970.‡

G.412 "Salo: Taidetta työpaikoille" (Salo: Art to the workplaces). *Turun Päivälehti*, 2 Apr. 1970.‡

G.413 "Nykytaiteen Museon näyttely Pirkkalaan" (The [Tampere] Modern Art Museum exhibition to Pirkkala). *Aamulehti*, 4 Apr. 1970.‡

G.414 Paavola, Pekka. "Kimmo Kaivanto: Lahjakkain taiteilija" (Kimmo Kaivanto: The most gifted artist). *Aamulehti*, 5 Apr. 1970.†

G.415 "Useita näyttelyjä Nykytaiteen Museossa" (A number of exhibitions at the [Tampere] Modern Art Museum). *Aamulehti*, 11 Apr. 1970.‡

G.416 Siukola, Kalle. "Kaivannon näyttely Lundissa" (Kaivanto's exhibition in Lund). *Uusi Suomi*, 1 May 1970.

G.417 Paavola, Pekka. "Mitä maisemassa tapahtuu?" (What is happening in the landscape?). *Aamulehti*, 13 May 1970.‡

G.418 "La peinture finlandaise contemporaine" (Finnish contemporary painting). *La Cité*, 14 May 1970.‡

G.419 Lindsten, Leo. "Korkeatasoista formalismia" (Formalism of a high standard). *Kansan Uutiset*, 21 May 1970.‡

G.420 Kovanen, Tapani. "Juhlataidetta" (Festival art). *Suomen Sosialidemokraatti*, 24 May 1970.‡

G.421 Könönen, Seppo. "Keväinen näyttelykierros Helsingissä" (Spring exhibition circuit in Helsinki). *Karjalainen*, 24 May 1970.†

G.422 "Neljä taidenäyttelyä Jyväskylän Kesässä" (Four exhibitions at the Jyväskylä Summer [Festival]). *Aamulehti*, 25 May 1970.‡

G.423 Routio, A.I. "Taidehallin tutka-asema" (The radar station of the [Helsinki] Art Hall). *Uusi Suomi*, 27 May 1970.‡

G.424 "Debytantteja ja muita näyttelyjä Jyväskylään" (Debuting artists and other exhibitions to Jyväskylä). *Helsingin Sanomat*, 28 May 1970.†

G.425 Paavola, Pekka. "Liikkeen, valon, äänen katselmus" (A survey of motion, light, sound). *Aamulehti*, 29 May 1970.‡

G.426 "Jokamiehen taidenäyttely koko kesän Taidemuseossa" (Every man's exhibition open all summer at the Art Museum). *Hämeen Yhteistyö*, 4 June 1970.‡

G.427 Paavola, Pekka. "Juhlailmettä, silti tasoa" (Festive, yet of a high standard). *Aamulehti*, 4 June 1970.‡

G.428 H[ögström], S[irkka]. "Aikamme kuva taiteessa" (The image of our time in art). *Vaasa*, 17 June 1970.‡

G.429 Routio, A.I. "Vaasan Kesän kuvataide" (Visual arts at the Vaasa Summer [Festival]). *Uusi Suomi*, 18 June 1970.‡

G.430 "Jyväskylän Kesän taidetta" (Art at the Jyväskylä Summer [Festival]). *Kansan Uutiset*, 2 July 1970.

G.431 Pablo. "Mukkulassa nyt kuvakesä" (The Mukkula Art Summer [Festival]). *Itä-Häme*, 2 July 1970.‡

G.432 Mikkola, Kaisu. "Jyväskesän näyttelyistä" (About exhibitions at the Jyväskylä Summer [Festival]). *Kaleva*, 4 July 1970.

G.433 Heinonen, Aulis. "Jyväskylän Kesän Näyttelyt" (Exhibitions at the Jyväskylä Summer [Festival]). *Iisalmen Sanomat*, 5 July 1970.

G.434 Routio, A.I. "Jyväskylän Kesän kuvat" (The pictures of the Jyväskylä Summer [Festival]). *Uusi Suomi*, 5 July 1970.†

G.435 Vuorela, Erkki. "Kuvataide Jyväskylän Kesässä" (Visual arts at the Jyväskylä Summer [Festival]). *Vaasa*, 7 July 1970.†

G.436 Sorjonen, K. "Kaivannon kirkkautta ja luontoa kuvataiteessa" (Kaivanto's brightness and nature). *Keski-Suomen Iltalehti*, 8 July 1970.

G.437 Paavola, Pekka. "Batman hymyilee niskaamme" (Batman smiles behind our back). *Aamulehti*, 9 July 1970.

G.438 Selin, Helmer. "Kesän näyttelykierros" (Summer exhibition circuit). *Keskisuomalainen*, 10 July 1970.

G.439 Eirto, Eero. "Jyväskylän kesän kuvat" (Pictures of the Jyväskylä Summer [Festival]). *Kouvolan Sanomat*, 12 July 1970.†

G.440 Paavola, Irmeli. "Kaivannon esineitä" (Kaivanto's objects). *Satakunnan Kansa*, 12 July 1970.

G.441 Wargh, Carl. "Sommarutställningar" (Summer exhibitions). *Hufvudstadsbladet*, 13 July 1970.

G.442 "Taidevieras Amsterdamista" (The art visitor from Amsterdam). *Aamulehti*, 11 Aug. 1970.‡

G.443 Routio, A.I. "Kuvia, taitoa, kukkakimppuja" (Pictures, skill, bunches of flowers). *Uusi Suomi*, 23 Sept. 1970.‡

G.444 Paavola, Pekka. "Tavanomaista, pari yllätystä" (Ordinary, but a couple of surprises). *Aamulehti*, 26 Sept. 1970.‡

G.445 Siukola, Kalle. "'Pikkuateneum' Hatanpäähän" ("Miniateneum" to Hatanpää). *Uusi Suomi*, 27 Sept. 1970.‡

G.446 Kalemaa, Kalevi. "Juhlanäyttely vailla yllätyksiä" (Jubilee exhibition without surprise). *Keskisuomalainen*, 6 Oct. 1970.‡

G.447 P., P. "Tamperelaiset juhlallisina" (Tampere artists in a festive mood). *Satakunnan Kansa*, 8 Oct. 1970.‡

G.448 PR., Heikki. "Veteraanien kuvajuhlaa: Nuorekasta mausteeksi" (The picture festival of veterans: The younger to add spice to it). *Kansan Lehti*, 10 Oct. 1970.†

G.449 "Aalto-museon yläkerrassa on Lavosta, alhaalla oman kokoelman parhaita paloja" (Lavonen exhibition on the top floor of the Aalto Museum, the best pieces of the Aalto Museum Collection downstairs). *Keskisuomalainen*, 10 Oct. 1970.‡

G.450 "Näyttelyt Ruovedellä, Orivedellä" (Exhibitions at Ruovesi, Orivesi). *Aamulehti*, 27 Oct. 1970.‡

G.451 "Bildens budskap på Lovisa museum" (A picture's message at the Loviisa Museum). *Kotka Nyheter*, 5 Nov. 1970.‡

G.452 Heiniö, Heli. "Tervakosken Taiderenkaan kokoelma Riihimäellä" (The Tervakoski Art Ring Collection in Riihimäki). *Hämeen Sanomat*, 25 Nov. 1970.‡

G.453 "650 teosta valtion taidekilpailussa" (650 works in the State Art Competition). *Turun Sanomat*, 13 Dec. 1970.‡

1971

G.454 "Kimmo Kaivanto ja 'Sormet pelissä'" (Kimmo Kaivanto and "Fingers at play"). *Aamulehti*, 17 Jan. 1971.

G.455 "Julkilausuma kuvataide- ja apurahapolitiikastamme" (A declaration concerning our visual arts and grant politics). *Uusi Suomi*, 24 Jan. 1971.‡

G.456 R[outio], A.I. "Pamppu ja perhonen" (A big guy and the butterfly). *Uusi Suomi*, 4 Feb. 1971.

G.457 "Kaivanto håller blå utställning" (Kaivanto's blue exhibition). *Hufvudstadsbladet*, 4 Feb. 1971.

G.458 S., L. "Fingrar på AA-museet" (Fingers at the Amos Anderson Art Museum). *Nya Pressen*, 5 Feb. 1971.

G.459 Heiniö, Heli. "Tampereen nykytaiteen museo vierailee Hämeenlinnassa" (The Tampere Modern Art Museum in Hämeenlinna). *Hämeen Sanomat*, 6 Feb. 1971.‡

G.460 R[outio], A.I. "Sunnuntain kuvat" (Sunday pictures). *Uusi Suomi*, 7 Feb. 1971.†

G.461 "Terävät päät" (The clever heads). *Aamulehti*, 7 Feb. 1971.†

G.462 Laine, Osmo. "Kaivannon sormifonia" (Kaivanto's finger symphony). *Turun Sanomat*, 12 Feb. 1971.

G.463 Viitala, Raimo. "Kimmo Kaivanto: Sormet pelissä" (Kimmo Kaivanto: Fingers at play). *Tyrvään Sanomat*, 13 Feb. 1971.

G.464 [Kruskopf], Erik. "Blåmålarens händer" (The hands of the blue painter). *Hufvudstadsbladet*, 14 Feb. 1971.

G.465 Valkonen, Markku. "Sormet ovat maailmanselitys" (Fingers are the explanation of the world). *Helsingin Sanomat*, 14 Feb. 1971.

G.466 Paavola, Pekka. "Sormet, linnut, horisontit" (Fingers, birds, horizons). *Aamulehti*, 20 Feb. 1971.

G.467 W., B. "Konst i blått" (Art in blue). *Västra Nyland*, 20 Feb. 1971.

G.468 Kps. "Helsingissä nähtyä" (Seen in Helsinki). *Keskipohjanmaa*, 25 Feb. 1971.

G.469 Ropponen, Pirkko. "Aihe ajaton ja ajassa" (A timeless and timely motif). *Kauppalehti*, 26 Feb. 1971.

G.470 Karlsson, Raija. "Kimmo Kaivannon ostalgiat ja metapoliittinen todellisuus" (Kimmo Kaivanto's "ostalgies" and the meta-political reality). *Uusimaa*, 27 Feb. 1971.

G.471 Mallander, Jan-Olof. "Goldfingers pekfinger: En konflikts anatomi" (Goldfinger's forefinger: The anatomy of a conflict). *Hufvudstadsbladet*, 28 Feb. 1971.

G.472 Reinikainen, Raimo. "Vaaleansinisiä ajatuksia" (Light blue thoughts). *Kansan Uutiset*, 28 Feb. 1971.

G.473 Sinisalo, Soili. "Lyyrikon puheenvuoro" (A lyricist's turn to speak). *Uusi Suomi*, 28 Feb. 1971.

G.474 Heininen, Greta. "Sormet" (Fingers). *Satakunnan Kansa*, 3 Mar. 1971.

G.475 Karhunen, Eva-Liisa. "Kimmo Kaivannon näyttely" (Kimmo Kaivanto's exhibition). *Savo*, 5 Mar. 1971.

G.476 "Koivistoinen kumppaneineen" (Koivistoinen and his companions). *Aamulehti*, 7 Mar. 1971.†

G.477 "Kimmo Kaivanto viikon taiteilija tv 2:ssa" (Kimmo Kaivanto is the artist of the week on TV 2). *Keskisuomalainen*, 9 Mar. 1971.

G.478 "Kimmo Kaivannon 'Sormet pelissä' Nykytaiteen museoon" (Kimmo Kaivanto's "Fingers at play" to the [Tampere] Modern Art Museum). *Aamulehti*, 12 Mar. 1971.

G.479 "Sormet pelissä Tampereella" (Fingers at play in Tampere). *Aamulehti*, 13 Mar. 1971.

G.480 "Lahden taiteiden nykytaiteen kokoelma" (The Lahti Arts [Association] contemporary art collection). *Etelä-Suomen Sanomat*, 16 Mar. 1971.‡

G.481 Rusko, Jussi. "Sormien kosketus" (The touch of fingers). *Hämeen Yhteistyö*, 19 Mar. 1971.

G.482 Paavola, Irmeli. "Sormet tarttuvat peliin" (Fingers set to play). *Etelä-Suomen Sanomat*, 28 Mar. 1971.

G.483 "Sinisiä sormia kaupungintalossa" (Blue fingers at the [Helsinki] City Hall). *Ilta-Sanomat*, 29 Mar. 1971.

G.484 Järvinen, Seppo. "Tässä ja nyt" (Here and now). *Hämeen Kansa*, 9 Apr. 1971.

G.485 "Kimmo Kaivannon ennätysnäyttely: Yli 7000 kävijää"

(Kimmo Kaivanto's exhibition record: Over 7,000 visitors). *Aamulehti*, 15 Apr. 1971.

G.486 "Nuoren Voiman taidetta" (Art of the Young Force [Union]). *Kansan Lehti*, 29 Apr. 1971.‡

G.487 Heininen, Greta. "Pinnalan kesä" (The summer of Pinnala). *Satakunnan Kansa*, 4 June 1971.‡

G.488 "Suomalaista grafiikkaa esillä Lontoossa" (Finnish graphic art shown in London). *Helsingin Sanomat*, 11 June 1971.‡

G.489 "Uutta taidetta Kaupunginmuseossa" (New art at the City Museum). *Aamulehti*, 12 June 1971.‡

G.490 Heiniö, Heli. "Purnu-71." *Hämeen Sanomat*, 13 June 1971.†

G.491 Forsberg, Reino. "Ketju-veistos kuvaa asukkaiden yhteistyötä" ("Chain" sculpture depicts the co-operation between tenants). *Suomen Sosialidemokraatti*, 29 June 1971.

G.492 "SDP:n taidepolitiikka" (Art politics of the SDP [Finnish Social Democratic Party]). *Uusi Suomi*, 1 July 1971.‡

G.493 Mikkola, Kaisu. "Kuplaa ja enkeleitä" (The Bubble [exhibition] and the angels). *Kaleva*, 2 July 1971.‡

G.494 Valkonen, Markku. "Taidenäyttelyiden rutiinia" (The conventionality of art exhibitions). *Helsingin Sanomat*, 2 July 1971.‡

G.495 "Nykytaidettamme Länsi-Saksaan" (Our contemporary art to West Germany). *Kansan Uutiset*, 6 July 1971.‡

G.496 K[ruskopf], E[rik]. "Kaivanto presenterad i norsk konsttidskrift" (Kaivanto introduced in a Norwegian art journal). *Hufvudstadsbladet*, 11 July 1971.

G.497 Paavola, Pekka. "Purnun värit ja uudet ilmeet" (The colors and the new look of Purnu). *Aamulehti*, 25 July 1971.‡

G.498 "Kaivannon ketju valmistuu Helsingin kaupungintaloon" (Kaivanto's "Chain" sculpture for the Helsinki City Hall nearing completion). *Uusi Suomi*, 23 Oct. 1971.

G.499 "Tamperelaista kuvataidetta Esseniin" (Visual art from Tampere to Essen). *Aamulehti*, 26 Oct. 1971.‡

G.500 "Kaivannon jättityö valmistuu Tampereella" (Kaivanto's gigantic work nearing completion in Tampere). *Ilta-Sanomat*, 30 Oct. 1971.

G.501 Rauhala, Lasse. "Suomenselän viikon kuvataidenäyttelyä" (Visual arts exhibition at the Suomenselkä Festival). *Ilkka*, 10 Nov. 1971.‡

G.502 "Valtion apurahat kuvataiteilijoille" (State grants for artists). *Aamulehti*, 1 Dec. 1971.‡

1972

G.503 Paavola, Pekka. "Tamperelaiset Hämeenlinnassa" (Tampere artists in Hämeenlinna). *Aamulehti*, 12 Jan. 1972.‡

G.504 Paavola, Irmeli. "Isoveli vierailulla" (Big brother visits). *Etelä-Suomen Sanomat*, 16 Jan. 1972.‡

G.505 Vartiainen, Liisa. "Tamperelaiset taidemuseossa" (Tampere artists at the [Hämeenlinna] Art Museum). *Hämeen Sanomat*, 16 Jan. 1971.‡

G.506 Valkonen, Markku. "Kaupungintalon lävistäjä" (The diagonal of the [Helsinki] City Hall). *Helsingin Sanomat*, 21 Jan. 1972.

G.507 R[outio], A.I. "Isojen poikien Ketju" (The "Chain" of the big boys). *Uusi Suomi*, 22 Jan. 1972.

G.508 "Kimmo Kaivannon Ketju ja peilit" (Kimmo Kaivanto's "Chain" and mirrors). *Aamulehti*, 22 Jan. 1972.

G.509 Opstad, Gunvald. "Kimmo Kaivanto." *Faedrelandsvennen*, 19 Feb. 1972.

G.510 "Nuoren voiman näyttöjä" (The Young Force [Union] demonstrates). *Aamulehti*, 21 Feb. 1972.‡

G.511 "Ei enää taidekilpailuja Tampereella" (No more art competitions in Tampere). *Aamulehti*, [Feb./Mar.?] 1972.‡

G.512 Susiluoto, Ahti. "Kimmo Kaivanto, Artek." *Kansan Uutiset*, 10 Mar. 1972.

G.513 Sundell, Dan. "Utställningsronden" (Exhibition circuit). *Hufvudstadsbladet*, 11 Mar. 1972.†

G.514 Routio, A.I. "Juhlan tuntua Taidehallissa" (Festive mood at the [Helsinki] Art Hall). *Uusi Suomi*, 12 Mar. 1972.†

G.515 H[ögström], S[irkka]. "Ajan graafista anatomiaa" (Graphic anatomy of time). *Vaasa*, 14 Mar. 1972.‡

G.516 Widén, Gustaf. "Grafikexpon har: Mycket att säga" (Grapic art exhibition has a lot to say). *Åland*, 14 Mar. 1972.‡

G.517 "Menneen kesän kuvat" (Pictures of past summer). *Kansan Lehti*, 15 Mar. 1972.

G.518 Valkonen, Markku. "Näyttämön sivuilta" (From the stage wings). *Helsingin Sanomat*, 15 Mar. 1972.

G.519 Heiniö, Heli. "Vedos '72" (Print '72). *Hämeen Sanomat*, 17 Mar. 1972.†

G.520 Talvisilta, Riitta. "Vedos 72" (Print 72). *Hämeen Kansa*, 18 Mar. 1972.†

G.521 Kovanen, Tapani. "Näyttelyistä" (About exhibitions). *Suomen Sosialidemokraatti*, 19 Mar. 1972.

G.522 Orava, V.O. "Vielä ei keisari ole saanut vaatteita ylleen" (Emperor still has no clothes). *Karjalainen*, 19 Mar. 1972.†

G.523 Niemi, Risto. "Taidegrafiikan inflaatio" (The graphic art inflation). *Liitto*, 22 Mar. 1972.‡

G.524 Valkonen, Markku. "Nykygrafiikamme rautaisannos" (A big dose of our contemporary graphic art). *Helsingin Sanomat*, 26 Mar. 1972.‡

G.525 Heininen, Greta. "Suomalaisen grafiikan kuva" (The image of Finnish graphic art). *Satakunnan Kansa*, 2 Apr. 1972.‡

G.526 "Kuvataiteen suurkatselmus tänä kesänä Savonlinnassa" (A large survey of visual arts in Savonlinna this summer). *Itä-Savo*, 27 May 1972.‡

G.527 Wargh, Carl. "Nyrealistiska samhällskritiska tendenser i konst" (New realistic socially-critical tendencies in art). *Vasabladet*, 16 June 1972.‡

G.528 Hausén, Marika. "Nainen kuvataiteessa Picassosta Kaivantoon" (Woman in art from Picasso to Kaivanto). *Helsingin Sanomat*, 18 June 1972.†

G.529 Paavola, Irmeli. "Itämeri lainehtii Vaasassa" (The Baltic Sea rolls in Vaasa). *Etelä-Suomen Sanomat*, 22 June 1972.‡

G.530 Rep. "Kuultua ja nähtyä" (Heard and seen). *Suomenmaa*, 22 June 1972.‡

G.531 Heininen, Greta. "Aallon suunnittelema Villa Mairea erinomainen ympäristö suomalaisten taiteilijoiden luomuksille" (Villa Mairea by Aalto is an excellent environment for Finnish art). *Satakunnan Kansa*, 29 June 1972.‡

G.532 Paavola, Irmeli. "Kuvakesän ruohonkorsia" (Blades of grass of the art summer). *Vaasa*, 19 July 1972.‡

G.533 Franck, Marketta. "Kesän värejä, leikkimieltä" (Colors of the Summer, playfulness). *Aamulehti*, 27 July 1972.‡

G.534 "Suomen nykytaiteen katselmus Mossissa" (Survey of Finnish contemporary art in Moss). *Uusi Suomi*, 19 Nov. 1972.‡

G.535 Nuortio, Antti. "Pienoismaailma" (Miniworld). *Uusi Suomi*, 4 Dec. 1972.‡

G.536 "Kirjoita postikortti" (Send a postcard). *Hämeen Kansa*, 6 Dec. 1972.

G.537 Laine, Osmo. "Valtion taidekilpailu" (The State Art

Competition). *Turun Sanomat*, 10 Dec. 1972.‡

1973

G.538 Paavola, Pekka. "Kaivanto on korento" (Kaivanto is a dragonfly). *Etelä-Suomen Sanomat*, 4 Jan. 1973.

G.539 "Suomen kuvataidetta Yhdysvaltoihin" (Finnish visual arts to the U.S.A.). *Hämeen Kansa*, 6 Jan. 1973.‡

G.540 Seebra. "Monenlaisilla taiteilijoilla oli hauskaa" (Many kinds of artists had a good time). *Uusi Suomi*, 7 Feb. 1973.‡

G.541 "Vietnam-matinea" (Vietnam matinee). *Kansan Uutiset*, 18 Feb. 1973.‡

G.542 Svanbäck, Lennart. "Ett tvärsnitt av 60-talets konst" (A cross-section of art in the sixties). *Jakobstads Tidning*, 25 Feb. 1973.‡

G.543 "Tampere palkitsee kuvataiteilijoita" (Tampere awards prizes to artists). *Helsingin Sanomat*, 13 Mar. 1973.‡

G.544 "8 vandrar i Sverige" (8 wander in Sweden). *Nya Pressen*, 31 Mar. 1973.‡

G.545 "Ajatuksia kevään korvalle" (Spring thoughts). *Aamulehti*, 17 Apr. 1973.†

G.546 "Taidegrafiikkaa Karhulassa" (Graphic art at Karhula). *Eteenpäin*, 16 June 1973.‡

G.547 Kruskopf, Erik. "Konst i det gröna" (Art in the green). *Hufvudstadsbladet*, 17 June 1973.‡

G.548 Nuortio, Antti. "Purnun taideparatiisi" (Art paradise of Purnu). *Uusi Suomi*, 1 July 1973.‡

G.549 "Taidetapahtuma Kainuussa" (An art event in Kainuu). *Kainuun Sanomat*, 3 July 1973.‡

G.550 Susiluoto, Ahti. "Uusrealismi Suomessa: Porvariston myötäilyä vai paluu taisteluasemiin" (New Realism in Finland: Is it surrendering to bourgeoisie or returning to the barricades?). *Kansan Uutiset*, 8 July 1973.‡

G.551 Valkonen, Markku. "Purnu, kesänäyttelyiden emo" (Purnu, the mother of summer exhibitions). *Helsingin Sanomat*, 11 July 1973.‡

G.552 S., M. "Näyttely Tornikahvilassa" (Exhibition at the Tower Café [in Lahti]). *Etelä-Suomen Sanomat*, 15 July 1973.

G.553 Laurila, Mirja. "Purnu 73." *Kouvolan Sanomat*, 18 July 1973.‡

G.554 Suvioja, Mika. "Purnun kuvat" (Pictures of Purnu). *Etelä-Suomen Sanomat*, 29 July 1973.‡

G.555 "Keskustelu realismista kuvataiteessa" (A discussion concerning Realism in the visual arts). *Tiedonantaja*, 3 Aug. 1973.‡

G.556 Vartiainen, Liisa. "Purnun kesänäyttely" (Summer exhibition at Purnu). *Hämeen Kansa*, 9 Aug. 1973.‡

G.557 Laine, Osmo. "Tampereen kuvakesä" (Summer art season in Tampere). *Turun Sanomat*, 13 Aug. 1973.‡

G.558 Kovanen, Tapani. "Tuulenvirettä ja valonkimallusta" (Breath of air and a glimmering of light). *Suomen Sosialidemokraatti*, 2 Sept. 1973.

G.559 Sundell, Dan. "Parkkonsten är populär" (Public art is popular). *Hufvudstadsbladet*, 7 Sept. 1973.‡

G.560 Päivinen, Déak. "Kaivanto." *Etelä-Suomen Sanomat*, 14 Sept. 1973.‡

G.561 Heininen, Greta. "Tamperelaista grafiikkaa" (Graphic art from Tampere). *Satakunnan Kansa*, 5 Oct. 1973.‡

G.562 Julkunen, Pirjo. "Suomalaista grafiikkaa Haapasalon museossa" (Finnish graphic art at the Haapasalo Museum). *Länsi-Savo*, 8 Oct. 1973.‡

G.563 Laine, Osmo. "Neljäkymmentä vuotta graafista toimintaa" (Forty years of graphic art). *Turun Sanomat*, 13 Nov. 1973.†

G.564 "Kaivanto ja sormet" (Kaivanto and the fingers). *Ilta-Sanomat*, 14 Oct. 1973.

G.565 T., S. "40-vuotisjuhlaa" (40th anniversary jubilee [exhibition of the Graphic Artists of Turku]). *Turkulainen*, 22 Nov. 1973.‡

G.566 "Taidetta kirjastossa" (Art at the library). *Kunnallistiedote*, 23 Nov. 1973.‡

G.567 "Suomen taide Finnairin siivellä" (Finnish art on the wings of Finnair). *Uusi Suomi*, 30 Nov. 1973.

G.568 Räsänen, Anja K. "Realistisia kuvia" (Realistic pictures). *Hämeen Sanomat*, 5 Dec. 1973.‡

G.569 Routio, A.I. "Taidetta ja joulumieltä" (Art and the mood of Christmas). *Uusi Suomi*, 23 Dec. 1973.‡

1974

G.570 "Katsastusmatkalla Ranskasta" (On a journey of inspection from France). *Aamulehti*, 16 Jan. 1974.

G.571 Ahtola-Moorhouse, Leena. "Käkikellon sijasta taidetta" (Art instead of a cuckoo clock). *Hämeen Sanomat*, 23 Jan. 1974.‡

G.572 "Grafiikkanäyttely" (Exhibition of graphic art). *Iisalmen Sanomat*, 7 Feb. 1974.‡

G.573 Rantanen, Leena. "Ars 74." *Keskisuomalainen*, 24 Feb. 1974.‡

G.574 Aurell, Heikki. "Ahdistava Ars 74 auttaa näkemään" (Oppressive Ars 74 helps one to see). *Kotimaa*, 26 Feb. 1974.‡

G.575 Lindström, Ville. "Lännen ja idän kuvia" (Pictures from the west and the east). *Päivän Uutiset*, 27 Feb. 1974.‡

G.576 Routio, A.I. "Ateneumin ja Taidehallin julistajat" (The agitators of the Ateneum and the [Helsinki] Art Hall). *Uusi Suomi*, 10 Mar. 1974.‡

G.577 Laine Osmo. "Piirtäjät liikkeellä" (Draftsmen on the move). *Turun Sanomat*, 17 Mar. 1974.‡

G.578 Tuominen, Maila-Katriina. "Ars 74." *Aamulehti*, 20 Apr. 1974.‡

G.579 "Lapinlahtipäivät" (Lapinlahti Festival). *Matti ja Liisa*, 16 May 1974.

G.580 Rauhala, Lasse. "Kuvataidetta kaiken kesää Pirkanpohjassa" (Summer visual arts at Pirkanpohja). *Ilkka*, 30 May 1974.‡

G.581 Sorjonen, K. "Pirkanpohjan kesänäyttely" (Summer exhibition of Pirkanpohja). *Keskisuomalainen*, 1 June 1974.‡

G.582 H., S. "Maisemagrafiikan kesänäyttely" (Summer exhibition of landscape graphics). *Etelä-Suomen Sanomat*, 15 June 1974.‡

G.583 Prepula, Heikki. "Kansojen väkivallasta luonnon tuhoutumiseen" (From the violence of nations to the destruction of nature). *Iisalmen Sanomat*, 20 June 1974.

G.584 Valkonen, Markku. "Pala kesän näyttelykakkua" (A slice of summer exhibition cake). *Helsingin Sanomat*, 21 July 1974.

G.585 "Taidetta Ruovedellä" (Art at Ruovesi). *Aamulehti*, 18 July 1974.‡

G.586 "Museokokeilu käyntiin Hämeessä" (A museum experiment starts in Häme). *Aamulehti*, 10 Sept. 1974.‡

G.587 Kippola, Arvo. "Taidehistoriallinen pitkittäisleikkaus kolmelta vuosikymmeneltä" (Art historical cross-section of three decades). *Itä-Häme*, 14 Nov. 1974.‡

G.588 Laine, Osmo. "Ihminen nykyajan maailmassa" (Man at the present time). *Turun Sanomat*, 14 Nov. 1974.‡

G.589 P., R. "Kimmon ilot" (Kimmo's pleasures). *Iltaset*, 21 Nov. 1974.

G.590 Hämäläinen, Kalle. "Pienet ilot suuressa näyttelyssä" (Small pleasures at the large exhibition). *Helsingin Sanomat*, 24 Nov. 1974.

G.591 "Metsot taistelevat jälleen" (The wood grouses are fighting again). *Aamulehti*, 24 Nov. 1974.

G.592 Räty, Vieno. "Kimmo Kaivannon sinfonia epävälineelliselle ilolle" (Kimmo Kaivanto's symphony of pure pleasure). *Turun Sanomat*, 24 Nov. 1974.

G.593 Kuronen, Hannu. "Tuhon ja toivon enteitä" (Omens of destruction and hope). *Ilta-Sanomat*, 29 Nov. 1974.

G.594 Kovanen, Tapani. "Kuvataide" (Visual arts). *Suomen Sosialidemokraatti*, 30 Nov. 1974.

G.595 Susiluoto, Ahti. "Realismin kahdet kasvot" (Two faces of Realism). *Kansan Uutiset*, 1 Dec. 1974.

G.596 Tuominen, Maila-Katriina. "Omituista rykimistä ovat Kaivannon teokset" (Peculiar "ahem" are the works of Kaivanto). *Aamulehti*, 1 Dec. 1974.

G.597 Routio, A.I. "Pajupillin hento ääni hukkuu torvisoittoon" (The faint sound of a willow whistle is drowned out by the blare of trumpets). *Uusi Suomi*, 8 Dec. 1974.

G.598 Suvioja, Mika. "Syksyn tärkeä näyttely" (Important exhibition of this autumn). *Etelä-Suomen Sanomat*, 8 Dec. 1974.

G.599 Mallander, Jan-Olof. "Den tvehågsna handen" (The hesitant hand). *Hufvudstadsbladet*, 9 Dec. 1974.

G.600 Laine, Osmo. "Kimmon huilu soi" (Kimmo's flute is playing). *Turun Sanomat*, 10 Dec. 1974.

G.601 Bonsdorff, O. "Kimmo Kaivannon näyttely Helsingin Taidehallissa" (Kimmo Kaivanto's exhibition at the Helsinki Art Hall). *Etelä-Saimaa*, 12 Dec. 1974.

G.602 Valkonen, Markku. "Miinuskasvun taulut" (The figure of losses). *Helsingin Sanomat*, 13 Dec. 1974.

G.603 Kovanen, Tapani. "Kimmo Kaivannon näyttely" (Kimmo Kaivanto's exhibition). *Suomen Sosialidemokraatti*, 14 Dec. 1974.

G.604 Aurell, H. "Kimmo Kaivanto: Kuunteleva taiteilija" (Kimmo Kaivanto: Artist as a listener). *Savon Sanomat*, 15 Dec. 1974.

G.605 Ropponen, Pirkko. "Koko vuoden lahjavihjeet" (Gift ideas for the whole year). *Kauppalehti*, 20 Dec. 1974.†

1975

G.606 Suvioja, Mika. "Vuoden 1974 kuvataidetapahtumia" (Visual art events of 1974). *Etelä-Suomen Sanomat*, 3 Jan. 1975.‡

G.607 "Nokian Myllyhaan koulun pihalle kaksi veistosta" (Two sculptures to the Nokia Myllyhaka School playground). *Aamulehti*, 5 Feb. 1975.‡

G.608 Viitala, Raimo. "Sisäänlämpiävä vuosinäyttely nykytaiteen museossa" (A cliquish annual exhibition [of the Tampere Artists' Association] at the [Tampere] Modern Art Museum). *Tyrvään Sanomat*, 12 Feb. 1975.‡

G.609 Tuominen, Maila-Katriina. "Vuosinäyttely" (Annual exhibition [of the Tampere Artists' Association]). *Aamulehti*, 23 Feb. 1975.‡

G.610 "Tampere Film Festival 20.-23.2.1975." *Hufvudstadsbladet*, 25 Feb. 1975.

G.611 Anttikoski, Riitta. "Kimmo Kaivannolla on näköala kaupungin sydämeen" (Kimmo Kaivanto has a view of the heart of the city). *Aamulehti*, 13 Apr. 1975.

G.612 Penttinen, Anja. "Purnun viides on veistosten kesä" (Fifth Purnu is the summer of sculptures). *Keskisuomalainen*, 6 June 1975.‡

G.613 Erkkilä, Eila. "Käynti Purnussa on virkistävä kokemus" (Visit to Purnu is a refreshing experience). *Ilkka*, 20 June 1975.‡

G.614 Sundell, Dan. "Purnu-biennalen konstens grönbete" (Purnu Biennial is a pasture of art). *Hufvudstadsbladet*, 20 June 1975.‡

G.615 Tottijärven perillinen. "Siivellä" (On the wing). *Aamulehti*, 31 Aug. 1975.‡

G.616 "Kiitosta Ruotsista" (Thanks from Sweden). *Helsingin Sanomat*, 24 Sept. 1975.‡

G.617 "Radiointi ja näyttelyitä" (A broadcast and exhibitions). *Uusi Suomi*, 26 Sept. 1975.‡

G.618 "Konst" (Art). *Hufvudstadsbladet*, 30 Sept. 1975.‡

G.619 L., H. "Suomalaista nykytaidetta Forssassa" (Finnish contemporary art in Forssa). *Forssan Lehti*, 30 Oct. 1975.‡

G.620 "Maalauksia, grafiikkaa, veistoksia" (Paintings, prints, sculpture). *Eteenpäin*, 1 Nov. 1975.†

G.621 Rissa, Jouko. "Joken kulma" (Joke's corner). *Eteenpäin*, 6 Nov. 1975.

G.622 Hartikainen, Marjatta. "Piirtäjän viestit ihmiselle" (The draftsman's messages to the people). *Eteenpäin*, 9 Nov. 1975.

G.623 "Kööpenhaminan Galerie Asbackissa [sic]..." (At the Galerie Asbæk in Copenhagen...). *Uusi Suomi*, 18 Dec. 1975.‡

G.624 Joenniemi, Sirpa. "Viikon kuvat" (Pictures of the week). *Kansan Lehti*, 20 Dec. 1975.‡

G.625 "Ja me toivotamm' hyvää ja onnellista joulujuhlaa..." (We wish you a merry Christmas...). *Aamulehti*, 23 Dec. 1975.†

1976

G.626 Ilasmaa, Urpu. "Orvokit kukivat Pariisissa" (Violets bloom in Paris). *Karjalainen*, 8 Feb. 1976.‡

G.627 "Monumentti täynnä yksityiskohtia" (A monument full of details). *Aamulehti*, 17 Feb. 1976.

G.628 "Tori keskellä kylää" (A square in the heart of the village). *Aamulehti*, 9 Mar. 1976.

G.629 "Turku tänään" (Turku today). *Helsingin Sanomat*, 1 Apr. 1976.

G.630 Routio, A.I. "Terveisiä Italiasta" (Greetings from Italy). *Uusi Suomi*, 14 Apr. 1976.‡

G.631 Ermala, Olavi. "Turun taiteellakaan ei ole varaa torkkua" (Not even the art of Turku can afford to be drowsy). *Turkulainen*, 22 Apr. 1976.†

G.632 Laine, Osmo. "Piirtäjien ja graafikkojen taidemuseo" (Art museum of draftsmen and printmakers). *Turun Sanomat*, 23 Apr. 1976.

G.633 W., B. "Blommor och ögon" (Flowers and eyes). *Västra Nyland*, 9 May 1976.‡

G.634 M., E. "Yli 30 kukkataulua nyt taidehallissa" (More than 30 flower paintings now at the [Kajaani] Art Hall). *Kainuun Sanomat*, 8 Aug. 1976.‡

G.635 P., A. "Kimmo Kaivannon todella ensimmäinen grafiikan näyttely" (Really the first graphics exhibition of Kimmo Kaivanto). *Keskisuomalainen*, 17 Sept. 1976.

G.636 Kalliola, Rauha. "Kimmo Kaivanto Aalto-museolla" (Kimmo Kaivanto at the [Alvar] Aalto Museum). *Kansan Lehti*, 21 Sept. 1976.

G.637 Tuominen, Maila-Katriina. "Kirjava aluenäyttely" (An uneven exhibition). *Aamulehti*, 24 Sept. 1976.

G.638 Niiranen, Jussi. "Tori" (The Square). *Ilta-Sanomat*, 2 Oct. 1976.

G.639 Valonen, Anu. "Kimmo valvoi viimeisen yön Tori-monumentin kanssa" (Kimmo stayed up all night working on "The Square" last night). *Kansan Lehti*, 2 Oct. 1976.

G.640 "Kaivannon Tori sai paikkansa" (Kaivanto's "Square" got its place). *Helsingin Sanomat*, 4 Oct. 1976.

G.641 "Kokoontumispaikka, historian kehykset" (A meeting place, the framework of history). *Aamulehti*, 4 Oct. 1976.

G.642 Paavola, Pekka. "Ympyrä sulkeutuu" (The circle closes itself). *Etelä-Suomen Sanomat*, 8 Oct. 1976.

G.643 KARA. "Kertovat mukavia asioita" (They speak about nice things). *Aamulehti*, 23 Oct. 1976.†

1977

G.644 Sinisalo, Soili. "Taiteessa tapahtuu Kirkkonummellakin" (It happens to art in Kirkkonummi). *Länsi-Uusimaa*, 8 Feb. 1977.‡

G.645 "Taidenäyttely lapsille auki perjantaista lähtien" (Exhibition for children open from Friday on). *Valkeakosken Sanomat*, 22 Feb. 1977.‡

G.646 Routio, A.I. "Kolmen vuosikymmen taidetta" (Art of three decades). *Uusi Suomi*, 6 Mar. 1977.†

G.647 Valkonen, Markku. "Alkupalat TM-galleriassa" (First exhibition at the TM gallery). *Helsingin Sanomat*, 9 Mar. 1977.‡

G.648 Tuominen, Maila-Katriina. "Tamperelaiset Taidehallissa" (Tampere artists at the [Helsinki] Art Hall). *Aamulehti*, 16 Mar. 1977.‡

G.649 Sundell, Dan. "Återblick på Tfrskonst" (A survey of Tampere art). *Hufvudstadsbladet*, 17 Mar. 1977.‡

G.650 Valkonen, Markku. "Pirkkalaisilme piilossa" (Pirkkala expression hidden). *Helsingin Sanomat*, 18 Mar. 1977.†

G.651 Susiluoto, Ahti. "Omaperäistä Tampereelta" (Original [art] from Tampere). *Kansan Uutiset*, 19 Mar. 1977.‡

G.652 Heininen, Greta. "Kuvataidekentältä" (From the art field). *Satakunnan Kansa*, 20 Mar. 1977.‡

G.653 Bonsdorff, O. "Pohjolan taidegraafikkojen 40-vuotisjuhlasnäyttely" (40th anniversary exhibition of Nordic printmakers). *Etelä-Saimaa*, 12 Apr. 1977.‡

G.654 "Tampereen tiede ja taide saivat 192 800 markkaa" (Science and art got 192,800 marks in Tampere). *Aamulehti*, 22 Apr. 1977.‡

G.655 Pohjonen, Kirsti. "Tampere hyvä patsaskaupunki" (Tampere is a good town for statues). *Aamulehti*, 26 Apr. 1977.†

G.656 "Imaginarius." *Helsingin Sanomat*, 27 Apr. 1977.‡

G.657 Valkonen, Markku. "Itämeren nopein hotelli" (The fastest hotel of the Baltic). *Helsingin Sanomat*, 29 Apr. 1977.†

G.658 Tuominen, Maila-Katriina. "Taidemuseon näyttelyt" (Exhibitions at the [Tampere] Art Museum). *Aamulehti*, 30 Apr. 1977.‡

G.659 Tottijärven perillinen. "Siivellä: Suomalaisia kuvia" (On the wings: Finnish pictures). *Aamulehti*, 1 May 1977.†

G.660 S., K. "Selvä linja Lahden II julistebiennalessa" (The clear line of the second Lahti Poster Biennial). *Etelä-Suomen Sanomat*, 3 June 1977.‡

G.661 Tottijärven perillinen. "Siivellä" (On the wings). *Aamulehti*, 12 June 1977.‡

G.662 Kippola, Maija. "Suvi-Pinx" (The Summer at Pinx). *Itä-Häme*, 24 June 1977.‡

G.663 Tuominen, Maila-Katriina. "Vesivärejä ja tekstiilejä" (Watercolors and textiles). *Aamulehti*, 7 July 1977.‡

G.664 "10 000 mk." *Aamulehti*, 30 Aug. 1977.‡

G.665 "Kuvantekijän syksy" (The picture maker's autumn). *Aamulehti*, 13 Sept. 1977.

G.666 Jyväkorpi, Pirkko. "Kaivannon Tori nyt kaikkien nähtäville" (Kaivanto's "Square" on public view). *Kansan Lehti*, 16 Sept. 1977.

G.667 Kaitala, Veli-Matti. "Kuvat" (Pictures). *Kansan Lehti*, 16 Sept. 1977.†

G.668 Paavola, Pekka. "Mitä tapahtui kun kuningas Kustaa III oli 33-vuotias?" (What happened when King Gustavus III was 33 years old?). *Aamulehti*, 23 Sept. 1977.

G.669 S., I. "Tori Tampereella Kaivannon silmin" (The Tampere Square through the eyes of Kimmo Kaivanto). *Suomenmaa*, 1 Nov. 1977.

G.670 Anttila, Leena. "Grafiikka kuuluu kansalle" (Graphic art belongs to the people). *Warkauden Lehti*, 30 Nov. 1977.‡

G.671 "Taiteilijat tutuiksi" (Get acquainted with the artists). *Oriveden Sanomat*, 1 Dec. 1977.‡

G.672 Hyvärinen, Pekka. "Taide: Hyvärinen ei kysy" (Art: Hyvärinen doesn't ask). *Liitto*, 6 Dec. 1977.‡

G.673 Stenbäck, Aulis. "Juhlanäyttelyn tiimoilta" (Concerning the jubilee exhibition). *Kaleva*, 29 Dec. 1977.‡

1978

G.674 Niemi, R. "Itsenäisyyden 60-vuotisjuhlanäyttely" (60th anniversary jubilee exhibition of independence). *Liitto*, 5 Jan. 1978.‡

G.675 Keinänen, Timo. "Meri, aina uusi" (The sea, always new). *Länsi-Suomi*, 15 Jan. 1978.‡

G.676 "Nykytaiteen näyttely Lappeenrannassa" (Contemporary art exhibition in Lappeenranta). *Kouvolan Sanomat*, 3 Feb. 1978.‡

G.677 "Kimmo Kaivanto lavastamaan Punainen viiva-oopperan" (Kimmo Kaivanto to design stage sets for "The Red Line" opera). *Kansan Lehti*, 8 Mar. 1978.

G.678 Kallio, Kyllikki. "Taidetuen mallia" (A model for art support). *Savon Sanomat*, 10 Mar. 1978.‡

G.679 "Sadan taiteilijan kesänäyttely" (Summer exhibition of 100 artists). *Tyrvään Sanomat*, 18 Apr. 1978.‡

G.680 "Tampere täyttää 200 vuotta" (Tampere turns 200). *Hämeen Sanomat*, 2 June 1978.‡

G.681 "F 15 kertoo Tampereesta" (The F 15 tells about Tampere). *Aamulehti*, 13 June 1978.‡

G.682 "Liput, viirit, mitallit" (Flags, banners, medals). *Aamulehti*, 12 Sept. 1978.‡

G.683 "45. kerta, ennätysvuosi" (The 45th time, a record year). *Aamulehti*, 29 Sept. 1978.‡

G.684 Eteläpää, Heikki. "Aulis Sallisen Punainen viiva" ("The Red Line" by Aulis Sallinen), *Uusi Suomi*, 26 Nov. 1978.†

G.685 Lampila, Hannu-Ilari. "Laulumelodia: Sallisen uusin aluevaltaus" (Melody to sing: Sallinen's newest territorial conquest). *Helsingin Sanomat*, 2 Dec. 1978.†

G.686 Wahlström, Erik. "Sallinens nya opera" (Sallinen's new opera). *Hufvudstadsbladet*, 2 Dec. 1978.†

G.687 Kovanen, Tapani. "Kuvataide" (Visual art). *Suomen Sosialidemokraatti*, 9 Dec. 1978.†

G.688 "Juhlakuutio nousi katolle Tampereella" (The festive cube rose to the roof in Tampere). *Aamulehti*, 21 Dec. 1978.

G.689 Nieminen-Helenius, Marja. "Kaivannon mustat viivat" (Kaivanto's black lines). *Ilta-Sanomat*, 27 Dec. 1978.

G.690 Tuominen, Maila-Katriina. "Neljätoista runoilijaa, neljätoista taiteilijaa" (Fourteen poets, fourteen artists). *Aamulehti*, 28 Dec. 1978.‡

1979

G.691 Routio, A.I. "Suomen osuus Allende-museoon" (The Finnish portion to the Allende Museum). *Uusi Suomi*, 14 Jan. 1979.‡

G.692 Valkonen, Markku. "Omantunnon työt" (Works of conscience). *Helsingin Sanomat*, 14 Jan. 1979.‡

G.693 Lahdenperä, Osmo. "Sara Hildénin taidemuseo avattiin" (Sara Hildén Art Museum opened). *Uusi Suomi*, 11 Feb. 1979.‡

G.694 Lehtola, Erkka. "Juhlakirja lahjaksi juhlavuoden lapsille" (A jubilee book as a present for the children of jubilee year). *Aamulehti*, 9 Mar. 1979.†

G.695 Savolainen, Maisa. "Taidetta Tampereelta" (Art in Tampere). *Hämeen Sanomat*, 22 Mar. 1979.‡

G.696 "Kimmo Kaivannon suunnittelema juhlavuoden tunnus..." (The symbol of [Tampere's] bicentennial designed by Kimmo Kaivanto...). *Kansan Uutiset*, 4 Apr. 1979.

G.697 Routio, A.I. "Juttu juoksee Tampereesta" (Stories about Tampere). *Uusi Suomi*, 23 Apr. 1979.†

G.698 Viitala, Raimo. "Tamperelaistaiteen tusina" (A dozen Tampere artists). *Tyrvään Sanomat*, 10 May. 1979.‡

G.699 Tuominen, Maila-Katriina. "Tampereen kuva puhuu" (The picture of Tampere speaks). *Aamulehti*, 12 May 1979.‡

G.700 "Orvokkimeren paikka tyhjänä" (The place of the Violet Sea empty). *Uusi Suomi*, 19 May 1979.‡

G.701 Elimäki, Kati. "Harkiten valittua tamperelaistaidetta" (Carefully chosen art from Tampere). *Hämeen Yhteistyö*, 24 May 1979.‡

G.702 Lehtola, Erkka. "Ooppera Lontoossa" (The [Finnish National] Opera in London). *Aamulehti*, 12 June 1979.†

G.703 Sundell, Dan. "Trivsel kring Purnu-konst" (Enjoy Purnu art). *Hufvudstadsbladet*, 15 June 1979.‡

G.704 Valkonen, Markku. "Kesätaiteen kirjavat kasvot" (Variegated face of summer art). *Helsingin Sanomat*, 16 June 1979.‡

G.705 Valkonen, Markku. "Suomalainen törmää omaan kuvaansa" (A Finn crashes into his own image). *Helsingin Sanomat*, 17 June 1979.‡

G.706 Ala-Outinen, Pertti. "Purnu-79" (Purnu 79). *Satakunnan Kansa*, 1 July 1979.‡

G.707 Paavola, Pekka. "Rostock on nykytaiteen tiivistymä" (Rostock consolidates contemporary art). *Aamulehti*, 3 Aug. 1979.‡

G.708 Tavela, Leena. "Tamperelaisittain" (As in Tampere). *Kunnallistiedote*, 3 Aug. 1979.†

G.709 Bucciarelli, Lea. "Kesäretki Purnun kuvamaailmaan" (An excursion to the picture world of Purnu). *Kansan Uutiset*, 4 Aug. 1979.‡

G.710 Laine, Osmo. "Helsinki osallistuu" (Helsinki takes part). *Turun Sanomat*, 4 Aug. 1979.‡

G.711 Ala-Outinen, Pertti. "Juhlavuoden kuvataidetta Tampereen taidemuseossa" (Art of [bicentennial] anniversary at the Tampere Art Museum). *Satakunnan Kansa*, 9 Aug. 1979.†

G.712 Maaltamuuttaja. "Moni kirja päältä kaunis" (A great many books have beautiful covers). *Hämeen Yhteistyö*, 11 Sept. 1979.†

G.713 "He rakensivat Tamperetta..." (They built Tampere). *Helsingin Sanomat*, 30 Sept. 1979.

G.714 Niiniluoto, Maarit. "Onko tampere kulttuurikaupunkina aikansa elänyt?" (Is Tampere a culture town anymore?) *Uusi Suomi*, 30 Sept. 1979.†

G.715 "Nyt kaikki voimat kulttuuriin!" (All the power for culture now!). *Aamulehti*, 30 Sept. 1979.†

G.716 Silvasti, Eero. "Pipopäinen kymmenluku" (Knitted cap headed decade). *Helsingin Sanomat*, 3 Oct. 1979.‡

G.717 Siltavuori, Eeva. "Muoviajan maahiset" (The earth spirits of the plastic time). *Helsingin Sanomat*, 19 Oct. 1979.‡

G.718 Routio, A.I. "Maalareiden suku koolla" (The painters' family gathering). *Uusi Suomi*, 21 Oct. 1979.‡

G.719 Suvioja, Mika. "Paikallinen perspektiivi jää yllättävän heikoksi" (Local perspective is surprisingly weak). *Etelä-Suomen Sanomat*, 21 Oct. 1979.†

G.720 Sundell, Dan. "Målarnas Tammerfors" (The painters' Tampere). *Hufvudstadsbladet*, 26 Oct. 1979.‡

G.721 "Kaivanto ja muotokuva" (Kaivanto and the portrait). *Aamulehti*, 11 Nov. 1979.

G.722 Paavola, Pekka. "Saari purjehtii merellä" (An island is sailing on the sea). *Ilkka*, 16 Nov. 1979.

G.723 Tuominen, Maila-Katriina. "Kimmo Kaivannon merimerkki" (Kimmo Kaivanto's buoy). *Aamulehti*, 25 Nov. 1979.

1980

G.724 "Kädet ovat Kimmo Kaivannon kädet, mutta..." (The hands are Kimmo Kaivanto's, but...). *Aamulehti*, 10 Jan. 1980.

G.725 Laaksonen, Riikka. "Punainen viiva syntyi Göteborgissa" ("The Red Line" was born in Göteborg). *Aamulehti*, 12 Jan. 1980.†

G.726 Perlström, Åke. "Tsarens röda streck, och björnens" (Tsar's red line, and the bear's). *Göteborgs-Posten*, 13 Jan. 1980.†

G.727 Tuominen, Maila-Katriina. "Taidemaalariliitto keski-iässä" (The Painters' Union reaches middle age). *Aamulehti*, 19 Jan. 1980.‡

G.728 Isomursu, Liisa. "Väri tv:stä taiteen perusteita." (The basics of art from color TV). *Uusi Suomi*, 22 Jan. 1980.†

G.729 Tuomainen, Väinö. "Monikasvoista kuvataidetta" (Multi-faceted visual arts). *Savon Sanomat*, 31 Jan. 1980.‡

G.730 Lehmussaari, Eeva. "Liikkeen ja rytmin kohtaaminen" (The meeting of movement and rhythm). *Etelä-Suomi*, 9 Feb. 1980.‡

G.731 Laine, Osmo. "Valaistu Tampere" (Tampere illuminated). *Turun Sanomat*, 24 Feb. 1980.‡

G.732 Puranen, Leena. "Tampere eilen ja tänään" (Tampere today and yesterday). *Savon Sanomat*, 24 Feb. 1980.†

G.733 Rauhala, Lasse. "Täysi tusina tamperelaisia" (A full dozen of Tampere artists). *Ilkka*, 7 Mar. 1980.‡

G.734 Högström, Sirkka. "Arvot puntarissa" (Values hanging in the balance). *Vaasa*, 12 Mar. 1980.‡

G.735 "Kriitikot ja kuvantekijät" (Critics and artists). *Aamulehti*, 13 Apr. 1980.‡

G.736 P., A. "Tamperelainen tusina" (A dozen Tampere artists). *Keskisuomalainen*, 14 Mar. 1980.†

G.737 Löfman, Anita. "Starkt personligt från Tammerfors" (Very individual from Tampere). *Vaasa*, 25 Mar. 1980.‡

G.738 "1,3 Mmk i kulturbidrag" (1.3 million marks for cultural grants). *Hufvudstadsbladet*, 15 Apr. 1980.‡

G.739 "Uusi laki vaatii" (The new law demands). *Aamulehti*, 30 Apr. 1980.†

G.740 Könönen, Seppo. "Tasokasta Tampereelta" ([Art of] a high level from Tampere). *Karjalainen*, 4 May 1980.†

G.741 Sundell, Dan. "Temakonst i Jyväskylä" (Thematic art in Jyväskylä). *Hufvudstadsbladet*, 3 June 1980.‡

G.742 Tuominen, Maila-Riitta. "Kuvakulkuja ihmisen ympäristössä" (Images floating in human environment). *Aamulehti*, 11 June 1980.‡

G.743 "Nykypäivien kuvataide" (Visual arts today). *Etelä-Suomen*

Sanomat, 20 June 1980.†

G.744 Pöykkö, Kalevi. "Muutoksen merkkejä" (Signs of change). *Keskisuomalainen*, 29 June 1980.†

G.745 Heiskanen, Seppo. "Kirjakansien kilpalaulanta" (The song contest of covers). *Suomen Sosialidemokraatti*, 1 July 1980.‡

G.746 Tuominen, Maila-Katriina. "Muutoksen merkkejä kuvassa" (Signs of change in the picture). *Aamulehti*, 3 July 1980.‡

G.747 Tallimäki, J. "Maailmankuva taiteen peilissä" (World picture in the mirror of art). *Etelä-Suomen Sanomat*, 5 July 1980.‡

G.748 Laine, Osmo. "Minne käy tuulen ilmassa tie..." (Where is the wind blowing...). *Turun Sanomat*, 20 July 1980.‡

G.749 "Kimmo Kaivannon työ kopioitiin luvatta: Neuvostohotelli nappasi teoksen" (Kimmo Kaivanto's work was copied without permission: A Soviet hotel snatched it). *Aamulehti*, 31 July 1980.

G.750 Eteläpää, Heikki. "Kimmo Kaivanto kesästään" (Kimmo Kaivanto's summer). *Uusi Suomi*, 3 Aug. 1980.

G.751 M-sela., K. "Ammattilaisten ja harrastajien taidetta esillä Noitakäräjillä" (Art of professionals and amateurs shown at the "Witch Trial"). *Ruovesi*, 16 Aug. 1980.‡

G.752 Savolainen, M. "Näyttely kuin oppitunti" (The exhibition like a lesson). *Hämeen Sanomat*, 17 Aug. 1980.‡

G.753 "...tulevaisus ei huolestuta" (...the future doesn't worry me). *Kansan Lehti*, 19 Sept. 1980.

G.754 Aare, Leif. "Finsk triumf" (Finnish triumph). *Dagens Nyheter*, 26 Sept. 1980.†

G.755 Routio, A. I. "Tampereellahan ei tunnelmoida" (They aren't in a sentimental mood in Tampere). *Uusi Suomi*, 28 Sept. 1980.‡

G.756 Tuominen, Maila-Katriina. "Nyt ovat ovet avoinna" (Now the doors are open). *Aamulehti*, 28 Sept. 1980.‡

G.757 Viitala, Raimo. "Tampereen Taiteilijaseuran juhlanäyttely" (Jubilee exhibition of the Tampere Artists' Association). *Tyrvään Sanomat*, 2 Oct. 1980.‡

G.758 "Herkkuja silmälle ja suulle" (Feasts for the eye and the mouth). *Uusi Suomi*, 18 Oct. 1980.‡

G.759 Paavola, Irmeli. "Tampereen Taiteilijaseura juhlii" (The Tampere Artists' Association is celebrating). *Etelä-Suomen Sanomat*, 23 Oct. 1980.‡

G.760 "Siirtolaisuuden maailmanennätys Södertäljessä" (The world record of imigrants in Södertälje). *Etelä-Saimaa*, 13 Dec. 1980.‡

1981

G.761 Kovanen, Tapani. "Kimmo Kaivanto." *Suomen Sosialidemokraatti*, 8 Jan. 1981.

G.762 Tyrkkö, Maarit. "Hyvät ystävät" (Dear friends). *Uusi Suomi*, 9 Jan. 1981.

G.763 "Kaivanto ställer ut" (Kaivanto's exhibition). *Jakobstads Tidning*, 21 Jan. 1981.

G.764 "Kimmo Kaivannon kokokuva Ruotsissa" (Full-length portrayal of Kimmo Kaivanto in Sweden). *Etelä-Suomen Sanomat*, 21 Jan. 1981.

G.765 MKT. "Kimmo Kaivannon näyttely Ruotsiin" (Kimmo Kaivanto's exhibition to Sweden). *Aamulehti*, 21 Jan. 1981.

G.766 "Kimmo Kaivanto Ruotsissa" (Kimmo Kaivanto in Sweden). *Turun Sanomat*, 22 Jan. 1981.

G.767 "Kaivannon kuvat Södertäljessä" (Kaivanto's pictures in Södertälje). *Uusi Suomi*, 23 Jan. 1981.

G.768 Carlsson, Kjell. "Finske Kimmo på Luna" (Finnish Kimmo at Luna). *Södertälje-kuriren*, no. 7 (1981).

G.769 "Kimmo Kaivanto ja silminnäkijät" (Kimmo Kaivanto and the Eyewitnesses). *Aamulehti*, 1 Feb. 1981.

G.770 Törnqvist, Arne. "Kimmo Kaivanto på Södertälje konsthall" (Kimmo Kaivanto at the Södertälje Art Hall). *Dagens Nyheter*, 3 Feb. 1981.

G.771 Sundell, Dan. "Kaivanto i Södertälje" (Kaivanto in Södertälje). *Hufvudstadsbladet*, 12 Feb. 1981.

G.772 Fleming, Katariina. "Kimmo Kaivanto pitämässä suurnäyttelyä Ruotsissa" (Kimmo Kaivanto's large exhibition in Sweden). *Eteenpäin*, 17 Feb. 1981.

G.773 "Kiihkeä keskustelu yleisön kanssa..." (A heated discussion with the audience...). *Aamulehti*, 21 Mar. 1981.

G.774 "Kaivannolla menestystä" (Kaivanto was a success). *Suomen Sosialidemokraatti*, 26 Mar. 1981.

G.775 "Kimmo Kaivannon mielimusiikkia" (Kimmo Kaivanto's favorite music). *Uusi Suomi*, 7 May 1981.

G.776 Drougge, Per. "Kaivantos 'Tänkaren'" (Kaivanto's "Thinker"). *Länstidningen*, 9 June 1981.

G.777 Jokinen, Pertti. "Vuoden taiteilija Kimmo Kaivanto" (Kimmo Kaivanto, Artist of the Year). *Kansan Uutiset*, 19 Nov. 1981.

G.778 "Kimmo Kaivanto on Vuoden taiteilija 1982" (Kimmo Kaivanto is Artist of the Year 1982). *Helsingin Sanomat*, 19 Nov. 1981.

G.779 "Kimmo Kaivanto Vuoden taiteilija" (Kimmo Kaivanto, Artist of the Year). *Vaasa*, 19 Nov. 1981.

G.780 "Kimmo Kaivanto Vuoden taiteilija-82" (Kimmo Kaivanto, Artist of the Year 1982). *Keskisuomalainen*, 19 Nov. 1981.

G.781 "Monitasoisesta Kimmo Kaivannosta Vuoden taiteilija" (The multi-talented Kimmo Kaivanto is Artist of the Year). *Uusi Suomi*, 19 Nov. 1981.

G.782 "Kimmo Kaivanto blev Årets konstnär 1982" (Kimmo Kaivanto became Artist of the Year 1982). *Hufvudstadsbladet*, 20 Nov. 1981.

G.783 "Taiteilijoiden rauhanjuna kiertää Suomen" (The artists' peace train goes around Finland). *Hämeen Sanomat*, 1 Dec. 1981.‡

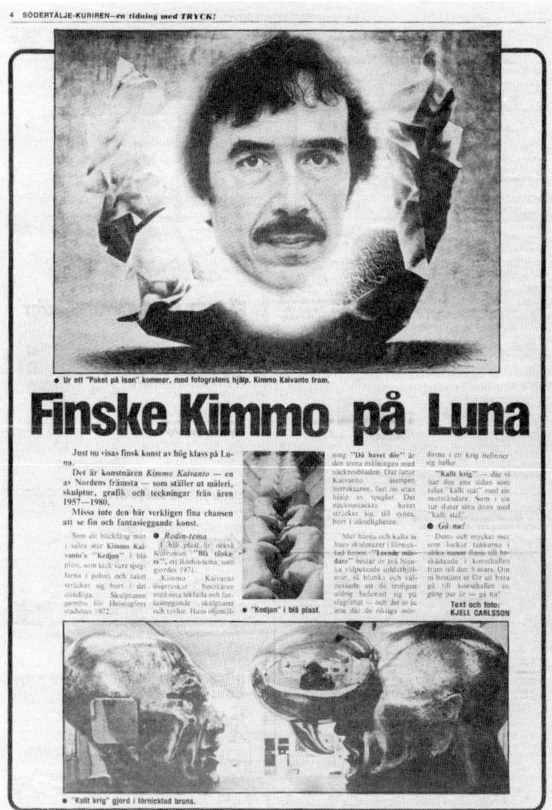

G.768

decades). *Kansan Uutiset*, 18 Aug. 1982.

G.796 Routio, A.I. "Vuoden taiteilija Kimmo Kaivanto" (Kimmo Kaivanto, Artist of the Year). *Uusi Suomi*, 20 Aug. 1982.

G.797 Tuominen, Maila-Katriina. "Näin sen koin" (This is how I experienced it). *Aamulehti*, 22 Aug. 1982.

G.798 Valkonen, Markku. "Kaipuun ja ahdistuksen sini" (The blue of longing and anxiety). *Helsingin Sanomat*, 22 Aug. 1982.

G.799 Helmiriitta. "Kimmo Kaivanto, Vuoden taiteilija" (Kimmo Kaivanto, Artist of the Year). *Päijät-Häme*, 25 Aug. 1982.

G.800 Kallio, Rakel. "Kimmo Kaivanto: Vuoden taiteilija" (Kimmo Kaivanto: Artist of the Year). *Ilkka*, 28 Aug. 1982.

G.801 Stålhammar, Leo. "Vuoden taiteilija Kimmo Kaivanto" (Kimmo Kaivanto, Artist of the Year). *Suomenmaa*, 28 Aug. 1982.

G.802 Huida, Jarmo. "Kaipuun kämmenenjälki" (The stamp of longing). *Satakunnan Kansa*, 29 Aug. 1982.

G.803 Susiluoto, Ahti. "Kimmo Kaivannon tilinpäätös" (Kimmo Kaivanto's balance sheet). *Kansan Uutiset*, 29 Aug. 1982.

G.804 Ropponen, Pirkko. "Vuoden taiteilija Kimmo Kaivanto" (Kimmo Kaivanto, Artist of the Year). *Hyvinkään Sanomat*, 31 Aug. 1982.

G.805 Sandqvist, Tom. "Kimmo Kaivanto, Årets konstnär" (Kimmo Kaivanto, Artist of the Year). *Hufvudstadsbladet*, 31 Aug. 1982.

G.806 Arell, Bernt. "Kimmo Kaivanto på festspelen" (Kimmo Kaivanto at the [Helsinki] Festival). *Västra Nyland*, 5 Sept. 1982.

G.807 Remes, Jukka. "Muistiinmerkintöjä ajasta" (Notes on the moment). *Hämeen Sanomat*, 5 Sept. 1982.

G.808 Välinoro, Anne. "Vuoden taiteilijan puolustuspuhe" (A speech in defence of Artist of the Year). *Iisalmen Sanomat*, 5 Sept. 1982.

G.809 Kivirinta, Marja-Terttu. "Kimmo Kaivannon maisema" (Kimmo Kaivanto's landscape). *Helsingin Sanomat*, 6 Sept. 1982.

G.810 Andersson, Jan-Erik. "Massiv bildsatsning på Hfors festspel" (A large quantity of art at the Helsinki Festival). *Åbo Underrättelser*, 10 Sept. 1982.

G.811 Leskelä, Esa. "Juhlaviikkojen näyttelyantia" (Exhibitions at the [Helsinki] Festival). *Kansan Tahto*, 10 Sept. 1982.

G.812 Suomela, Aamos. "Kuin medion käsi" (Like the hand of a medium). *Kaleva*, 10 Sept. 1982.

G.813 Laine, Osmo. "Vuosien taiteilija" (Artist of the Years). *Turun Sanomat*, 11 Sept. 1982.

G.814 Castrén, Hannu. "Tapahtumien silminnäkijä" (The eyewitnesses of the case). *Keskisuomalainen*, 12 Sept. 1982.

G.815 Kalaja, Marja-Leena. "Kimmo Kaivannon laaja näyttely" (Kimmo Kaivanto's large exhibition). *Länsiväylä*, 12 Sept. 1982.

G.816 Suvioja, Mika. "Kimmo Kaivanto kaikkine vaiheineen" (Kimmo Kaivanto in all his phases). *Etelä-Suomen Sanomat*, 12 Sept. 1982.

G.817 Unho, Pirkko. "Kaivannon vaihtuvat kaudet" (The changing periods of Kaivanto). *Tiedonantaja*, 15 Sept. 1982.

G.818 Jern, Åsa. "Högklassig konst under festspelen" (Art of a high level at the [Helsinki] Festival). *Vasabladet*, 16 Sept. 1982.

G.819 "Helsingin Taidehallissa Kimmo Kaivanto: Taide on elämä, elämä on taide" (Kimmo Kaivanto at the Helsinki Art Hall: Art is life, life is art). *Kamppi*, [date unknown, Aug./Sept.?] 1982.

G.820 "Kaivannon näyttelyssä kävi lähes 40 000" (Nearly 40,000 people visited Kimmo Kaivanto's exhibition). *Etelä-Suomen*

G.784 Kinnunen, Pirkko. "Vuoden taiteilija Kimmo Kaivanto" (Kimmo Kaivanto, Artist of the Year). *Ilta-Sanomat*, 12 Dec. 1981.

1982

G.785 Räty, Vieno. "Kimmo Kaivanto." *Turun Sanomat*, 20 Feb. 1982.

G.786 "Punaisen viivan uusi ilme" (A new look of "The Red Line"). *Aamulehti*, 7 July 1982.†

G.787 Lampila, Hannu-Ilari. "Holmbergin Punainen viiva" (Holmberg's "Red Line"). *Helsingin Sanomat*, 9 July 1982.†

G.788 Fleming, Katriina. "Kimmo Kaivannon kiireinen kesä" (The hurried summer of Kimmo Kaivanto). *Kansan Lehti*, 20 July 1982.

G.789 Eteläpää, Heikki. "Vuoden taiteilija Kimmo Kaivanto" (Kimmo Kaivanto, Artist of the Year). [Newspaper unidentified], 1 Aug. 1982.

G.790 "Vuoden taiteilija Kimmo Kaivanto" (Kimmo Kaivanto, Artist of the Year). *Hämeen Sanomat*, 12 Aug. 1982.

G.791 "Vuoden taiteilija Kimmo Kaivanto" (Kimmo Kaivanto, Artist of the Year). *Turun Sanomat*, 12 Aug. 1982.

G.792 Seppälä, Arto. "Kimmo Kaivanto, vuoden taiteilija" (Kimmo Kaivanto, Artist of the Year). *Aamulehti*, 15 Aug. 1982.

G.793 "Pelkistetty katsaus Kaivannon taiteesta" (A no-frill survey of Kimmo Kaivanto's art). *Helsingin Sanomat*, 18 Aug. 1982.

G.794 Pirtola, Erkki. "Kimmo Kaivanto Taidehallissa" (Kimmo Kaivanto at the [Helsinki] Art Hall). *Ilta-Sanomat*, 18 Aug. 1982.

G.795 Vuori, Hilkka. "Kaivannon vuosikymmenet" (Kaivanto's

Sanomat, 29 Sept. 1982.

G.821 Tuominen, Maila-Katriina. "Dramatiikkaa, työtä ja haikeutta" (Drama, work and sadness). *Aamulehti*, 1 Oct. 1982.

G.822 Larpo, Maire. "Kimmo Kaivannon näyttely kotikaupungissa" (Kimmo Kaivanto's exhibition in his hometown). *Hämeen Yhteistyö*, 2 Oct. 1982.

G.823 Heräjärvi, Aira. "Sinisten ajatusten totuus" (The truth about blue thoughts). *Koillis-Häme*, 9 Oct. 1982.

G.824 "Kimmo Kaivanto: Sairaaloihin abstraktisia töitä" (Kimmo Kaivanto: Abstract art to hospitals). *Ilta-Sanomat*, 9 Oct. 1982.

G.825 Viitala, Raimo. "Kimmo Kaivanto Sara Hildén museossa" (Kimmo Kaivanto at the Sara Hildén Museum). *Tyrvään Sanomat*, 9 Oct. 1982.

G.826 Kotirinta, Pirkko. "Kaivanto ja tuhon kauneus" (Kaivanto and the beauty of destruction). *Vaasa*, 10 Oct. 1982.

G.827 "Kaivanto fick Tammerforspris" (Kimmo Kaivanto received the Tampere Prize). *Vasabladet*, 11 Oct. 1982.

G.828 Joenniemi, Sirpa. "Ajan virrassa" (At the current of time). *Kansan Lehti*, 14 Oct. 1982.

G.829 Rusko, Jussi. "Kimmo Kaivannon kuvalliset merkit" (The illustrated signs of Kimmo Kaivanto). *Hämeen Yhteistyö*, 16 Oct. 1982.

G.830 Remes, Jukka. "Kimmo Kaivanto." *Hämeen Sanomat*, 17 Oct. 1982.

G.831 "Täydennystä Kimmo Kaivannon näyttelyyn" (A supplement to Kimmo Kaivanto exhibition). *Kansan Lehti*, 21 Oct. 1982.

G.832 Tuominen, Maila-Katriina. "Kadotettua ihmistä löytämässä" (Finding the lost man). *Aamulehti*, 30 Oct. 1982.

G.833 Svanbäck, Lennart. "Årets konstnär, K Kaivanto" (Kimmo Kaivanto, Artist of the Year). *Jakobstads Tidning*, 2 Nov. 1982.

G.834 "Kaivannosta luennoidaan" (A lecture on Kaivanto). *Tamperelainen*, 3 Nov. 1982.

G.835 "Kimmo Kaivanto." *Porin Lehti*, 10 Nov. 1982.

G.836 Wettenhovi, Hannu-P. "Kimmo Kaivanto tekee ja osaa" (Kimmo Kaivanto can and does). *Kalajokilaakso*, 18 Nov. 1982.

G.837 Vainionpää, Marja-Leena. "Toinen teos" (Another work). *Aamulehti*, 19 Nov. 1982.†

G.838 Kovanen, Tapani. "Siveltimellä ja kynällä" (With brush and pen). *Suomen Sosialidemokraatti*, 23 Nov. 1982.

G.839 "Eikö kirkko ole osa kulttuuria" (Isn't the church a part of culture?). *Etelä-Suomen Sanomat*, 25 Nov. 1982.

G.840 "Kirja joka ei unohdu" (An unforgettable book). *Aamulehti*, 1 Dec. 1982.†

G.841 "Mitä itsenäisyys on Pekka Kuuselle, Riitta Auviselle, Heinäsirkalle, Kimmo Kaivannolle ja minulle…" (What independence means to Pekka Kuusi, Riitta Auvinen, Heinäsirkka, Kimmo Kaivanto and me…). *Uusi Suomi*, 6 Dec. 1982.†

1983

G.842 Pennanen, Ulla. "Puunveistäjien pojanpoika: Kimmo Kaivanto" (Grandson of the wood carvers: Kimmo Kaivanto). *Karjalainen*, 4 Jan. 1983.

G.843 Kruskopf, Erik. "Bildtänkare i blått" (A picture thinker in blue). *Hufvudstadsbladet*, 20 Feb. 1983.

G.844 Henahan, Donald. "Music: Finnish Opera Offers Sallinen's 'Red Line'." *New York Times*, 28 Apr. 1983.†

G.845 Goodman, Peter. "Finns Shine in 'The Red Line'." *Newsday*, 29 Apr. 1983.†

G.846 O'Reilly, Warren. "Finns Win New Acclaim with Sallinen's 'Red Line'." *Washington Times*, 29 Apr. 1983.†

G.847 Roos, James. "The 'Opera Wave' of Finland Makes Met Debut." *Miami Herald*, 1 May 1983.†

G.848 "Kimmo Kaivanto koristaa Forumin valopihan" (Kimmo Kaivanto decorates the Forum's light well). *Helsingin Sanomat*, 2 June 1983.

G.849 Saukkomaa, Harri. "Tyhmät kysymykset" (Stupid questions). *Helsingin Sanomat*, 14 June 1983.

G.850 "Kalle Holmberg: Ei meistä tarvitse pitää, mutta olemme me aika hyviä" (Kalle Holmberg says "You need not like us, but we are pretty good anyway"). *Aamulehti*, 5 July 1983.†

G.851 Vuojola, Antti. "Kimmo Kaivanto on tapausten silminnäkijä" (Kimmo Kaivanto is the eyewitness of the case). *Turun Päivälehti*, 16 July 1983.

G.852 "Kaivannon ensimmäistä näyttelyä suunnitellaan" (First exhibition of Kaivanto [in the U.S.] being planned). *Aamulehti*, 15 Sept. 1983.

1984

G.853 "Aikaansa edellä" (Ahead of his time). *Ilta-Sanomat*, 27 Jan. 1984.

G.854 Auréen, Bo. "Kimmo Kaivanto." *Keskipohjanmaa*, 29 Jan. 1984.

G.855 Enbom, Carla. "Arkitektonisk spegling" (Architectural reflections). *Hufvudstadsbladet*, 3 Feb. 1984.

G.856 "Kimmo Kaivanto loi Sokerille tilateoksen" (Kimmo Kaivanto has created an installation for Finn Sugar). *Helsingin Sanomat*, 3 Feb. 1984.

G.857 "Zefyros on tilateos" (Zefyros is an installation). *Aamulehti*, 3 Feb. 1984.

G.858 "Kaivannon tilateos Tapiolaan" (Kaivanto's installation for Tapiola). *Uusi Suomi*, 4 Feb. 1984.

G.859 Pietiläinen, Tuomo. "Makeaa taidetta sokerista" (Sweet art out of sugar). *Länsiväylä*, 11 Mar. 1984.

G.860 Vähäkylä, Liisa. "Kimmo Kaivanto Lopella" (Kimmo Kaivanto at Loppi). *Hämeen Sanomat*, 14 Apr. 1984.

G.861 Manner, Eeva-Liisa. "Punainen viiva" (The Red Line). *Aamulehti*, 15 Apr. 1984.†

G.862 "Kimmo Kaivanto kirjallisuuspiirin vieraana" (Kimmo Kaivanto visited the literary circle). *Lopen Lehti*, 18 Apr. 1984.

G.863 Vainio, Irene. "Minuun tämä teki mahtavan vaikutuksen" (This had a powerful effect on me). *Kainuun Sanomat*, 10 July 1984.

G.864 Seppälä, Arto. "Punainen viiva saapui Suomussalmelle" ("The Red Line" came to Suomussalmi). *Aamulehti*, 10 Aug. 1984.†

G.865 "Kaivanto, Kanerva, Pohjola." *Kansan Lehti*, 17 Nov. 1984.†

G.866 Viitala, Raimo. "kolmen taitajan yhteisnäyttely" (Group exhibition of three masters). *Tyrvään Sanomat*, 22 Nov. 1984.†

G.867 Ryynänen, Hannu. "Mältinrannassa esillä kolmen miehen mysteerit" (Mysteries of three men shown at Mältinranta). *Tamperelainen*, 25 Nov. 1984.†

G.868 Tuominen, Maila-Riitta. "Vanhat toverit" (Old comrades). *Aamulehti*, 29 Nov. 1984.†

G.869 Rusko, Jussi. "Kuvataiteen trio" (The trio of visual arts). *Hämeen Yhteistyö*, 30 Nov. 1984.†

1985

G.870 Helin, Pekka. "Pyhäniemi." *Hämeen Sanomat*, 11 Aug. 1985.‡

G.871 Karo, Leena. "Viikon kasvo" (The week's face). *Helsingin Sanomat*, 15 Aug. 1985.

G.872 Suvioja, Mika. "Mallikkaasti kahdessa tilassa" (Stylishly in two rooms). *Etelä-Suomen Sanomat*, [Aug.?] 1985.‡

G.873 "Agentin raportti" (Agent's report). *Tamperelainen*, 29 Sept. 1985.†

G.874 Sinerkari, Kaarina. "Forumin valot syttyvät ensi viikolla" (The Forum will be lit up next week). *Helsingin Sanomat*, 31 Oct. 1985.‡

G.875 Pirtola, Erkki. "Meillä kaikilla on vapaa värisielu" (Each of us has a free color-soul). *Ilta-Sanomat*, 5 Nov. 1985.†

G.876 "Champagneporl i nya Forum" (Champagne bubbles at the new Forum). *Hufvudstadsbladet*, 6 Nov. 1985.†

G.877 Perttula, Marja. "Forum on vihreää ja valkoista" (Forum is green and white). *Uusi Suomi*, 6 Nov. 1985.‡

G.878 Routio, A.I. "Pikku kuvaelma nimeltä exlibris" (A short scene named exlibris). *Uusi Suomi*, 7 Nov. 1985.

G.879 Kovanen, Tapani. "Takaisinko Informalismiin?" (Back to Informalism?). *Suomen Sosialidemokraatti*, 9 Nov. 1985.

G.880 Sundell, Dan. "Lekar för ögat" (Delight for the eyes). *Hufvudstadsbladet*, 9 Nov. 1985.

G.881 Tuominen, Maila-Katriina. "Kuningas ja Pyhän Sebastianin sääriluu" (The king and Saint Sebastian's shin). *Aamulehti*, 13 Nov. 1985.

G.882 Sarje, Kimmo. "Vallan semiotiikkaa" (The semiotics of power). *Helsingin Sanomat*, 14 Nov. 1985.

G.883 Sundell, Dan. "Synliga Monument" (Public monument). *Hufvudstadsbladet*, 14 Nov. 1985.†

G.884 Kivirinta, Marja-Terttu. "Taideteokset luovat hiljaisuutta" (Art works into calm). *Helsingin Sanomat*, 15 Nov. 1985.†

G.885 Holmila, Paula. "Forumin veistokset" (Sculptures at the Forum). *Uusi Suomi*, 16 Nov. 1985.†

G.886 Engeström, Georg. "Uutta viiniä uudessa leilissä" (New wine in a new bottle). *Suomenmaa*, 21 Nov. 1985.†

G.887 Paavilainen, Maija. "Forum † art." *Kotimaa*, 21 Nov. 1985.†

G.888 Sundell, Dan. "Konsten fick sitt" (Art has got to fit). *Hufvudstadsbladet*, 5 Dec. 1985.†

G.889 "Taidetta aidan takaa" (Art from behind the fence). *Helsingin Sanomat*, 8 Dec. 1985.

G.890 Aapro, Pirkko. "Kiihkeää työskentelyä, omakohtaisia kriisejä" (Hard work, personal crisis). *Keskisuomalainen*, 16 Dec. 1985.

G.891 Helin, Pekka. "Kolme erilaista taiteilijaa" (Three different kinds of artists). *Hämeen Sanomat*, 24 Dec. 1985.†

1986

G.892 "Kimmo Kaivanto Linnan muotokuvasta" (Kimmo Kaivanto on the portrait of Linna). *Ilta-Sanomat*, 26 Nov. 1986.

G.893 Tuominen, Maila-Katriina. "Kimmo Kaivannon pitkä kypsyttely" (The long maturing of Kimmo Kaivanto). *Aamulehti*, 27 Nov. 1986.

G.894 "Väinö Linna kuin Robert de Niro" (Väinö Linna likes Robert de Niro). *Ilta-Sanomat*, 27 Nov. 1986.

G.895 "Väinö Linnan muotokuva paljastettin" (Portrait of Väinö Linna unveiled). *Kansan Lehti*, 27 Nov. 1986.

G.896 "Väinö Linnan muotokuva paljastettiin Tampereella" (The portrait of Väinö Linna unveiled in Tampere). *Helsingin Sanomat*, 27 Nov. 1986.

G.897 "Eloisa muotokuva Väinö Linnasta" (The lively portrait of Väinö Linna). *Kotikaupunki*, 30 Nov. 1986.

G.898 Lahdenperä, Osmo. "Näkijän sininen katse" (The blue gaze of the prophet). *Uusi Suomi*, 30 Nov. 1986.

G.899 [Cartoon] "Viimeisen kerran, Kimmo..." (Last call, Kimmo...). *Kotikaupunki*, 30 Nov. 1986.

1987

G.900 "100 suomalaista vaikuttajaa" (100 Finnish men of consequence). *Uusi Suomi*, 11 Jan. 1987.‡

G.901 Halmekoski, Tuija. "Nuori taiteilija ei mene muotokuvan kehyksiin" (A young artist doesn't go to the frame of a portrait). *Suomen Sosialidemokraatti*, 13 Feb. 1987.†

G.902 Heikkilä, Ulla-Maija. "Peilejä maailma tarvitsee" (The world needs mirrors). *Liitto*, 7 Mar. 1987.

G.903 "Kaivantoa Taidemuseossa" (Kaivanto at the [Oulu] Art Museum). *Oulu-lehti*, 8 Mar. 1987.

G.904 Kastemaa, Heikki. "Kimmo Kaivannon tuotantoa kymmenlukujen vuoropuhelussa" (Kimmo Kaivanto's art in a dialogue of the decades). *Kaleva*, 9 Mar. 1987.

G.905 Ollila, Timo. "Hän on täällä tänään" (He is here today). *Kansan Tahto*, 14 Mar. 1987.

G.906 "Vale-Kaivanto sai vankeutta" (False Kaivanto landed in jail). *Aamulehti*, 28 Mar. 1987.

G.907 Puusti, Artturi. "Osallistuva taiteilija" (A participating artist). *Liitto*, 29 Mar. 1987.

G.908 Tikkinen, Hannele. "Kaivanto Kuopion taidemuseossa" (Kaivanto at the Kuopio Art Museum). *Savon Sanomat*, [Date unknown]. 1987.

G.909 Miettinen, Marja. "Kimmo Kaivanto Kuopiossa" (Kimmo Kaivanto in Kuopio). *Iisalmen Sanomat*, 3 Apr. 1987.

G.910 Siltari, Aimo. "Kuopion kääntöpiiri" (Tropic of Kuopio). *Savon Sanomat*, 5 Apr. 1987.†

G.911 "Kaivanto on täällä" (Kaivanto is here). *Uutis-Kukko*, 9 Apr. 1987.

G.912 Tikkinen, Hannele. "Kimmo Kaivannon näyttely Kuopion taidemuseossa" (Kimmo Kaivanto's exhibition at the Kuopio Art Museum). *Savon Sanomat*, 12 Apr. 1987.

G.913 Rossi, Leena-Maija. "Kimmo Kaivannon sininen huoli" (The blue concern of Kimmo Kaivanto). *Helsingin Sanomat*, 24 Apr. 1987.

G.914 "Aivan oikein..." (That's right...). *Kaleva*, 5 May 1987.

G.915 "Kaivanto maalaamastaan Väinö Linnan muotokuvasta" (Kimmo Kaivanto on the portrait of Väinö Linna). *Forssan Lehti*, 2 Aug. 1987.

G.916 "Muotokuva Linnan syntymäkuntaan" (Linna's portrait for his birth place). *Hämeen Sanomat*, 2 Aug. 1987.

G.917 "Muotokuvan selitys" (Explanation of the portrait). *Aamulehti*, 2 Aug. 1987.

G.918 Tirkkonen, Marja-Liisa. "Väinö Linna, Kimmo Kaivanto." *Iltalehti*, 3 Aug. 1987.

G.919 A., A-M. "Dynaaminen, levoton Väinnö Linna" (Dynamic, restless Väinö Linna). *Urjalan Sanomat*, 6 Aug. 1987.†

G.920 Timonen, Kaarina. "Kaljut kohtasivat kun Kassila filmasi jännäriään" (Baldies met when Kassila was filming his thriller). *Ilta-Sanomat*, 9 Aug. 1987.†

G.921 "Kimmo Kaivannon muistiinmerkintöjä" (Notes by Kimmo Kaivanto). *Aamulehti*, 18 Aug. 1987.

G.922 Kivirinta, Marja-Terttu. "Henkilökuva on matka Kimmo Kaivannon maisemaan" (Portrait is a journey into the landscape of Kimmo Kaivanto). *Helsingin Sanomat*, 18 Aug. 1987.

G.923 "Tampere-talo somistuu" (Tampere Hall will be decorated). *Aamulehti*, 6 Oct. 1987.

G.924 Heinonen, Kalervo. "Puoli vuosisataa mainosmaailmassa" (Half a century in advertising). *Aamulehti*, 8 Nov. 1987.†

G.925 "Poliisi, diiva ja taidemaalari" (Police, diva and painter). *Aamulehti*, 28 Nov. 1987.‡

G.926 Töyssy, Seppo. "Kohtaamisia luonnossa ja Ruoveden maisemissa" (Meetings in nature and in the landscape of Ruovesi). *Ruovesi*, 16 Dec. 1987.†

1988

G.927 Seppänen, Veikko. "Kaivannon ateljee Tammerkosken partaalle" (Kaivanto's studio on the Tammerkoski). *Kansan Lehti*, 20 Jan. 1988.

G.928 "Kaivanto kosken partaalla" (Kaivanto on the bank of the rapids). *Aamulehti*, 21 Jan. 1988.

G.929 "Sorsa matkustaa Keski-Amerikkaan" (Sorsa is going to leave for Central America). *Aamulehti*, 9 Mar. 1988.‡

G.930 "Rantanen toisi Tampereelle uuden tutkimuslaitoksen" (Rantanen would bring a new research institute to Tampere). *Aamulehti*, 16 Aug. 1988.‡

G.931 "Tampere-talon salat julki" (Out in the open with the secrets of Tampere Hall). *Aamulehti*, 10 Sept. 1988.‡

G.932 "Suomen Sokeri palasi Helsinkiin" (Finn Sugar returned to Helsinki). *Helsingin Sanomat*, 13 Sept. 1988.†

G.933 "Tilateos" (Installation). *Aamulehti*, 14 Sept. 1988.

G.934 Kunnas Jouko. "Kuvia synnyttämättömästä talosta" (Pictures of an unborn house). *Kaleva*, 21 Sept. 1988.‡

G.935 Koivisto, Raimo. "Tampere-talo ennakkoesittelyssä" (An advance presentation of Tampere Hall). *Kainuun Sanomat*, 29 Sept. 1988.‡

G.936 Lapintie, Kimmo. "Tampere-talon tavaramarkkinat" (Tampere Hall merchandise fair). *Aamulehti*, 29 Sept. 1988.‡

G.937 Rossi, Leena-Maija. "Tampereen omavarainen taidesyksy" (Tampere's own art autumn). *Helsingin Sanomat*, 8 Oct. 1988.†

G.938 Valkonen, Markku. "Taide pakenee sisätiloihin" (Art flees indoors). *Helsingin Sanomat*, 5 Nov. 1988.†

G.939 "Sininen kuva tekee minut onnelliseksi" (A blue picture makes me happy). *Ilta-Sanomat*, 10 Nov. 1988.

G.940 Kolsi, Eeva-Kaarina. "Kimmo Kaivanto näyttelynsä avajaisissa" (Kimmo Kaivanto at the opening of his exhibition). *Ilta-Sanomat*, 11 Nov. 1988.

G.941 Tirkkonen, Marja-Leena. "Kaivannon tärkein näyttely" (Kaivanto's most important exhibition). *Iltalehti*, 11 Nov. 1988.

G.942 Heiskanen, Seppo. "Punainen hevonen käsitteiden metsässä" (A red horse in the forest of conceptions). *Suomen Sosialidemokraatti*, 15 Nov. 1988.

G.943 Rinne, Matti. "Kirjanpito: Kaivanto puree" (Bookkeeping: Kaivanto bites). *Ilta-Sanomat*, 18 Nov. 1988.

G.944 Rouhiainen, Anne. "Taide näyttää vallan merkit" (Art shows the signs of power). *Uusi Suomi*, 19 Nov. 1988.

G.945 Pirtola, Erkki. "Art." *Ilta-Sanomat*, 22 Nov. 1988.†

G.946 Valjakka, Timo. "Pienikin viesti puree" (A short message also bites). *Helsingin Sanomat*, 26 Nov. 1988.

1989

G.947 Vainionpää-Palmgren, Marja-Leena. "Runoilija Eeva-Liisa Manner" (Eeva-Liisa Manner, the poet). *Kaleva*, 26 Feb. 1989.†

G.948 Tuominen, Maila-Katriina. "Maaliskuulaiset räjäyttivät padot" (The March Group blew up the dams). *Aamulehti*, 9 Mar. 1989.‡

G.949 Heiskanen, Seppo. "Maaliskuulaisten 60-luku Taidehallissa" (The sixties art of the March Group in the [Helsinki] Art Hall). *Suomen Sosialidemokraatti*, 15 Mar. 1989.‡

G.950 Tuominen, Maila-Katriina. "Radikaaleista tuli klassikoita" (Radicals became classics). *Aamulehti*, 18 Mar. 1989.‡

G.951 Valkonen, Markku. "Maaliskuulaisten 60-luku on säilyttänyt vetovoimansa" (The sixties art of the March Group maintains the power of attraction). *Helsingin Sanomat*, 19 Mar. 1989.‡

G.952 Routio, A.I. "Taidehallin maaliskuulaiset" (The March Group at the [Helsinki] Art Hall). *Uusi Suomi*, 23 Mar. 1989.‡

G.953 Sundell, Dan. "Martianerna i Konsthallen" (The March Group at the [Helsinki] Art Hall). *Hufvudstadsbladet*, 23 Mar. 1989.‡

G.954 Lahtonen, Katariina. "Maaliskuulaiset seisovat kahden kauden rajalla" (Artists of the March Group stand on the boundary between two periods). *Forssan Lehti*, 29 Mar. 1989.‡

G.955 "Tampere-taloon Kaivannon 200-metrinen betonityö" (Kaivanto's 200-meter-long work in concrete for the Tampere Hall). *Helsingin Sanomat*, 11 Apr. 1989.†

G.956 Nyrhinen, Tiina. "Kuoleman puutarha ja salasynnyttäjä" ("The Garden of Death" [by Hugo Simberg] and "Woman in a Secret Childbed" [by Akseli Gallén-Kallela]). *Helsingin Sanomat*, 9 June 1989.‡

G.957 "Suomen taidetta esillä Moskovassa" (Finnish art shown in Moscow). *Aamulehti*, 18 Nov. 1989.†

G.958 Teriö, Hannu. "Euroopan henkinen perintö rakentuu Siniseen suoraan" (The European intellectual heritage is incorporated in the Blue Line). *Aamulehti*, 31 Dec. 1989.

1990

G.959 "Suomalaistaide esittäytyy Oslossa" (Finnish art introduced in Oslo). *Helsingin Sanomat*, 13 Jan. 1990.‡

G.960 "Tampere-talon kuvataide ja esirippu julkistettiin" (The visual arts and the curtain of Tampere Hall on public view). *Helsingin Sanomat*, 11 May 1990.†

G.961 Välinoro, Anne. "Vähän, mutta hyvää" (Not much, but good). *Aamulehti*, 11 May 1990.†

G.962 "Mitä Tove Jansson piirsi lapsena?" (What did Tove Jansson draw in her childhood?). *Ilta-Sanomat*, 30 May 1990.‡

G.963 "Kimmo Kaivanto viihtyy Kaapelitehtaalla" (Kimmo Kaivanto gets on well at the [Nokia] cable factory). *Ilta-Sanomat*, 5 June 1990.

G.964 Tuominen, Maila-Katriina. "Kuokka vaihtui penseliin" (The hoe was changed to a brush). *Aamulehti*, 14 Sept. 1990.‡

G.965 Ikonen, Heikki. "Informalismi tuli ja meni" (Informalism came and went). *Aamulehti*, 30 Sept. 1990.‡

G.966 Honkavaara, Raila. "Arkadia-seurassa pohdittiin Helsingin keskustaa" (The center of Helsinki discussed at the Arkadia Club), *Iltalehti*, 22 Nov. 1990.‡

G.967 Korhonen, Hannele. "Musiikkia, valoa ja taidetta" (Music, lights and art). *Iltalehti*, 26 Nov. 1990.†

G.968 Heimo, Jussi. "Hyvä tunnus ei vanhene koskaan" (A fine mark never ages). *Aamulehti*, 20 Dec. 1990.

1991

G.969 "Lahjoitus tikan suojelijoille" (A donation for the protectors of the woodpecker). *Keskisuomalainen*, 23 Feb. 1991.†

G.970 Jaatinen, Hilkka. "Kaivannon sininen on onnenkaipuun väri" (Kaivanto's blue is a color of longing for happiness). *Kansan Lehti*, 8 Mar. 1991.

G.971 "Suomalaisissa on potentiaalia" (There is potential among the

Finns). *Helsingin Sanomat*, 16 June 1991.‡

G.972 "Kimmo Kaivannon ympäristöteos SOK:n kortteliin Vallilaan" (Kimmo Kaivanto's environmental work for the SOK Co-op at Vallila). *Helsingin Sanomat*, 26 Sept. 1991.

G.973 "Puhemies Sorsa muotokuvaksi" (The portrait of Kalevi Sorsa, the Speaker). *Helsingin Sanomat*, 11 Oct, 1991.

G.974 Ritolahti, Pentti. "Kirkon ja taiteen roolit" (The roles of church and art). *Kotimaa*, 22 Nov. 1991.

G.975 Nyrhinen, Tiina. "Intressien risteyskohdassa" (At the intersection of interests). *Helsingin Sanomat*, 14 Dec. 1991.†

H. Oral Documentation

1975

H.1 [Interview with the artist] Eini, Paavo. "Omatunto nimeltä Kimmo Kaivanto" (A conscience called Kimmo Kaivanto). Helsinki: Finnish Broadcasting Company, Apr. 1975.

I. Audio-Visual Documentation

1966

I.1 "Taiteilijan kesä" (An artist's summer). Ed. by Aila Rantala. Helsinki: Social Programs, Finnish Broadcasting Company TV 2, 7 July 1966.

1969

I.2 "Jos ja kun" (If and when). Produced by Heikki Ritavuori and Seppo Jokinen. Helsinki: Cultural Edition, Finnish Broadcasting Company TV 1, 6 Feb. 1969.

1970

I.3 "Filmikalenteri" (Film calendar). Directed by Leena Lohtander and ed. by Erkka Lehtola and Matti Rosvall. Helsinki: Documentary Edition, Finnish Broadcasting Company TV 2, 26 Feb. 1970.

1971

I.4 "Viikon taiteilija" (Artist of the week). Helsinki: Finnish Broadcasting Company TV 2, 8-14 Mar. 1971.

1973

I.5 "Kauneus ja tuho" (Beauty and destruction‡). Realized by Lisa Kuhlberg, Jorma Karhunen, Jorma Kuusisto and Anssi Mellblom. Helsinki: Documentary Edition, Finnish Broadcasting Company TV 2, 1 Jan.1973.

1976

I.6 "Kalevalaa kuvin" (The Kalevala in pictures). Ed. and directed by Lisa Hovinheimo. Helsinki: Documentary Edition, Finnish Broadcasting Company TV 2, 27 Feb. 1976.†

I.7 "Kulttuurikakkonen" (Cultural channel two). Produced and ed. by Lisa Hovinheimo. Helsinki: Documentary Edition, Finnish Broadcasting Company TV 2, 20 Jan. 1976.†

1977

I.8 "Kimmo Kaivanto ja Tori" (Kimmo Kaivanto and "The Square"). Ed. by Pirkko Leisti. Helsinki: Special Edition, Finnish Broadcasting Company TV 1, Jan. 1977.

1980

I.9 "Kerro, kerro kuvastin" (Mirror, mirror on the wall). Ed. by Eeli Aalto. Helsinki: Documentary Edition, Finnish Broadcasting Company TV 2, 22 Jan. 1980 and 5 Feb. 1980.

I.10 "Kansakunta kehyksissä" (The nation in frames). Scripted and directed Tuulikki Islander and Markku Valkonen. Helsinki: Cultural Edition, Finnish Broadcasting Company TV 1, 22 June 1980.

1981

I.11 "Musiikkiterveiset" (Musical greetings). Produced, directed and ed. by Matti Heinivaho. Helsinki: Music Programs, Finnish Broadcasting Company TV 2, 7 May 1981.

1982

I.12 "Muistiinpanoja 1941-82" (Notes 1942-82). Produced, scripted, directed and ed. by Tuulikki Islander. Helsinki: Cultural Edition, Finnish Broadcasting Company TV 1, 6 Sept. 1982.

Periodicals and newspapers cited in the bibliography

Listed by title (translation), city of publication

Aamulehti (Morning Paper), Tampere
Åbo Underrättelser (Turku News), Turku
Aika (Time), Helsinki
Åland (Ahvenanmaa), Ahvenanmaa
Anna (Anna), Helsinki
Ännä (N), Tampere
Apu (Help), Helsinki
Askel (Step), Vantaa
Astra (Star), Helsinki
Aviisi (Newspaper), Helsinki
Avotakka (Open Hearth), Helsinki
Blue Wings, Helsinki
Books from Finland, Helsinki
Dagens Nyheter (Today's News), Stockholm
Eeva (Eeva), Helsinki
Elanto-lehti (Elanto Magazine), Helsinki
Elias (Elias), Elias
Eteenpäin (Forward), Kotka
Etelä-Saimaa (South Saimaa), Lappeenranta
Etelä-Suomen Sanomat (Southern Finland News)
Etelä-Suomi (Southern Finland), Lahti
F 15 Kontakt (F15 Contact), Moss
Faedrelandsvennen (Patriot), Kristiansand
Finnish Business Report, Helsinki
Finnjet-kokousuutiset (Finnjet-Meeting News), Helsinki
Folktidningen Ny Tid (People's Paper New Time), Stockholm
Form–Function–Finland, Helsinki
Forssan Lehti (Forssa Paper), Forssa
Gloria (Gloria), Helsinki
Göteborgs-Posten (Göteborg Post), Göteborg
Hämeen Kansa (People of Häme), Hämeenlinna
Hämeen Sanomat (Häme News), Hämeenlinna
Hämeen Yhteistyö (Collaboration of Häme), Tampere
Hämeenlinnan paikallislehti (Hämeenlinna Local Paper), Hämeenlinna
Helsingin Sanomat (Helsinki News), Helsinki
Helsingin Sanomat–Kuukausiliite (Helsinki News–Monthly Supplement), Helsinki
Hokki (Hokki), Helsinki
Hopeapeili (Silver Mirror), Helsinki
Hufvudstadsbladet (Capital City Newspaper), Helsinki
Hymy (Smile), Helsinki
Hyvinkään Sanomat (Hyvinkää News), Hyvinkää
Iiris (Iris), Helsinki
Iisalmen Sanomat (Iisalmi News), Iisalmi
Ilkka (Ilkka), Vaasa
Ilta-Sanomat (Evening News), Helsinki
Iltalehti (Evening Paper), Helsinki
Iltaset (Evening Post), Tampere
Images from Finland: Poetry and Graphics, Helsinki
Itä-Häme (Eastern Häme), Heinola
Itä-Savo (Eastern Savo), Savonlinna
Jaana (Jaana), Helsinki
Jakobstads Tidning (Pietarsaari Paper), Pietarsaari
Kainuun Sanomat (Kainuu News), Kajaani
Kaks' plus (Two Plus), Tampere
Kalajokilaakso (Kajajokilaakso), Ylivieska
Kaleva (Kaleva), Oulu
Kamppi (Kamppi), Helsinki
Kansan Ääni (People's Voice), Vaasa
Kansan Lehti (People's Paper), Tampere
Kansan Tahto (People's Will), Oulu
Kansan Uutiset (People's News), Helsinki

Karjala (Karelia), Lappeenranta
Karjalainen (Karelian),
Katso (Watch), Helsinki
Kaunis Koti (Beautiful Home), Helsinki
Kauppa ja Koti (Business and Home), Helsinki
Kauppalehti (Business Paper), Helsinki
Keski-Suomen Iltalehti (Central Finland Evening Paper)
Keskipohjanmaa (Central Ostrobothnia), Kokkola
Keskipohjanmaa, 29 Jan. 1984.
Keskisuomalainen (Central Finland), Jyväskylä
Kinski (Kinski), Tampere
Koillis-Häme (North-Eastern Häme), Jämsä
Kotikaupunki (Hometown), Tampere
Kotiliesi (Home Hearth), Helsinki
Kotimaa (Homeland), Helsinki
Kotka Nyheter (Kotka News), Kotka
Kouluohjelmat (School Programs), Helsinki
Kouvolan Sanomat (Kouvola News), Kouvola
Kunnallistiedote (Communal Bulletin), Helsinki
Kunst og Kultur (Art and Culture), Oslo
Kurikka (Batlet), Helsinki
Kuvaposti (Illustrated Post), Helsinki
Kymen Sanomat (Kyme News), Hamina
Kymppi (Ten), Helsinki
La Cité, Brussels
Lääkäri ja Vapaa-aika (Doctor and Leisure), Espoo
Lahti (Lahti), Lahti
Länsi-Savo (West Savo), Mikkeli
Länsi-Suomi (West Finland), Rauma
Länsi-Uusimaa (West Uusimaa), Lohja
Länsiväylä (Western Highway), Espoo
Länstidningen (Provincial Paper), Stockhom
Lentosuunta (Flight Direction), Vantaa
Liitto (Union), Oulu
Look at Finland, Helsinki
Lopen Lehti (Loppi Paper), Loppi
Louisiana Revy (Louisiana Review), Humlebæk
Maaseudun Tulevaisuus (Countryside Future), Helsinki
Mainosuutiset (Advertisement News), Helsinki
Markkinointi (Marketing), Helsinki
Matti ja Liisa (Matti and Liisa), Helsinki
Me (We), Helsinki
Me Naiset (We Women), Helsinki
Mestari-Tappara (Master Tappara), Tampere
Näköpiiri (Range of Vision), Helsinki
Nutida Musik (Contemporary Music), Stockholm
Nya Argus (New Argus), Helsinki
Nya Pressen (New Press), Helsinki
Öljyposti (Oil Post), Espoo
Om Konst och Annat i Stockholms Län (About Art and Else in Stockholm Province), Stockholm
Oma Markka (Own Mark), Helsinki
Oriveden Sanomat (Orivesi News), Orivesi
Orja (Slave), Tampere
Oulu-lehti (Oulu Paper), Oulu
Päijät-Häme (Häme of Päijänne), Vääksy
Päivän Sanomat (Daily News), Helsinki
Päivän Uutiset (Today's News), Helsinki
Paletten (Palette), Göteborg
Porin Lehti (Pori Paper), Pori
Radar (Radar), Berlin
Ruovesi (Ruovesi), Ruovesi
Sanomalehtimies/Journalisten (Journalist), Helsinki

Satakunnan Kansa (People of Satakunta), Pori
Savo (Savo), Kuopio
Savon Sanomat (Savo News), Kuopio
Seura (Company), Helsinki
Södertälje-kuriren (Södertälje Courier), Södertälje
Sokeri Pohjalla (Sugar at Bottom), Helsinki
Sosialistinen Aikakausilehti (Socialist Periodical), Helsinki
Status (Status), Tampere
Suomalainen (Finn), Helsinki
Suomen Kuvalehti (Illustrated Magazine of Finland), Helsinki
Suomen Sanomat/Finlandsnytt (Finnish News), Helsinki
Suomen Sosialidemokraatti (Finnish Social Democratic Paper), Helsinki
Suomen Sosialidemokraatti (Finnish Social Democrat), Helsinki
Suomenmaa (Country of Finland), Helsinki
Suomi-Finland USA (Finland-Finland USA), Helsinki
Svenska Dagbladet (Swedish Daily News), Stockholm
Sydsvenska Dagbladet (South Sweden Daily), Malmö
Taide (Art), Helsinki
Tammerkoski (Tammerkoski), Tampere
Tamperelainen (People of Tampere), Tampere
Teatteri (Theater), Helsinki
Tehy (Tehy), Helsinki
Tiedonantaja (Informer), Helsinki
Turkulainen (People of Turku), Turku
Turun Päivälehti (Turku Daily Paper), Turku
Turun Sanomat (Turku News), Turku
Turun Ylioppilaslehti (Turku Student Paper), Turku
Tyrvään Sanomat (Tyrvää News), Tyrvää
Urjalan Sanomat (Urjala News), Urjala
Uuden Ajan Aura (Plough of New Time), Helsinki

Uudenmaan Sanomat (Uusimaa News), Porvoo
Uusi Aika (New Time), Helsinki
Uusi Anna (New Anna), Helsinki
Uusi Aura (New Plough), Helsinki
Uusi Nainen (New Woman), Helsinki
Uusi Suomi (New Finland), Helsinki
Uusimaa (Uusimaa), Porvoo
Uutis-Kukko (News-Cock), Kuopio
Vaasa (Vaasa), Vaasa
Valkeakosken Sanomat (Valkeakoski News), Valkeakoski
Valokuva (Photograph), Helsinki
Vartija (Guard), Järvenpää
Vasabladet (Vaasa Newspaper), Vaasa
Västra Nyland (Western Uusimaa), Tammissari
Veikkaaja (Bettor), Helsinki
Veikkaus ja Lotto (Betting and Lottery), Helsinki
Viikko Sanomat (Weekly News), Helsinki
Viikkolehti (Weekly Magazine), Helsinki
Vilkku (Flash), Tampere
VIP (VIP), Helsinki
Warkauden Lehti (Varkaus Paper), Varkaus
Welcome to Finland, Helsinki
Yhdyslanka (Connecting Thread), Tampere
Yhteishyvä (Common Good), Helsinki
Ylä-Vuoksi (Upper Vuoksi), Imatra
Yliopisto (University), Helsinki
Yliopisto Uutiset (University News)
Ylioppilaslehti (Student Paper), Helsinki
YV (YV), Helsinki
Yykoo (Yykoo), Tampere